Stairway to Heaven

通往天堂的阶梯

Stairway to Heaven

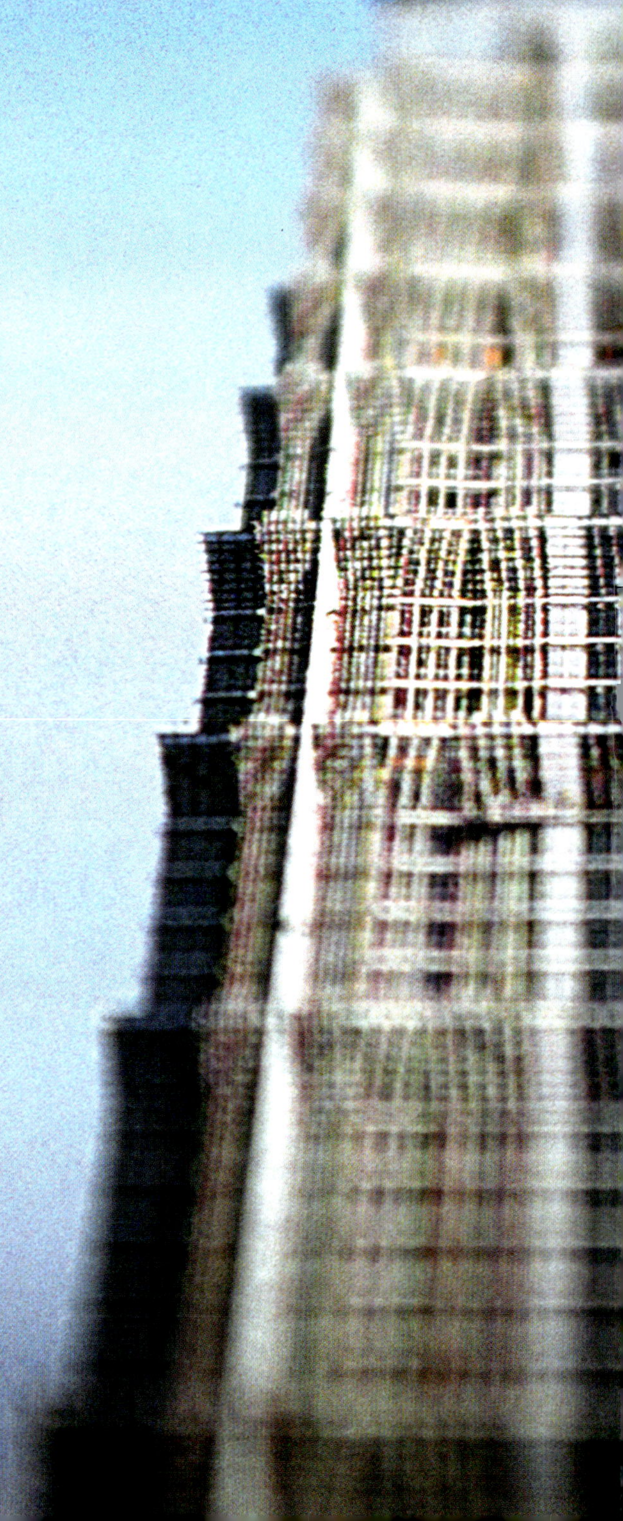

通往天堂的阶梯

FROM

CHINESE STREETS

TO MONUMENTS

AND SKYSCRAPERS

从中国的街道到

纪念碑和摩天楼

MARK H. C. BESSIRE

UNIVERSITY PRESS OF NEW ENGLAND

Hanover and London

In association with

BATES COLLEGE MUSEUM OF ART

Lewiston, Maine

Stairway to Heaven is originated by
the Bates College Museum of Art and the
H & R Block Artspace at the Kansas City Art
Institute and curated by Mark H. C. Bessire
and Raechell Smith.

Published by
University Press of New England,
One Court Street, Lebanon, NH 03766
www.upne.com

© 2009 by Bates College Museum of Art
Printed in Singapore

5   4   3   2   1

Library of Congress
Cataloging-in-Publication Data
Bessire, Mark.
From Chinese streets to monuments
and skyscrapers / Mark H. C. Bessire.
p. cm.
Chinese and English.
Catalog of an exhibition of photographs
from 17 Chinese artists, including Ai Weiwei
and others.
"In association with Bates College Museum
of Art, Lewiston, Maine."
Includes bibliographical references.
ISBN 978-1-58465-728-6 (pbk.: alk. paper)
1. Street photography—China—Exhibitions.
2. Art and popular culture—China—
Exhibitions. 3. Cities and towns—China—
Growth—Exhibitions. I. Bates College
(Lewiston, Me.). Museum of Art. II. Title.
TR659.8.B47   2009
779'.451—dc22
2009006562

CONTENTS

Chinese translations immediately follow the English essays in this book.

Introduction 1
Mark H. C. Bessire

STREETS 街道
　Chen Shaoxiong 陈劭雄 17
　Gu Zheng 顾铮 19
　Liang Weiping 梁卫平 29
　Liu Bolin 刘勃麟 33
　Lu Yuanmin 陆元敏 35
　Zhang Dali 张大力 37

From the Street to the Skyscraper:
Notes on the Relationship
between Urban Space and Chinese
Contemporary Photography 41
Gu Zheng 顾铮

MONUMENTS 纪念碑
　Ai Weiwei 艾未未 49
　Gu Wenda 谷文达 51
　Hong Lei 洪磊 52
　Luo Yongjin 罗永进 54
　Ma Liuming 马六明 64
　Wang Jing 王净 65
　Zhu Feng 朱锋 68

China Spectacle 69
Gan Xu 徐淦

SKYSCRAPERS 摩天楼
　Weng Fen 翁奋 79
　Xing Danwen 邢丹文 81
　Yang Yongliang 杨泳梁 91
　Yening 也宁 93
　Zhu Feng 朱锋 95

An Interview with
Luo Yongjin 罗永进,
Xing Danwen 邢丹文,
and Zhang Dali 张大力 97
Raechell Smith

Artist Biographies 125
Works in Exhibition 133
Acknowledgments 137

Stairway to Heaven

通往天堂的阶梯

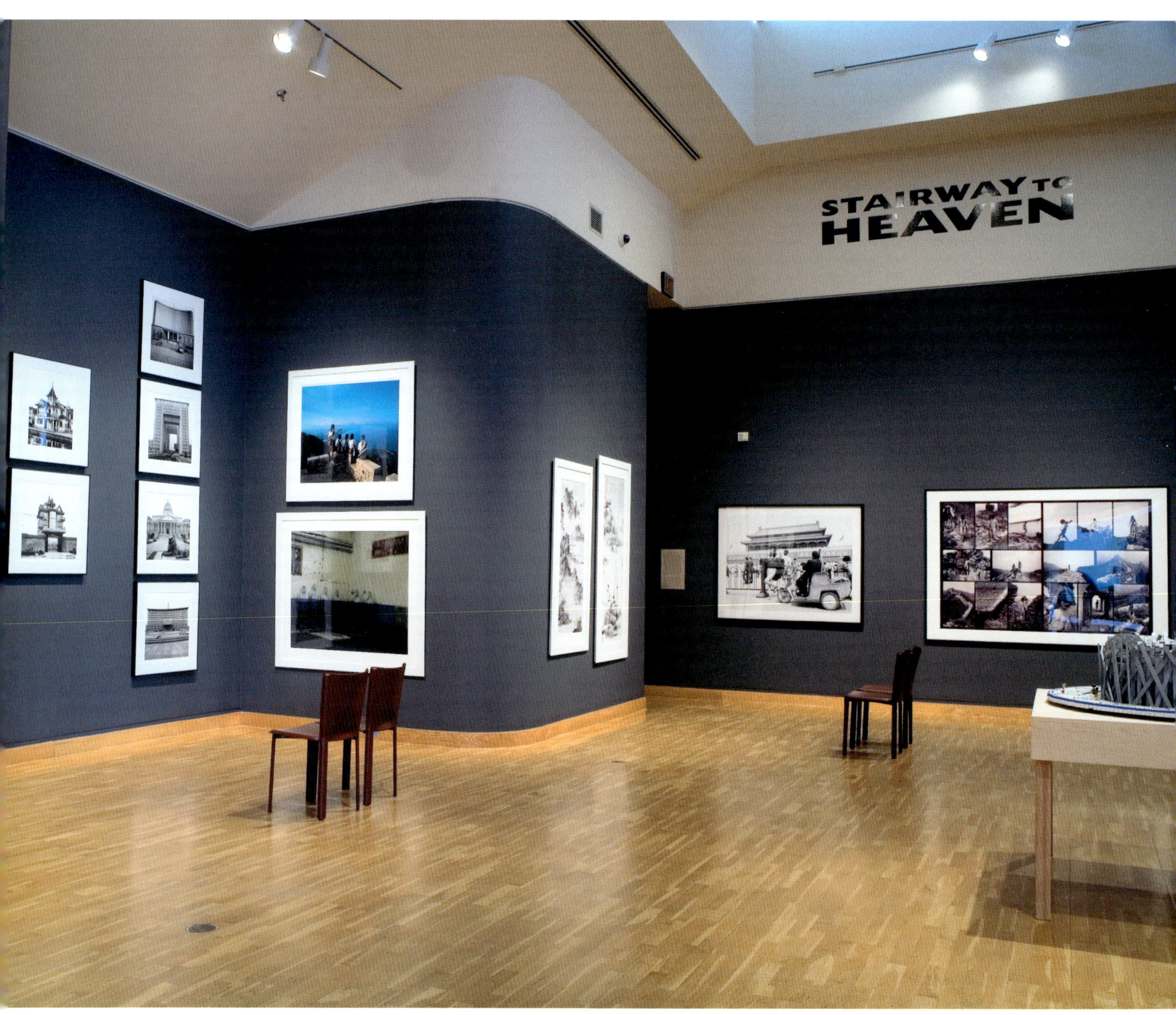

STAIRWAY TO
HEAVEN

MARK H. C. BESSIRE

Stairway to Heaven is an exhibition of contemporary art analyzing the changing streets and urban landscapes of China. The work in the exhibition responds to traditional monuments and the unparalleled growth in skyscrapers within the context of cultural transformation. The artists provide an intimate look at how new histories are constructed and old histories are erased in a country that assiduously recorded its history through the arts until the Maoist era, which was dominated by propaganda. It is a remarkable opportunity to watch art history unfold in real time during this extraordinary moment in Chinese history when the country's transformation has realigned with a resurgence in Chinese art. Just as Germany tore down the Berlin wall during a building boom that left little trace of the nation's history, China is dismantling its urban history on an unprecedented scale. While the country is building skyscrapers, the artists are recording and critiquing old and new histories alike as they unfold at alarming speed.

This exhibition presents layers of diversity through the multiple voices, strategies, and techniques of seventeen Chinese artists: Ai Weiwei, Chen Shaoxiong, Gu Wenda, Gu Zheng, Hong Lei, Liang Weiping, Liu Bolin, Lu Yuanmin, Luo Yongjin, Ma Liuming, Wang Jing, Weng Fen, Xing Danwen, Yang Yongliang, Yening, Zhang Dali, and Zhu Feng. Organized thematically, the exhibition focuses on the changing relationships between artists and streets, monuments, and skyscrapers with a subtext exploring the multifaceted art boom in China. The loci are sites where artists are digesting and processing an overload of cultural, philosophical, economic, and technological changes in a condensed period of time.

As the twenty-first century develops, China is becoming the next dominant global culture. Yet, in 2008 the world is still curious about what role China wants to play. In the lead-up to the Olympics, the government of China has spent more time defending its policies than reveling in its accomplishments. International public opinion has condemned its Tibetan policy, questions its currency policy, and is outraged by shoddy manufactured products, lead-contaminated toys, and tainted food products; yet the government seems more interested and responsive to domestic opinion. They are well aware that as the economy and culture have been opened, people have higher expectations about their relationship with government.

When the horrible earthquake in Sichuan Province on May 12, 2008 killed up to 50,000 people and displaced millions, the spotlight was put on the Chinese gov-

Stairway to Heaven, Bates College Museum of Art, Installation images by Luc Demers.

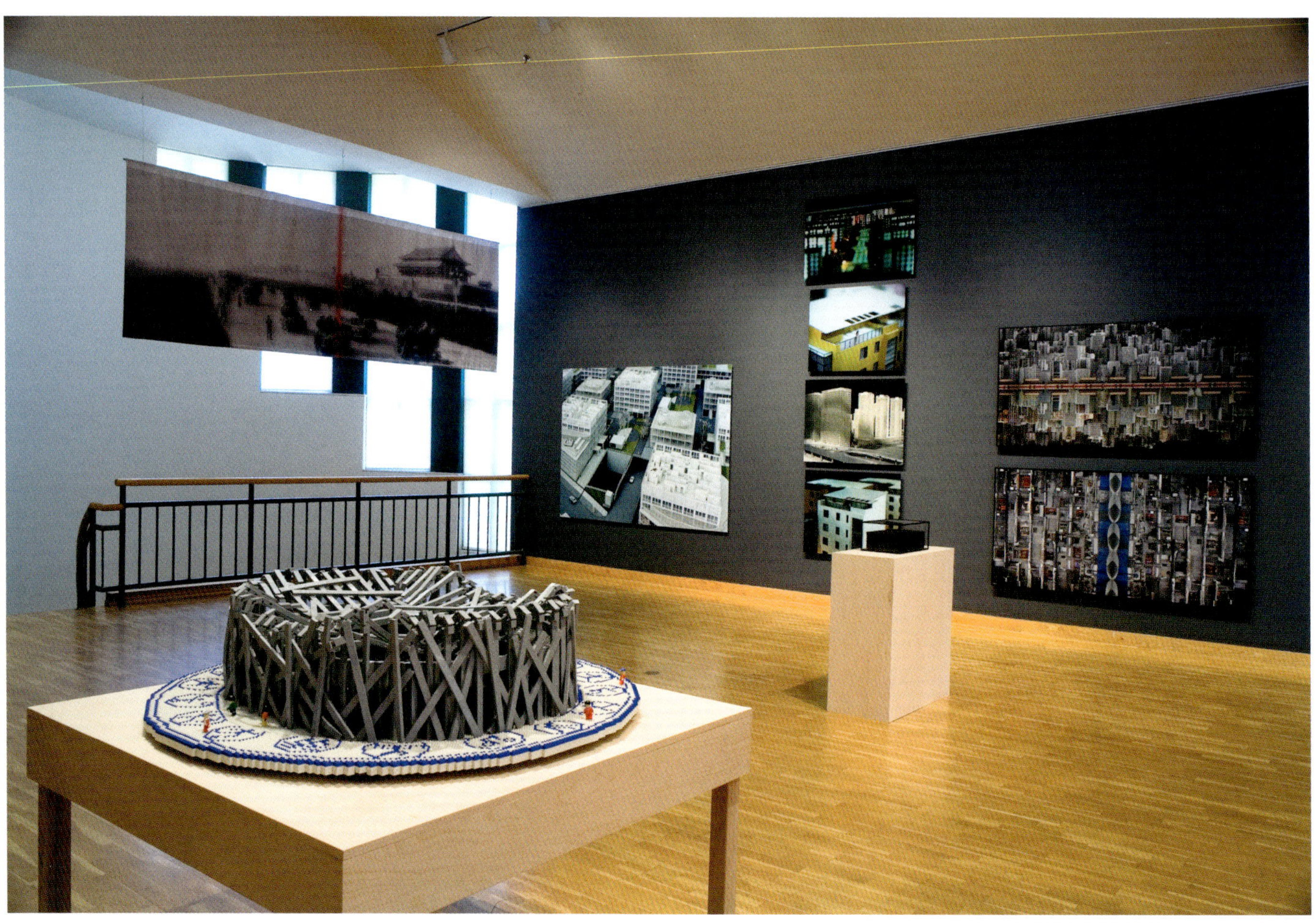

ernment again. This time international opinion has proved extremely sympathetic, and the government has for the first time welcomed international support and offered access to the disaster area to international aid organizations and the media. What is most interesting is to watch the leadership of China take on responsibility and accountability for rescue efforts and be put to task by citizens for the alarming death toll at poorly built schools. Also, for the first time in many years, people are taking personal responsibility by rushing to Sichuan to offer help, sending money, and challenging the government response, which by many accords has been quite responsive. Yet as the mechanisms of government become more open, people are demanding more and more accountability.

The best way to gauge the future path of a culture is through its art. For years contemporary artists have been questioning the leadership and responsibility of the Chinese government, and it seems that in the year that the government was to show the world the greatness of China, the people are embracing the critical spirit of contemporary Chinese art by forcing greater accountability. Another new history is being scripted as you view the art in this exhibition, which foretold the transformative political environment today in China. As China's political and economic policies continue to become the focus of the international scene during the 2008 Beijing Olympics, *Stairway to Heaven* offers a unique context and opportunity to present the response of Chinese artists to China's resurgence.

Stairway to Heaven refers to the search for an experience that may define the expectations and dreams of the Chinese people. In the context of the Olympics, it recognizes that as athletes strive for gold, they are searching for "heaven" and that each Chinese citizen is also trying to find her piece of "heaven" in the new China. The artists in the exhibition explore where heaven may or may not be found: from traditional to neon street life, to the top floors of skyscrapers, to a home with a family or a visit to cultural or spiritual monuments. They also look at the mechanization of change and contemplate how their landscape is being changed by machinery and technology. What does it mean for Chinese culture to become more urban than rural and more conceptual than representational? How will this influence Chinese history? It is a fascinating time and as the world focuses on China during the Beijing Olympics, it is an important moment to illuminate the culture created by rapid economic and social growth.

What signifies a period or a site with an abundance of great art for the ages? What made the art and culture of the Sacred Valley of the Inca, Renaissance Italy, seventeenth-century Holland, fin de siècle Paris, the Kingdom of Benin, and other great art regions or moments significant? Will this moment of Chinese art transcend time and place, joining the canon of art history? Or is it merely a trend exploiting social, historical, and economic conditions? Or are the social, historical, and economic conditions providing a perfect storm for producing the unprecedented burst of artistic creativity that is currently dominating the global art world?

After years of Mao's subjugation of the arts, including his complete control and exploitation of photography, today there is a confluence of an incredible rebirth of classic Chinese art with a culture yearning for the nonlinear and open-ended possibilities provided by postmodernism and global contemporary art. Chinese contemporary art was originally supported and driven by an international market but has now been embraced by curators, collectors, and universities in China, providing the market with a depth and breadth transcending the fickle and trendy international market. Combined with excellent scholarship, major museum exhibitions, burgeoning art schools, and new museums in China, it seems that this period of Chinese art will remain significant well past this moment in time. Yet there are questions to be answered. The unprecedented rate of cultural and economic acceleration provides opportunity and often contradictions, as seen in the celebration of the new and mourning of the old. For example, in the mid-1990s some artists trained in traditional Chinese art such as ink painting, quickly adopted the digital camera because of its immediacy and ability to document the rapid changes in China, as well as the possibilities of postproduction alteration. Yet in many ways the digital camera is a product of globalization, industrialization, and urbanization, making it very interesting that artists are choosing it as their medium of choice for expressing what they perceive as negative changes in their society. It is also interesting how these artists are creating work that mourns aspects of the past and critiques the present but does not offer alternatives for the future.

The art in *Stairway to Heaven* is a testament to the transformation and creative potential brewing within a culture whose rich art traditions were stifled by generations of political upheaval. Today Chinese culture is experiencing a gamut of complementary and contradictory emotions and conditions that are providing new generations with obstacles and opportunities, including wealth, poverty, alienation, competition, and confusion. Unlike the clarity of propaganda unveiled during the Olympics, these artists provide a less-structured environment that invites questions and offers challenging and provocative critiques.

For three years Raechell Smith, Gu Zheng, Gan Xu, and I have seen a repetition of themes, streets, monuments, and skyscrapers in photographs we saw during studio visits and exhibitions. With so many exhibitions of Chinese art concentrating on the same artists, we were looking for a more diverse and lesser-known group. These themes provided an exhibition platform to include artists from different backgrounds and using diverse strategies and techniques. It includes recent graduates, professors, international art stars, conceptual and street photographers, and those who use digital manipulation as well as gelatin silver-printing methods. The diversity of these artists comes alive in the essays "From the Street to the Skyscraper: Notes on the Relationship between Urban Space and Chinese Contemporary Photography" by Gu Zheng, "China Spectacle" by Gan Xu, and Raechell Smith's interviews with Luo Yongjin, Xing Danwen, and Zhang Dali.

Scholar, international curator, critic, and one of China's preeminent street photographers, Gu Zheng provides an insider's diary of the development of street photography as an art form in China. Except for colonial photography and a brief time in the 1930s when Chinese photographers aimed their lenses at the nascent skyscrapers like the Park Hotel, twentieth-century China was framed by propaganda

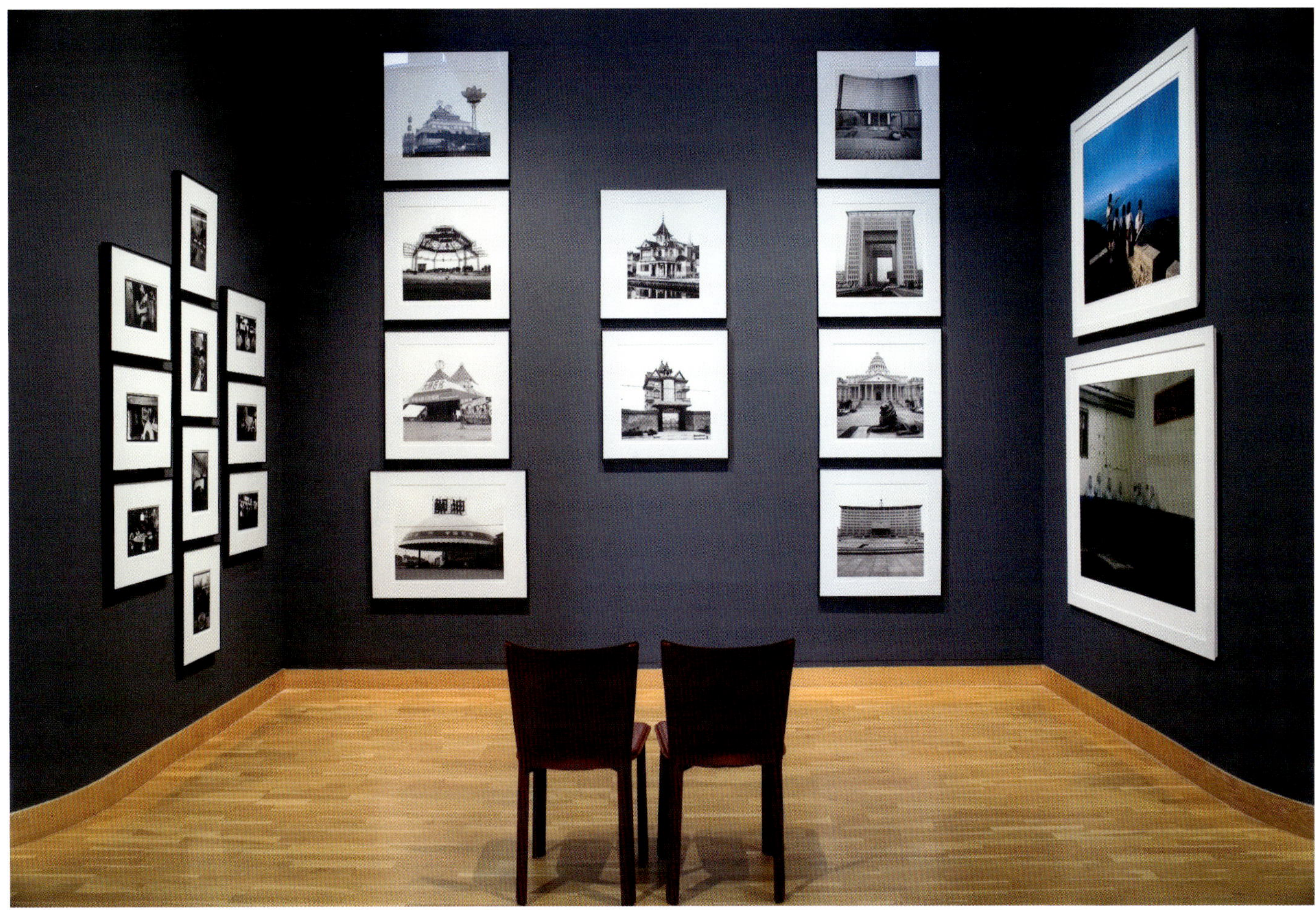

photography. Coming alive in the late 1980s, street photography, Gu Zheng explains, was such a stark contrast to the exoticized and often racist images created by colonial "outsiders" and the politically staged images of the Maoist propaganda machine. The new style of photography was exciting and *real,* reflecting a new urban culture transformed from state-sponsored production centers to commercial/consumer centers. The force behind street photography, Gu Zheng suggests, was the street itself, and the best way to document change was photographing people in these new spaces. With a new freedom for self-expression through fashion and consumption, the people in the street were the art. It became a unique moment where artist, camera, and people on the street all reveled in the early performative dance of constructing new identities after years of subjugation. By the 1990s photographers were experimenting with flashing light, super fish-eye and noncompositional techniques, and the photographer's angle and conceptual nature increasingly crept into the lens as seen through photo manipulation and large-format prints. At the same time the skyscraper began to epitomize the transformation of Chinese urban culture and its shift from a horizontal to a vertical culture. Ironically, while the skyscraper made photographs look modern, as it did for Lang Jingshan and Ao Enhong in the 1930s, the 1990s verticality is more of a challenge to the establishment than a celebration. Today the horizontal street life of Shanghai with its limited buildable properties is disappearing as life goes vertical, and every inch of available land is being torn down for skyscrapers. In response, urban photography seems to be becoming more and more performance-based and conceptual. *Stairway to Heaven* documents this extraordinary case study of artistic production, making the viewer feel like she is living art history as it unfolds. Within that context, Gan Xu's essay explores the pertinence of art history to the artists and their work in the exhibition.

Gan Xu grew up in China during the Maoist period, attended graduate school in the United States, and teaches art history at Maine College of Art in Portland, Maine. He was one of the first Chinese scholars in many years to receive a Ph.D. in art history outside of China; yet he always stayed in touch with artists and scholars in China and now lives in both Shanghai and Portland. He brings an insider and outsider perspective to his essay on the relationship between monuments and skyscrapers in contemporary Chinese photography. Weaving his own voice and intimate familiarity with the artists in the exhibition, he mines the conflict, tragedy, and hypocrisy of mourning and celebrating that seems to be the common theme in China. Placing the current phase of Chinese history in context, Gan Xu reflects on the new skyscraper architecture of China in relation to Mao's "Great Leap Forward" and "Cultural Revolution," the "Open Door Policy" of Deng Xiaoping, Pure Land Buddhist traditions, and fifth-century poetry. He wonders if the skyscraper has become the popular equivalent to historical utopian visions and dreams of China. Whether or not the apartment in the sky is the updated "Chinese Dream" whose traditions are much older than the "American Dream," we learn that as an icon of change it has become a magnet for positive and negative developments in China. In an excellent critique Gan Xu suggests that Liang Weiping's image of factories that have since been demolished represents a fading history of the few early successes of industrialization. And in Yang Yongliang's work the digitally altered images reveal how the cranes of progress are building skyscrapers that are trampling China's 5,000-year-old civilization. As the skyscrapers rise on the remnants of the past, the Great Wall of China in Ma Liuming's famous performative walk is crumbling, the Forbidden Temple is being encroached on in Zhang Dali's *Demolition* series, and history is being erased by blood in the images of Hong Lei. Yening's series *Dream in the Deserted Peking* documents skyscraper development, mourning the past and

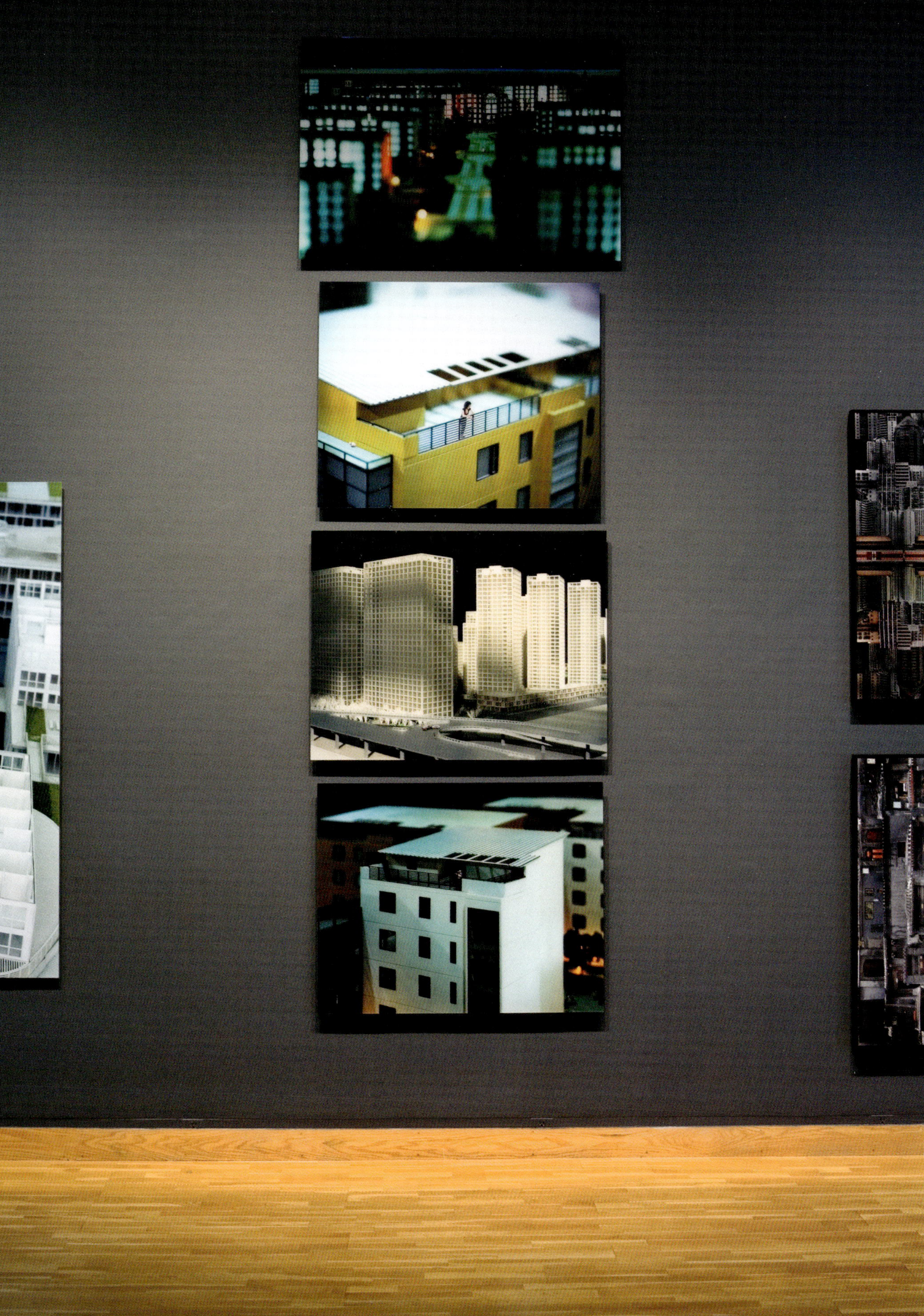

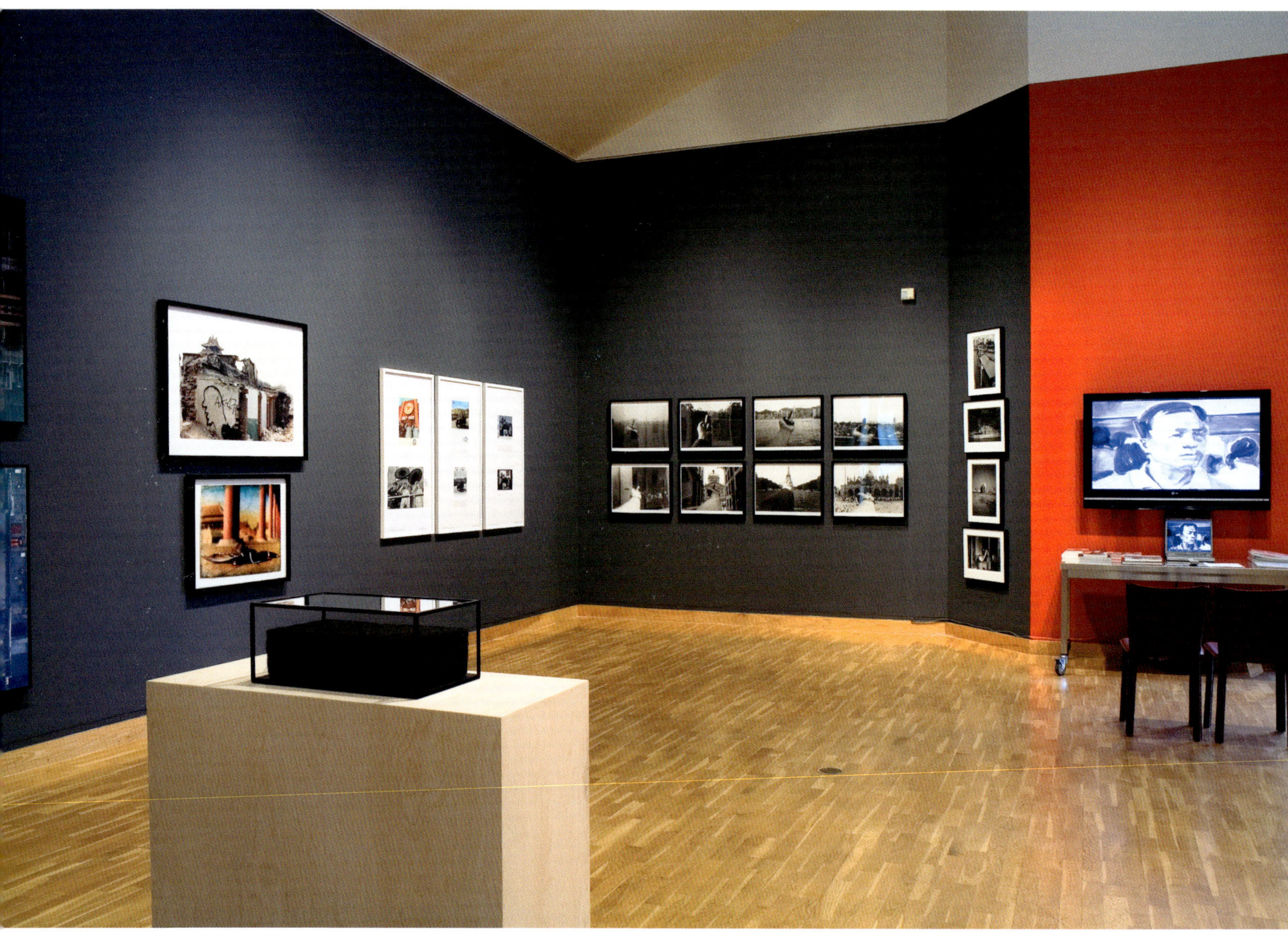

wondering what the future will hold for her in a city she no longer recognizes. In a clinical photo exploration, Luo Yongjin captures the demise of the spectacular gas stations that competed for customers through uniqueness but are now being replaced by sterile gas stations that can be seen throughout the world. Even in brilliant color there is no denying the sterile atmosphere in Xing Danwen's *Urban Fiction* series of life in a gated or restricted urban development. The dark side of the new heaven in the skies may in fact be alienation and despair, where the utopian ideals of the collective are erased.

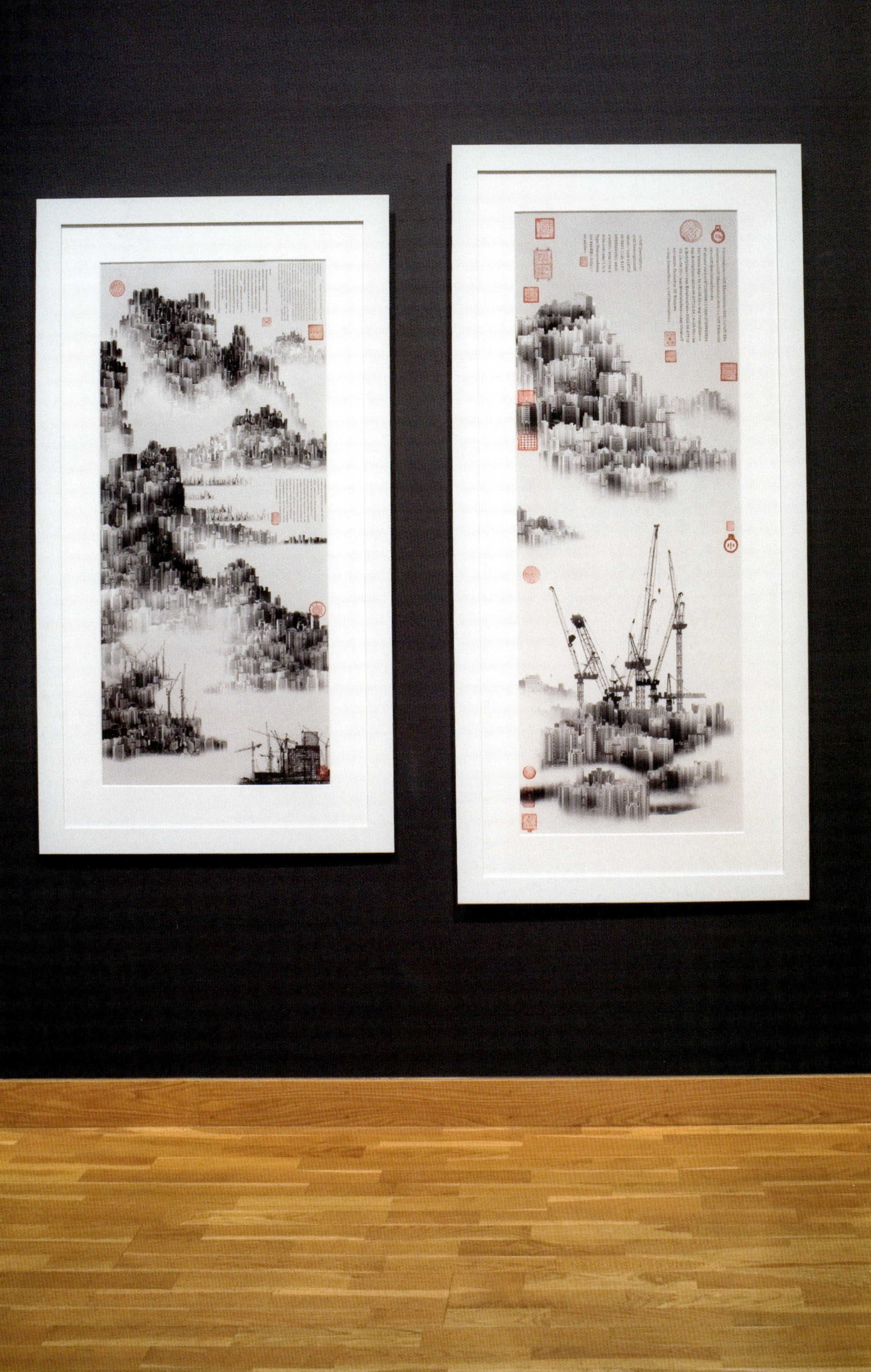

In candid interviews with Luo Yongjin, Xing Danwen, and Zhang Dali, curator Rae-chell Smith invited the artists to place their work and lives within the context of phenomenal changes in China. They discuss how the digital world and internet have made them more efficient and aware, but Zhang Dali suggests he views them as tools that do not change his understanding of art but provide more possibilities. What has really changed their making of art is the urban landscape where they live: the danger in riding a bike, Beijing's population growth from four to thirteen million, the destruction of old neighborhoods, architectural development, the free and mass movement of people from the country to the city, and generally better living standards, to name a few. All three artists view their work as connecting to the past through the present, offering critical insight for the future, and they hope that their current work will indeed transcend this era, enabling those in the future to understand our present and their past. As radical as the art is within the context of recent Chinese history, the artists do lament some of the sacrifices made for greater prosperity and mobility, such as community for anonymity and Chinese culture for a homogenous global culture.

Much of the dialogue, which includes technology, changing surroundings, urbanization, capitalism, the art market, and the role of history, often returns to architecture and the causes and results of the changing urban spaces. "I hope," Luo Yongjin explains, "that people will understand that in the beginning of the twenty-first century, there were some sensitive artists who were both suspicious and sarcastic about the trendy architecture of the day, and yet they were able to turn these tasteless structures into tasty works of art." What could be more tasty than Wang Jing's wonderful installation *The China Food in 2008,* which is a riff on Olympic architecture and Chinese food?

I believe that the art of this period in China will always be recognized for its immense creative output following an incredibly controlled and fallow period of art making under Mao, who stifled the nations' great art traditions. Who would have thought that after so much isolation Chinese artists would emerge with the energy and creativity to place Chinese art at the forefront of a global art world in less than a generation?

Many thanks to curatorial assistants Emily Monty and Rachel Tofel for their exhibition research, which has informed the introduction.

MARK H. C. BESSIRE

《通往天堂的阶梯》是一个现代艺术展览，它汇集了变化中的中国街头与城市景观。从参展作品中我们看到了处于文化变迁过程中的传统纪念碑建筑和与之不协调的急剧增加的摩天楼建筑。艺术家们从个人视角向我们展示了这个国家的历史新篇章是如何构造起来的，她的旧的一页是如何消失的。在艺术为宣传所操控的毛泽东时代之前，这个国家一直勤勉于以艺术形式记录自己的历史。这个国家的变革正伴随着中国艺术的复活而重新组合。能够在中国历史上这一不平凡的瞬间及时关注中国的艺术发展对我们来说难能可贵。正如德国拆除柏林墙之际急迫发展，几乎没有留下一丝历史痕迹一样，中国也正在以空前的规模摈弃它的城市历史。当中国忙于建设摩天大楼的时候，艺术家们也在匆忙地记录和评价着以惊人速度展现着的一页页旧的和新的历史篇章。

本次展览通过十七位中国艺术家的多种声音、手法和技巧充分体现了多样化的特点。这些艺术家包括：艾未未、陈劭雄、谷文达、顾铮、洪磊、梁卫平、刘勃麟、陆元敏、罗永进、马六明、王净、翁奋、邢丹文、杨泳梁、也宁、张大力和朱峰。展览紧紧围绕主题，作品聚焦于艺术家与街道之间、纪念碑和摩天楼之间不断变化的关系，它潜在地探究中国艺术迅速繁荣时期的多个层面。摄影场景则选取了艺术家们超负荷消化和处理在一段浓缩的时间内文化、哲学、经济和技术的变化的一个个场地。

随着二十一世纪的发展，中国正在成为下一个在全球占有优势的文化大国。2008年全世界仍然在观注着中国在新的二十一世纪里将要扮演什么样的角色。在迎接奥运会之际，相比于迷醉它的成就，中国政府把时间更多地花费在维护它的政策上。国际舆论谴责其西藏政策，质疑其现行政策，迁怒于其劣质产品、含铅玩具和受到污染的食品，而政府好象更注重国内舆论。他们充分意识到，随着经济和文化的开放，人民对他们与政府之间关系的期望值日益增高。

5月12日发生在四川省的强烈地震夺去了五万人的生命，使几百万人失去家园，世界的焦点再次集中于中国政府。国际舆论此时极具同情心，政府也史无前例地对国际援助表示欢迎，并为国际援助组织和媒体提供了去往灾区的通道。最有意义的是看到中国领导阶层担负起抗震救灾的责任和期望，并受任于公民去面对因劣质学校建筑而造成的惊人的死亡数字。与此同时，普通百姓多年来第一次自发地承担起个人责任奔赴四川帮助灾民，他们捐财献物，并挑战政府的反应，而此次政府的反应得到众口一词的好评。当然，政府机制越公开化，人民的期望也越来越高。

艺术是估量一个文化将来去向的最佳方式。多年来，现代艺术一直在质疑中国政府的领导和责任。在政府急于向世界展示中国成就的这一年度，民众在接受中国现代艺术批评精神的同时强加给政府更多的责任。当你在参观展览中这些预示着今日中国变革了的政治环境的艺术品时，一段新的历史正被载入史册。当中国的政府及其经济政策在2008年北京奥运会期间继续成为国际局势的焦点时，《通往天堂的阶梯》提供了一个独一无二的背景与机会，向我们展示中国艺术家对中国复兴的反响。

《通往天堂的阶梯》反应了中国人对期待与梦想的追求。在奥林匹克的大环境下，这个展览给我们的启示是，运动员们在为金牌而拼搏的时候，他们也在寻求"天堂"，同样，每一个中国公民也在新生的中国寻求属于他自己的一片"天堂"。艺术家们在作品中探讨哪里可能有或者可能没有"天堂"可寻：从传统生活到霓虹绚烂的街头生活，到摩天楼顶，到一个家庭居住的房子，或是一次对文化和精神纪念碑的参观。艺术家们也观注变化的机械性并思索他们的景观如何通过机器和技术得以转换。中国文化从乡村化变得更加都市化，从具象主义变得更加概念化，这意味着什么呢？这些变化将如何影响中国的历史？这一瞬间让人着迷。随着世界的焦点因北京奥运而聚集于中国，在这个重要的历史时刻，经济和社会的急剧发展将带动一个什么样的文化历程，我们将拭目以待。

在以往的岁月中，是什么让某个时期或某个地区的艺术繁荣久负盛名？从印加的神圣峡谷到文艺复兴时期的意大利、十七世纪的荷兰、世纪末危机中的巴黎以及贝宁王国，是什么使得这些时期和地区的艺术和文化如此辉煌？当前这一时期的中国艺术能否超越时空，最终作为经典载入艺术史册？或者它仅仅是一种趋势，引导着我们去开发和利用社会、历史和经济环境？或者说，这一时期的社会、历史和经济局势将带给我们一阵风暴似的动荡，从而引发一场空前的、主导着全球艺术世界的艺术创造力的爆发？

经过了毛泽东对艺术的多年压制，包括他对摄影艺术的全面控制和操纵之后，今天我们看到了中国古典艺术的重生，它汇合了后现代主义及全球现代艺术为我们营造的追求无限度可能性的文化氛围。中国的现代艺术最初的形成是为了迎合国际市场的需要，但它目前已经受到中国国内博物馆、收藏家和大学的青睐，而正是这些博物馆、收藏家和大学为现代艺术提供了一个较之浮燥而变幻无常的国际市场而更具深度和广度的市场。结合了中国国内优越的学术成就、大型博物馆展览、萌芽时期的艺术学校和新兴的博物馆，这一时期的中国艺术将保持史上前所未有的影响力。当然，还有一些问题需要解答。文化和经济以空前的进度加速发展给我们带来机遇也让我们面对辞旧迎新所不可避免的种种矛盾。比如说，在上一世纪九十年代中，象水墨画家那样受过传统训练的艺术家们迅速接纳了数码相机，因为它能直接记录快速变化的中国，同时还具备后期裁剪制作功能。当然，从很多方面来说，数码相机是全球化、工业化和城市化的产物。颇具意味的是，这些艺术家们选择了数码相机作为媒介手段来表现在他们看来对社会具有负面影响的变化。同样有意思的是，这些艺术家用作品哀悼过去和批评现在，却没有提供对于未来的选择。

中国文化的深厚传统，曾因历年的政治动荡而饱受压抑。《通往天堂的阶梯》中作品的艺术性则是对蕴含于中国文化中的革新与创造潜力的一个很好的证明。　今天的中国文化正在经历一场情感与形势上的苦辣酸甜，这些错综复杂的情感与形势既相辅相成又充满矛盾，从而以财富、贫穷、疏离感、竞争和迷惑等种种形式为新的一代人设置了障碍也带来机遇。与奥运宣传的目的明确相反，这些艺术家为我们创造了一种更为松散的环境，允许我们去怀疑，并允许我们提出兼具挑战性和刺激性的批评意见。

　　在三年多的时间里，Raechell Smith、顾铮、徐淦和我在艺术家工作室和展览中看到摄影家们重复使用一些同样的主题：街道、纪念碑和摩天大楼。在众多的中国艺术展均出自同一些艺术家之手这种情形下，我们试图寻找一组另类的而且不太出名的艺术家。这些主题为我们提供了一个展示平台，使得我们能够发现来自不同背景并使用不同手法与技巧的艺术家。这个群体包括刚刚走出校门的学生，还有教授和国际艺术界的新星、观念摄影家和街头摄影家，以及那些既会使用数码技术、又懂得银－明胶合剂冲印方法的艺术家。在顾铮的《从街道到摩天楼 — 关于城市空间与中国现代摄影之关系的笔记》、徐淦的《中国景观》和Raechell Smith对罗永进、邢丹文和张大力的采访这几篇文章中，我们可以看到艺术家的多元化。

　　身为学者、国际策展人、评论家和中国最优秀的街头摄影家之一的顾铮从局内人的视角为我们讲述了街头摄影这一艺术形式在中国的发展状况。除了殖民地时期和上个世纪三十年代一段短暂时期摄影家把镜头对准"公园饭店"一类初期的摩天楼以外，二十世纪的中国摄影一直是宣传的工具。顾铮说，自八十年代末开始恢复生气的街头摄影与过去殖民者创建的具有异国情调和种族色彩的影象，以及毛泽东的宣传机器所创建的政治舞台影象形成了鲜明的对比。新的摄影风格真实而令人振奋，它反应了一种由国营产业中心向商业与消费中心转换的新的城市文化特征。顾铮认为，街头摄影之后所隐藏的力量，恰恰来自街道本身，而能够最好地记录转变的方式就是在这一全新的空间拍摄人群。街头群众通过时尚和消费来自由地表现自己，他们自身就是艺术。历经了多年的压迫之后，艺术家、镜头和街头的人群都在欣喜若狂地创建自己新的身份。到了九十年代，摄影家们开始试用闪光灯、超广角镜头和非构图拍摄等技巧，他们的视角和观念也更多地通过镜头呈现出来，这些从他们对图片的处理和对大幅面冲印技术的应用中不难看到。与此同时，摩天楼也开始勾勒出中国城市文化的变革和它由平面文化到立体文化的转变。具有讽刺意义的是，尽管摩天楼让照片看起来更现代，如同三十年代郎静山和敖恩洪的照片看起来很现代一样，九十年代照片的垂直化与其说是对现代建筑的赞颂，不如说是在向它挑战。今天，随着生活变得越来越垂直化，以及地盘一寸寸地让位于摩天楼，在可建地有限的上海，扁平化的街头生活正在消失。作为回应，城市摄影似乎变得越来越以表现力为本，也越来越显得观念化。《通往天堂的阶梯》记录了这一非凡的对艺术创造的个案研究，使参观者感到他们如同生活在层层展现开的艺术历史中。针对这样一种背景，徐淦的文章探讨了艺术史与艺术家及其作品的相关性。

　　徐淦生长于毛泽东时代的中国，后来到美国读研究生。他目前任教于缅因州的波特兰缅因艺术学院。徐淦是历年来第一位从国外大学获得艺术史博士学位的中国人。尽管如此，他多年来一直与中国的艺术家和学者保持着紧密的联系，他现在仍然不断往返于上海与波特兰之间。他在文章中从局内者与局外者的双重角度阐述了现代中国摄影中纪念碑与摩天楼的关系。他融合了自己的观点和对这些艺术家的直接了解，深入挖掘目前中国这一最常见的主题，即哀悼与欢庆的冲突及其悲剧性和伪善性。徐淦将中国历史中当前这一幕置于他的讨论范围，结合了毛泽东的"大跃进"与"文化大革命"、邓小平的"开放政策"、净土宗传统与五世纪的诗歌来研究中国的新的摩天建筑。他试图弄清楚，摩天大楼是否已经成为大众的历史性的中国式乌托邦幻想和梦想的翻版。无论高耸入云的公寓楼是否标志着新版的比"美国梦"更具悠久传统的"中国梦"，我们都看到了摩天楼作为变革的象征已经成为中国发展的正面的和负面的核心所在。徐淦在一篇出色的评论文章中指出，梁卫平创作的，后来已经被拆除了的那些工厂的影象，代表了当初一段为数不多的成功的工业化的历史，现在那段历史已经褪色了。而杨泳梁的作品中经数码技术处理过的影象揭示了行进中的起重机如何筑起摩天大楼，却践踏了中华民族的五千年文明。当摩天楼升起在历史残垒之上时，中国的长城却在马六明那著名的行为艺术中碎成废片。在张大力的《拆》系列中紫禁城中的庙宇正在受到侵犯；在洪磊创造的影象中，历史被鲜血抹去。也宁的《游园京梦》系列记录了摩天楼的发展，哀悼着历史，憧憬着她已不再熟悉的城市将为她保留什么。罗永进以他客观冷静的图片剖析，记录了那些一度以特色服务取胜的大型加油站如何让位于毫无生气的世界上随处可见的加油站。在邢丹文的《都市演绎》中，亮丽的色彩并不能掩饰发展受到阻碍过程中城市生活的单调乏味。空中新的天堂中阴暗的一面实际上很可能正是对乌托邦式集体理想主义的疏离与绝望。

在对罗永进、邢丹文和张大力的直接采访中，策展人Raechell Smith引导艺术家们将他们自己的作品与生活放置于中国形势的巨变之中。他们讨论了数码世界与互联网如何使他们更有效更清醒地工作。但张大力认为，他把数码技术与互联网看成工具，这些工具的使用并不影响他对艺术的理解，相反却为他提供了更多的可能。真正改变了他们艺术创作的是他们处于其中的城市景观本身：骑自行车所面对的危险、北京人口从四百万到一千三百万的剧增、老居民区的拆迁、建筑的发展和农村人口自由大量地涌入城市，简而概之就是总体生活水平的提高。三位艺术家无一例外地认为他们的作品是通过现在连接过去，为我们评判和洞察未来。他们希望他们今天的作品将超越时代，让未来的观众了解我们的现在和他们的过去。做为中国艺术史一部分的近期的中国艺术是如此地激进，艺术家们确实感慨他们为了艺术更加繁荣更具流动性而做出的牺牲，有时他们不得不在社区利益与个人独立性、继承中国文化和维护全球统一文化之间做出权衡。

采访中讨论的诸多话题涉及了技术、变化的环境、城市化、资本主义、艺术市场及历史的角色等各个方面，却又不断地绕回到建筑和城市空间变化的因果关系这一主题。罗永进解释说，"我希望人们会明白，在二十一世纪开始之际，曾经有过一些感觉敏锐的艺术家，他们敢于嘲讽和怀疑时髦的建筑，却能将这些呆板的建筑物变成美味的艺术品。" 还有什么能比王净那绝妙的奥运会建筑与中国食物片段系列，《2008年中国食品》，更让人垂涎欲滴呢？

我相信，因毛泽东的压制饱受摧残而荒芜已久的中国艺术以其巨大的产量一定会得到人们的赞赏。谁能想到中国的艺术家们在离群索居之后，能在一代人之间迅速恢复他们的能量和创造力而将生机勃勃的中国艺术带入全球艺术世界的前沿呢？

衷心感谢策展助理Emily Monty和Rachel Tofel为展览所作的研究工作，使本篇介绍得以成形。

Streets 街道

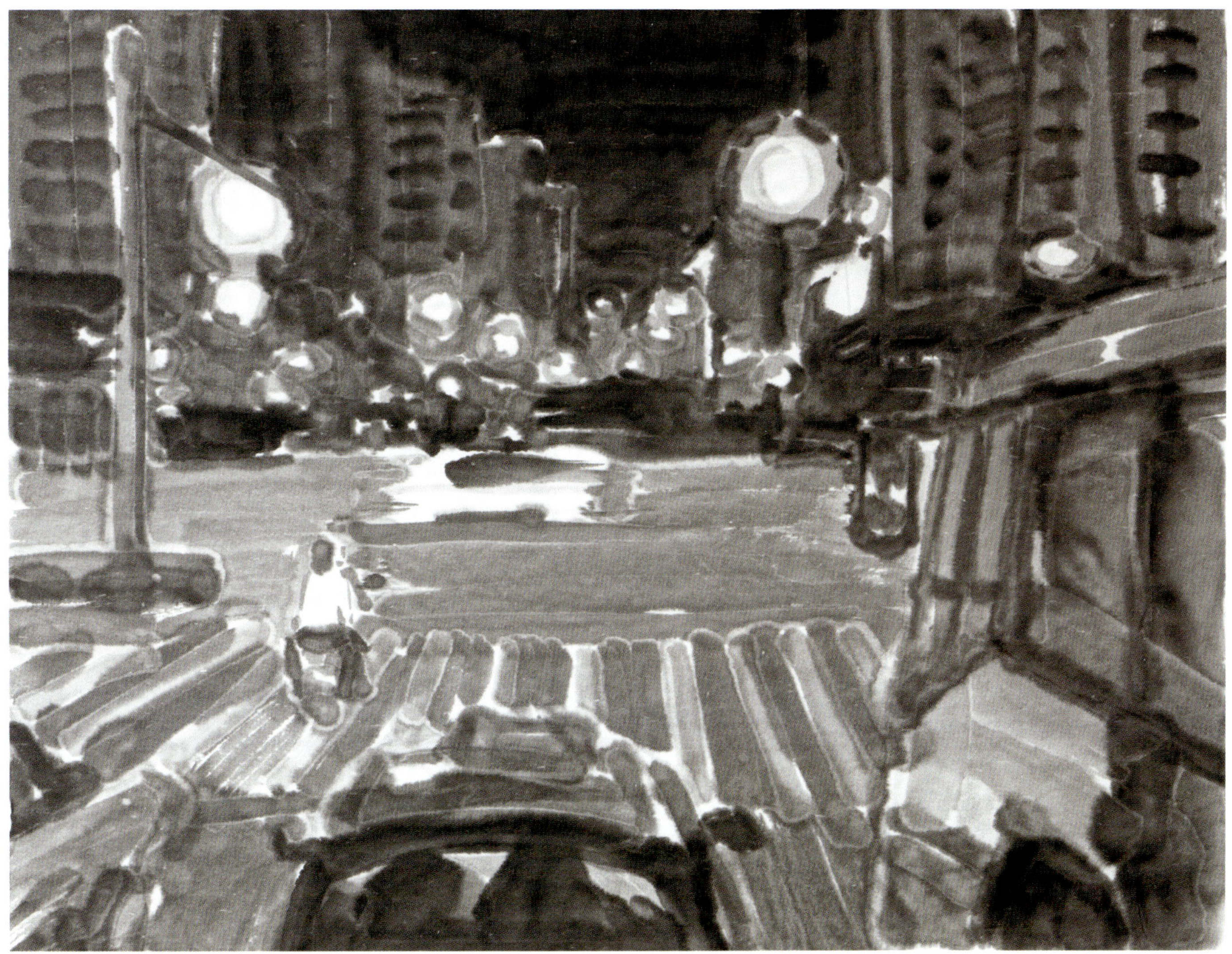

CHEN SHAOXIONG 陈劭雄 *Ink City*, 2005

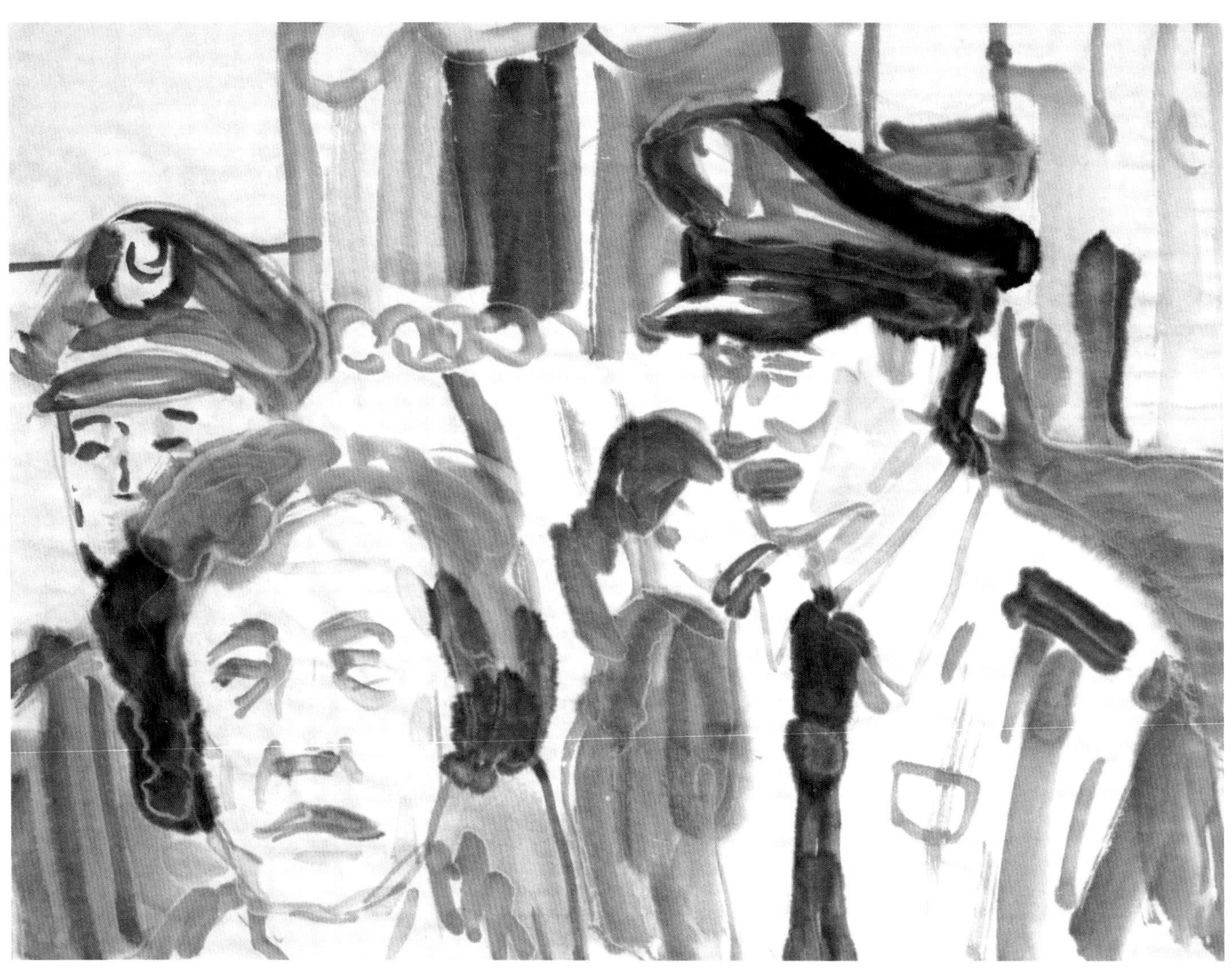

CHEN SHAOXIONG 陈劭雄 *Ink City*, 2005

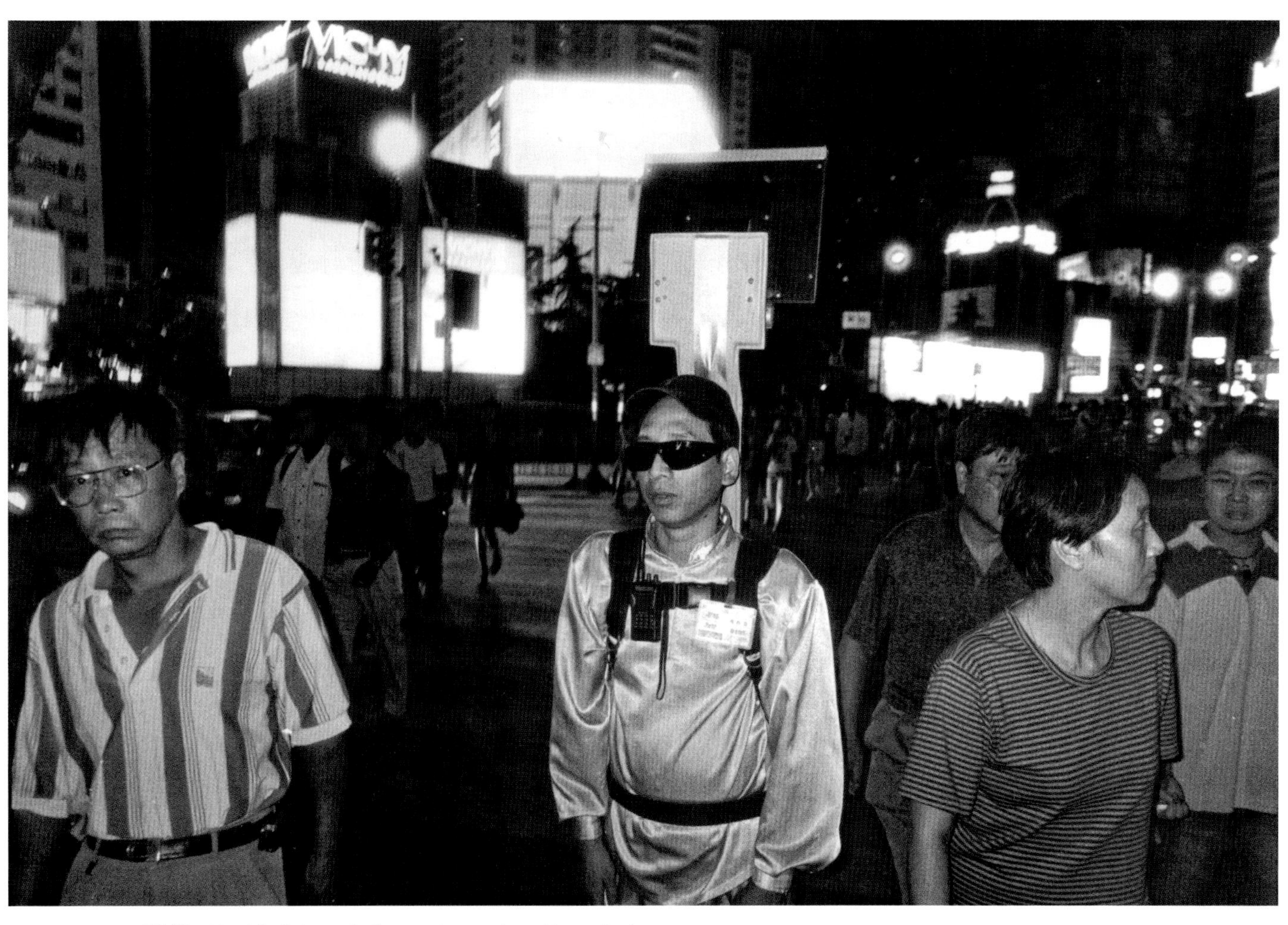

GU ZHENG 顾铮 *Untitled (no. 1)*, from the series *Shanghai*, 2004

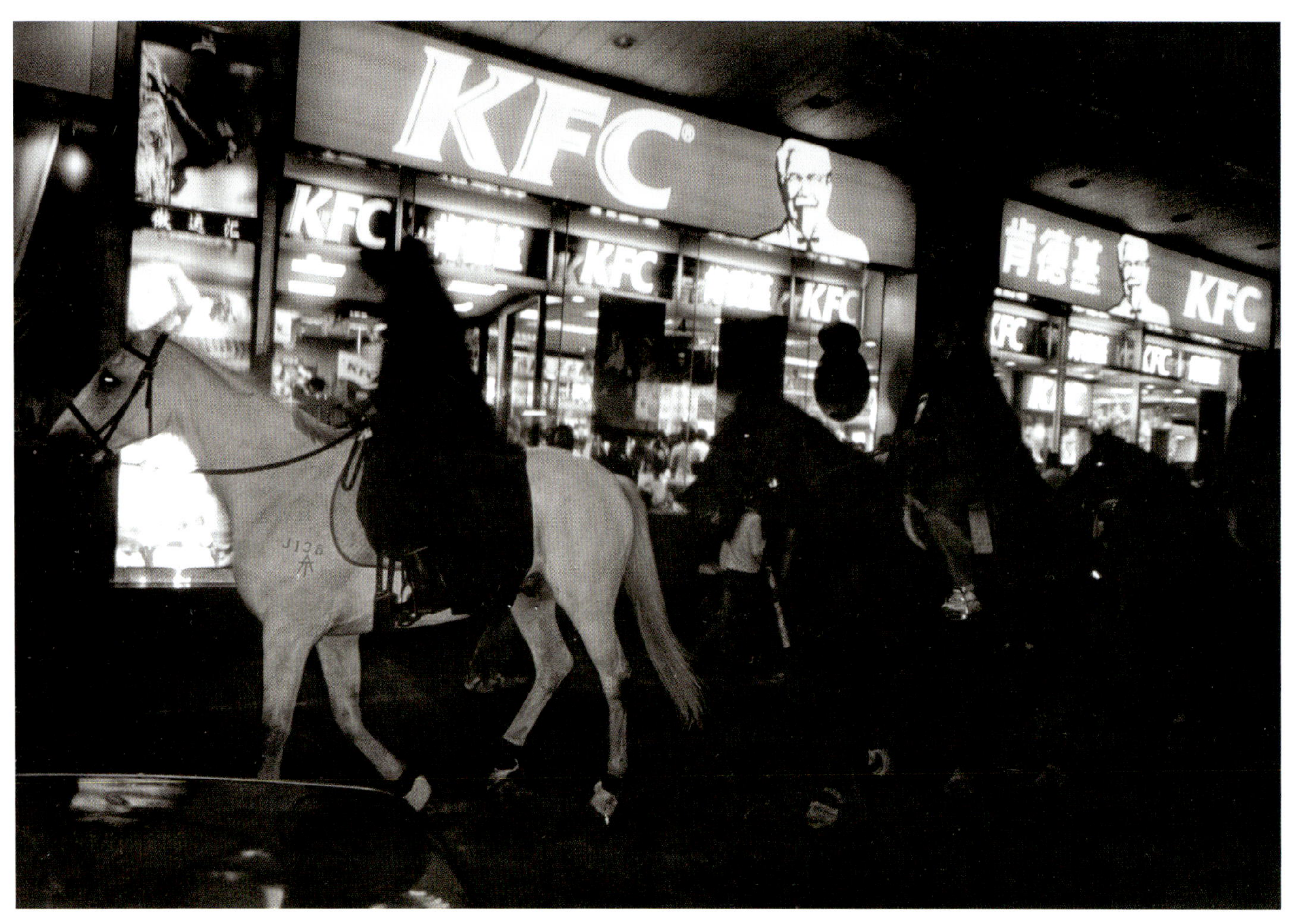

GU ZHENG 顾铮 *Untitled (no. 4)*, from the series *Shanghai*, 2004

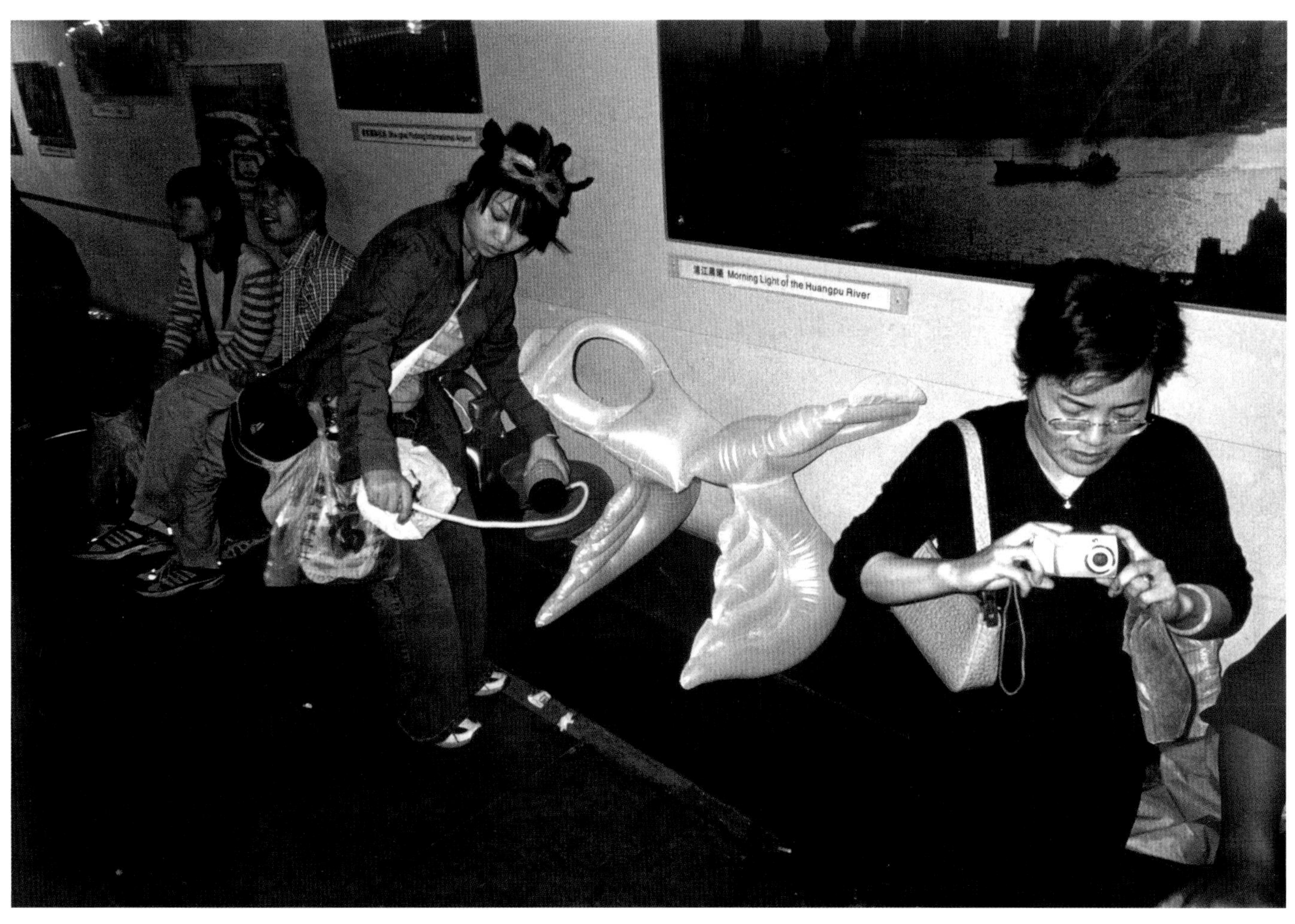

GU ZHENG 顾铮 *Untitled (no. 5)*, from the series *Shanghai*, 2004

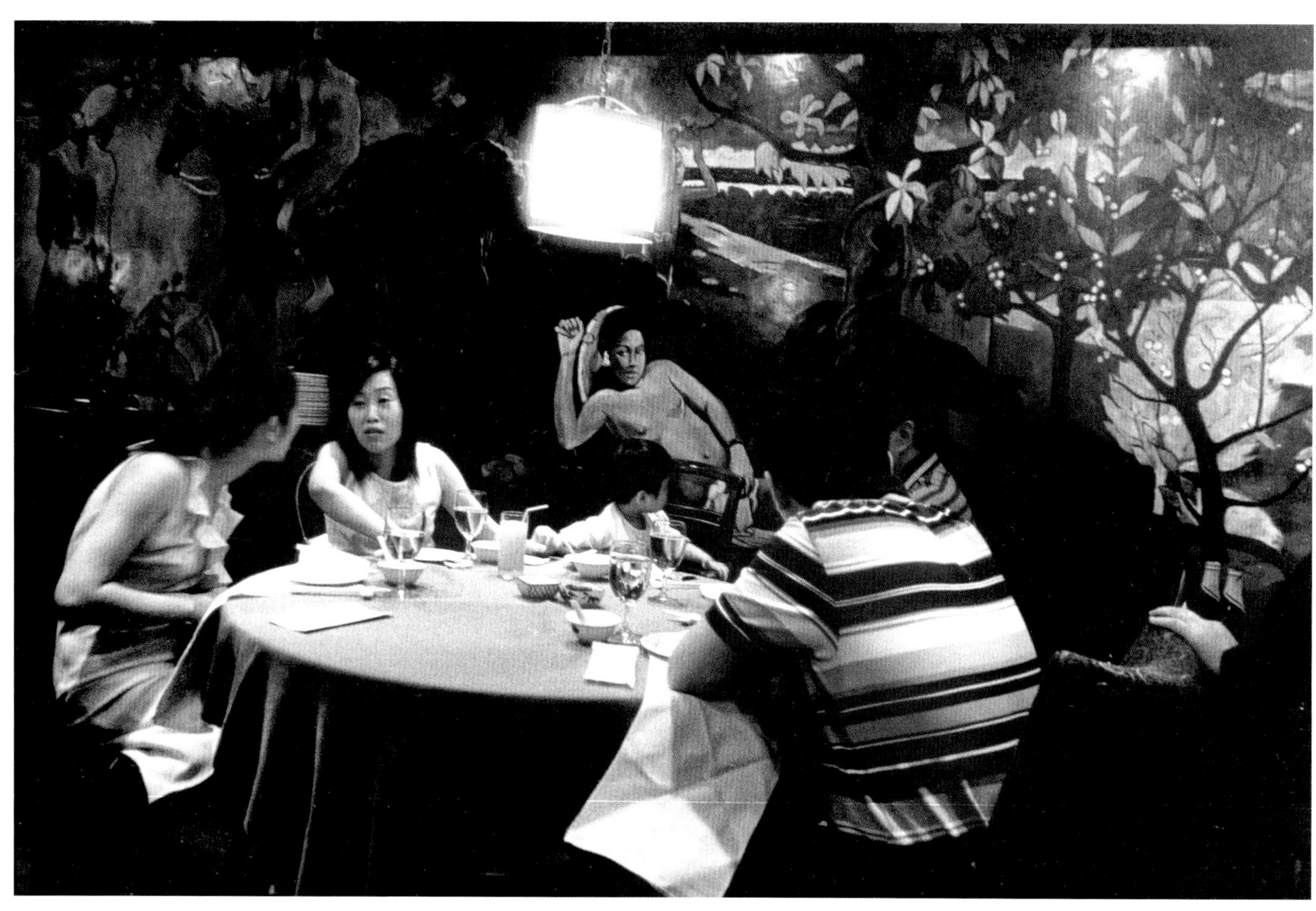

GU ZHENG 顾铮 *Untitled (no. 6)*, from the series *Shanghai*, 2004

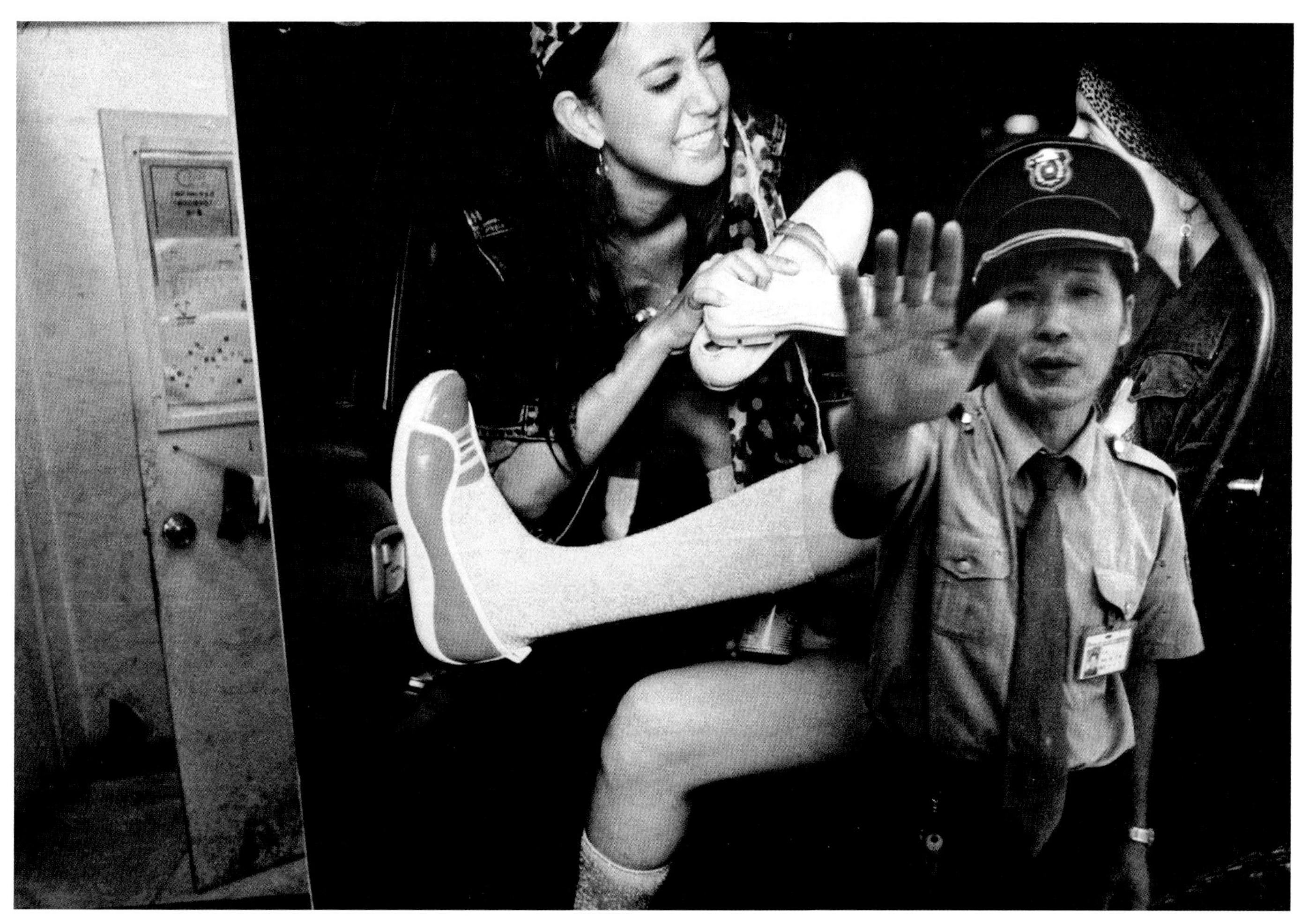

GU ZHENG 顾铮 *Untitled (no. 7)*, from the series *Shanghai*, 2004

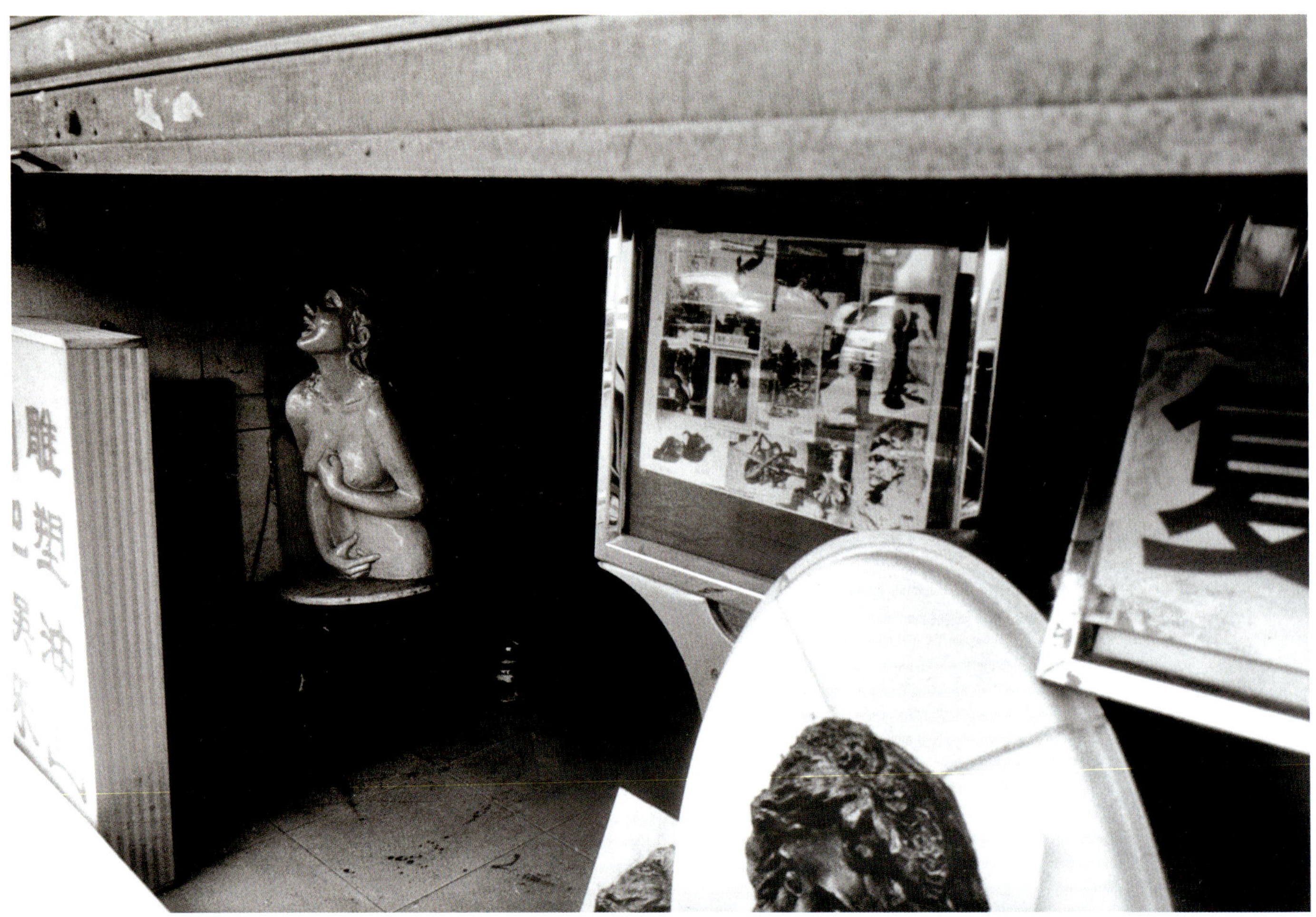

GU ZHENG 顾铮 *Untitled (no. 10)*, from the series *Shanghai*, 2004

24

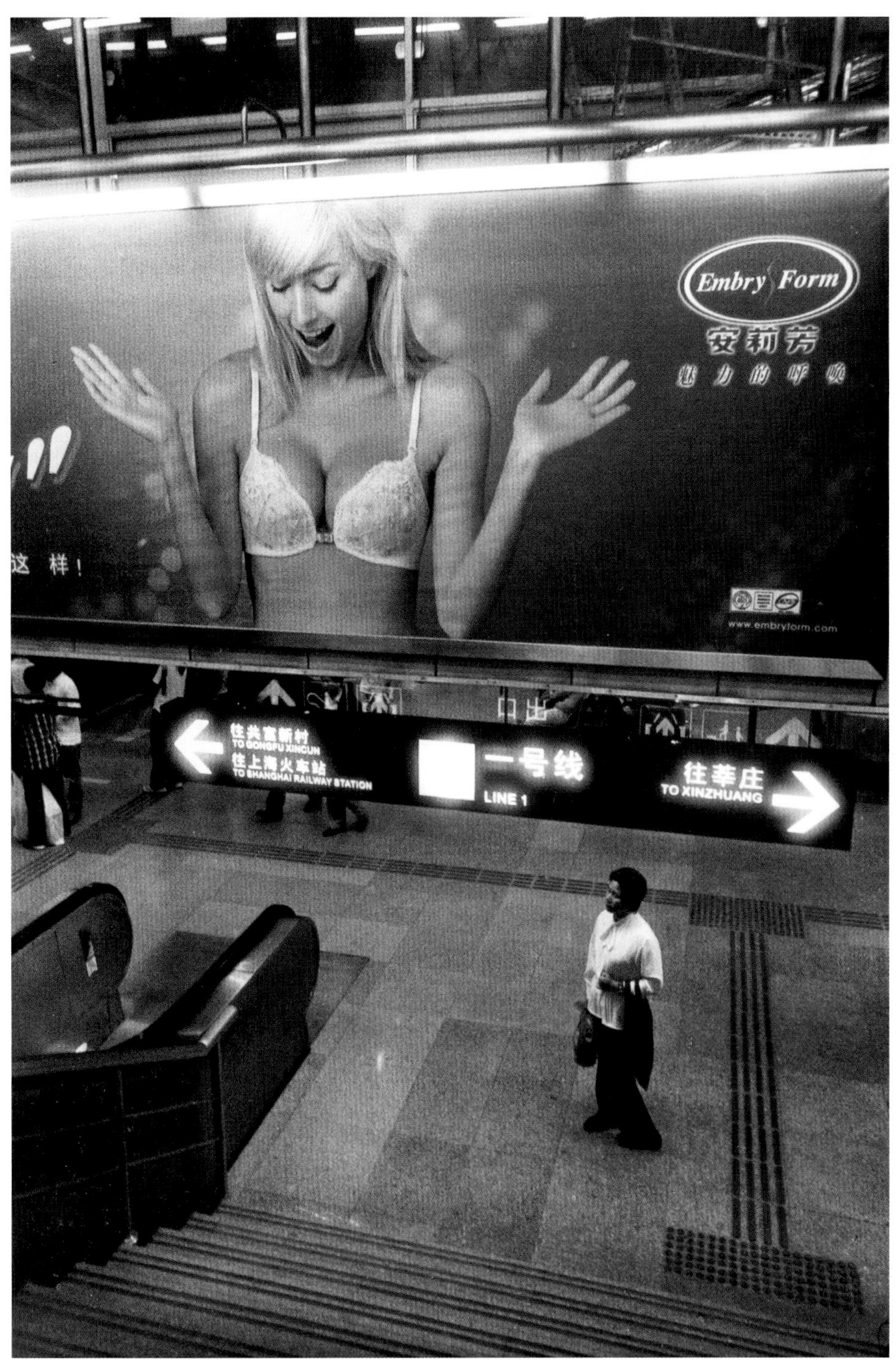

GU ZHENG 顾铮 *Untitled (no. 2)*, from the series *Shanghai*, 2004

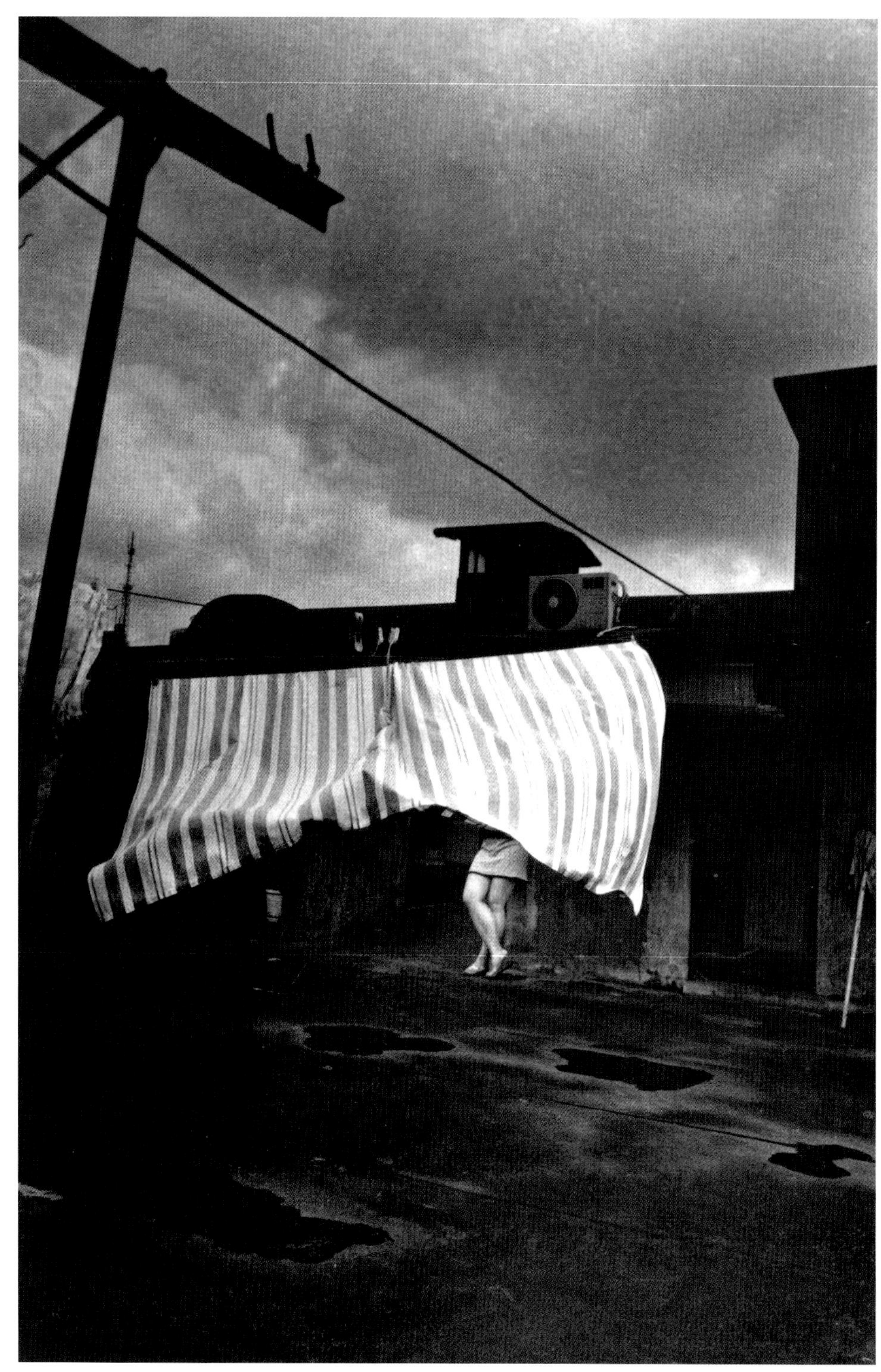

GU ZHENG 顾铮 *Untitled (no. 3),*
from the series *Shanghai*, 2004

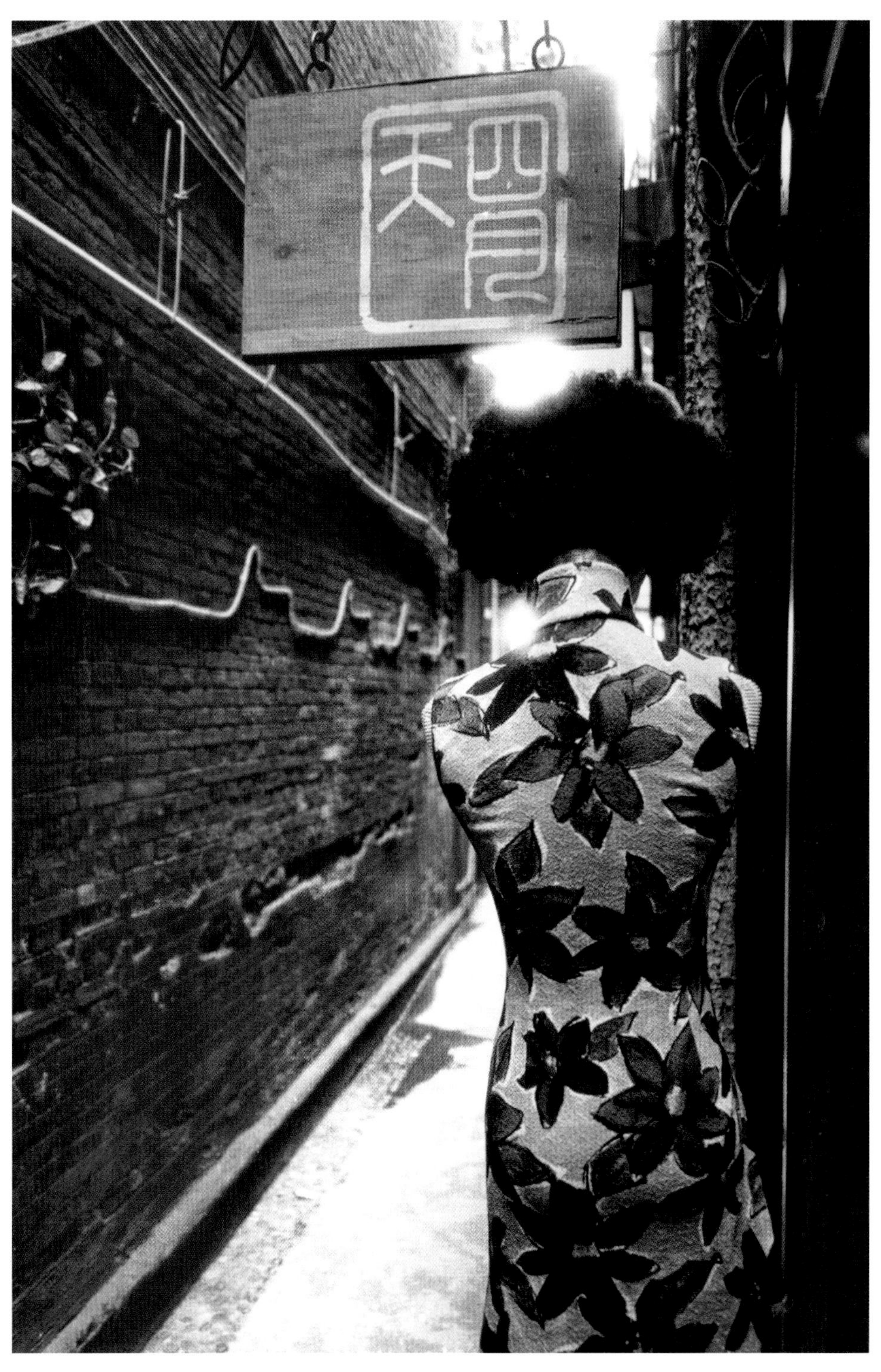

GU ZHENG 顾铮 *Untitled (no. 8)*,
from the series *Shanghai*, 2004

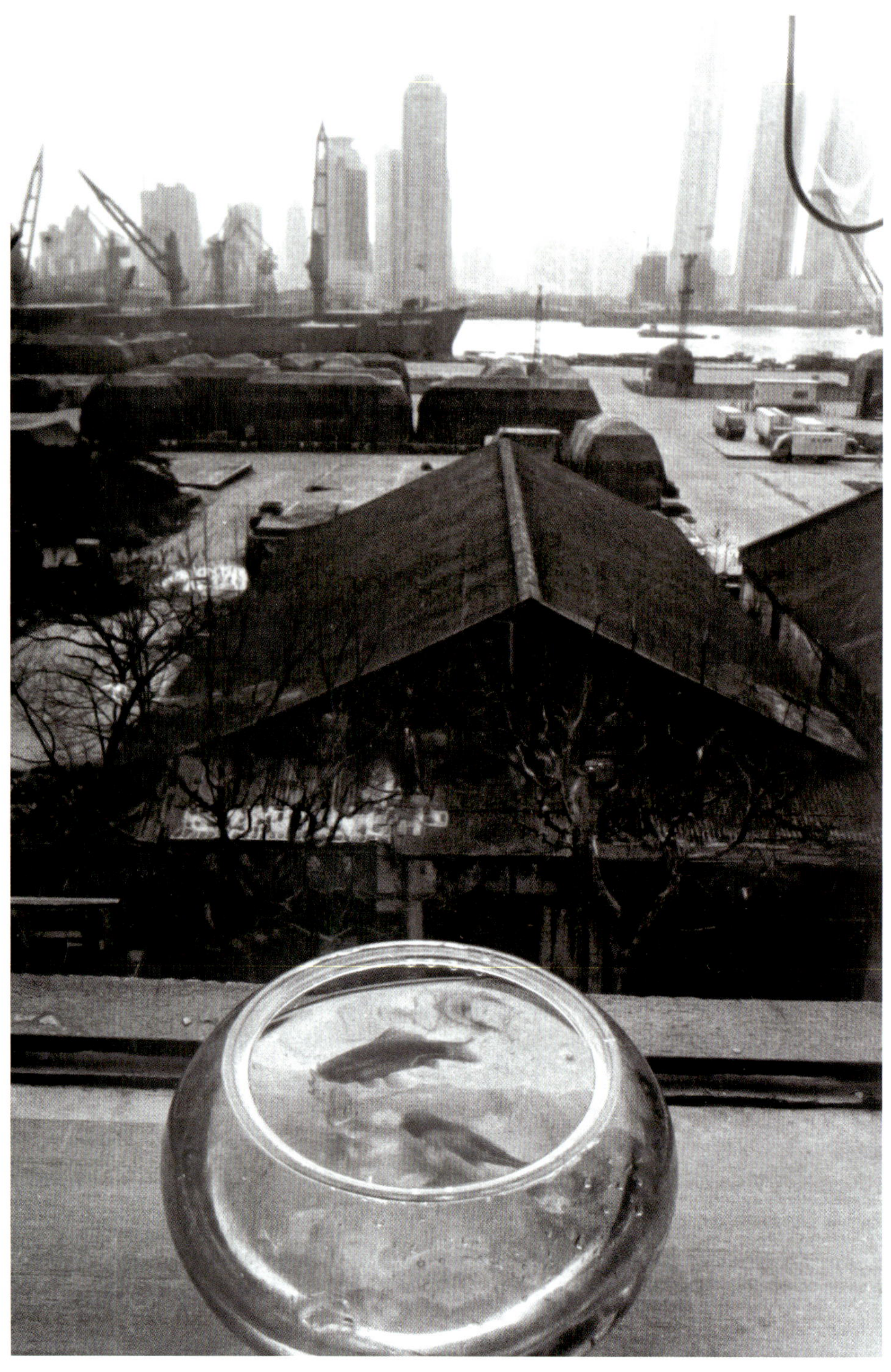

28

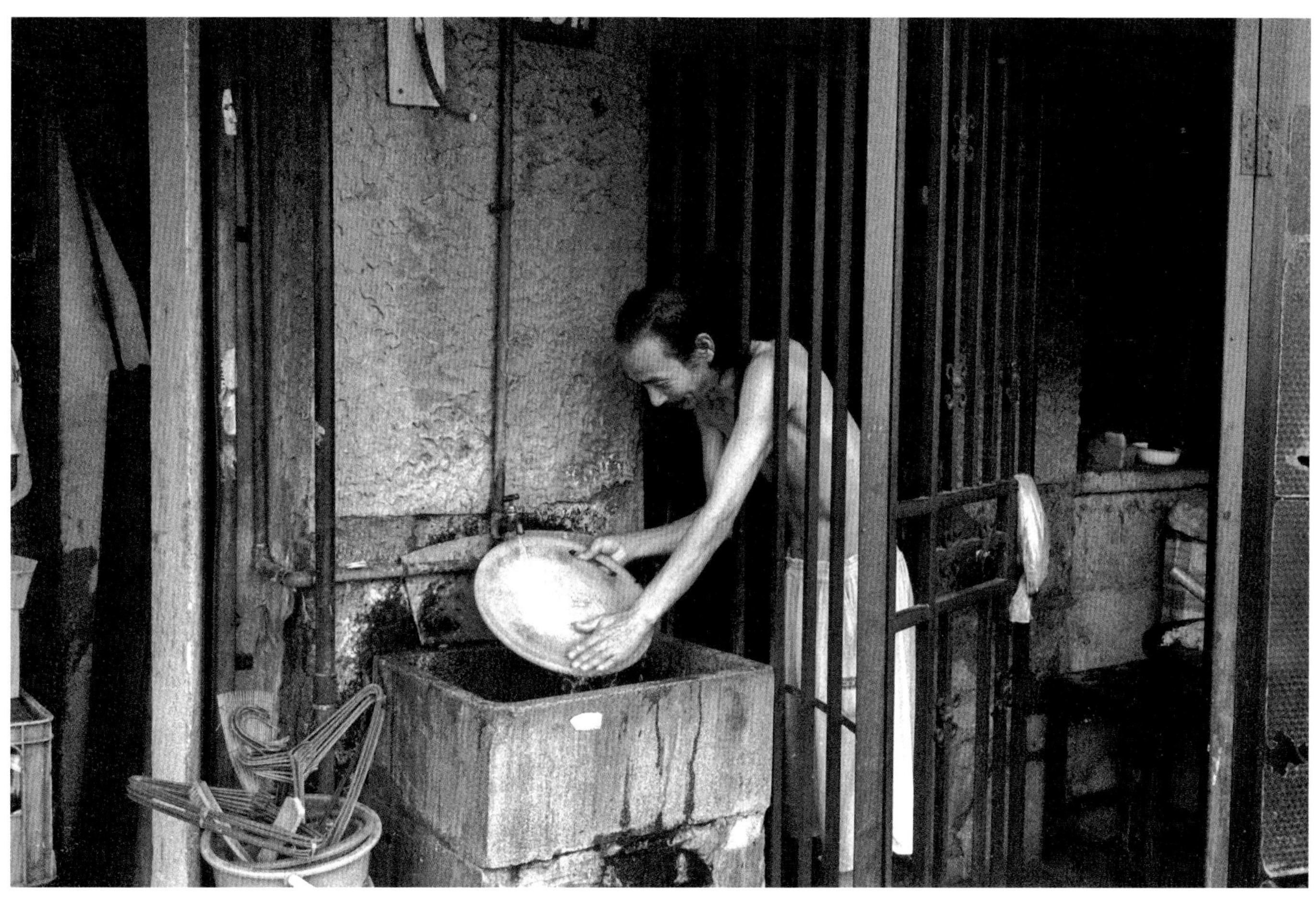

LIANG WEIPING 梁卫平 *Untitled (no. 2)*, 2006

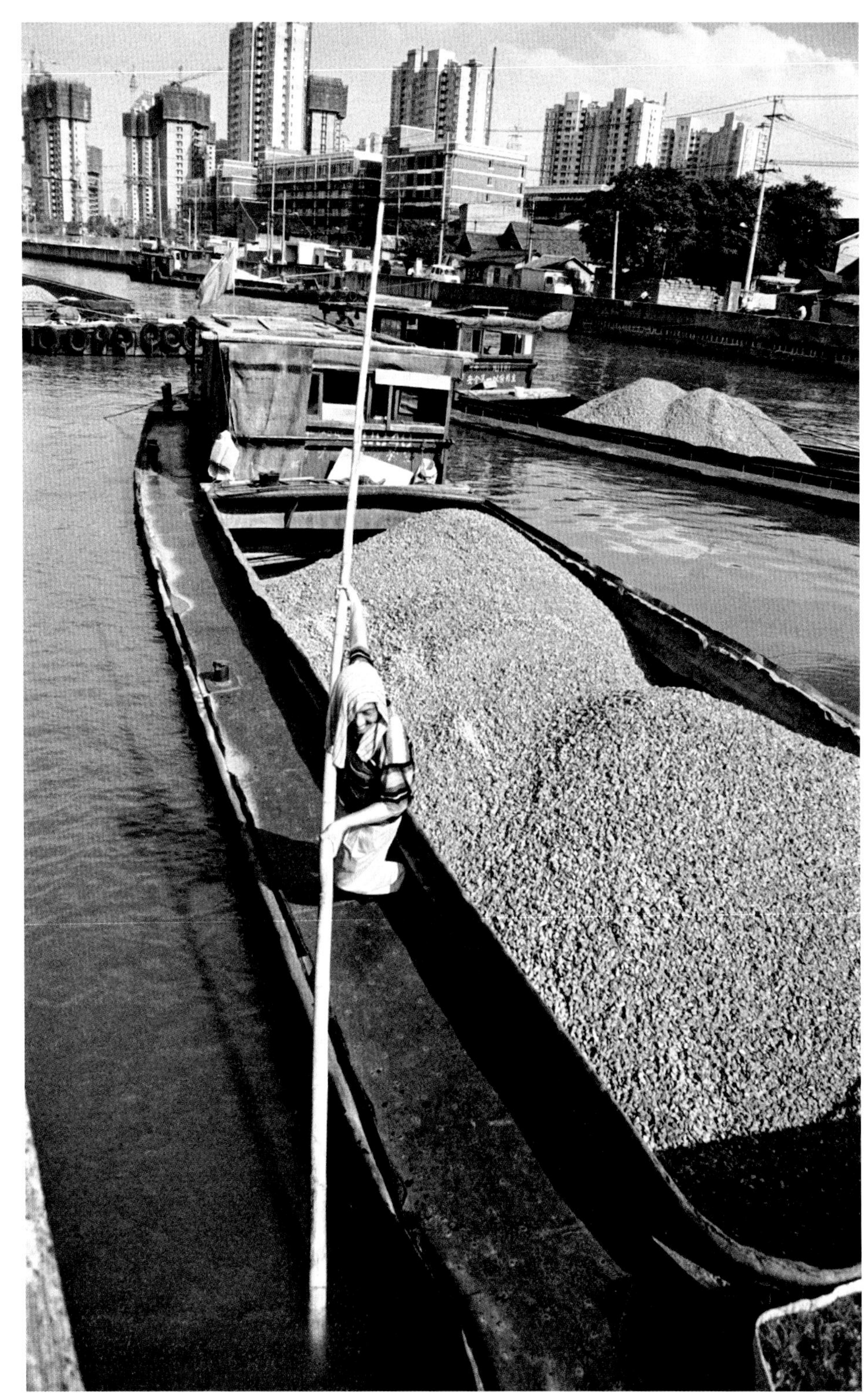

LIANG WEIPING 梁卫平 *Untitled*
(*no. 4*), 2006

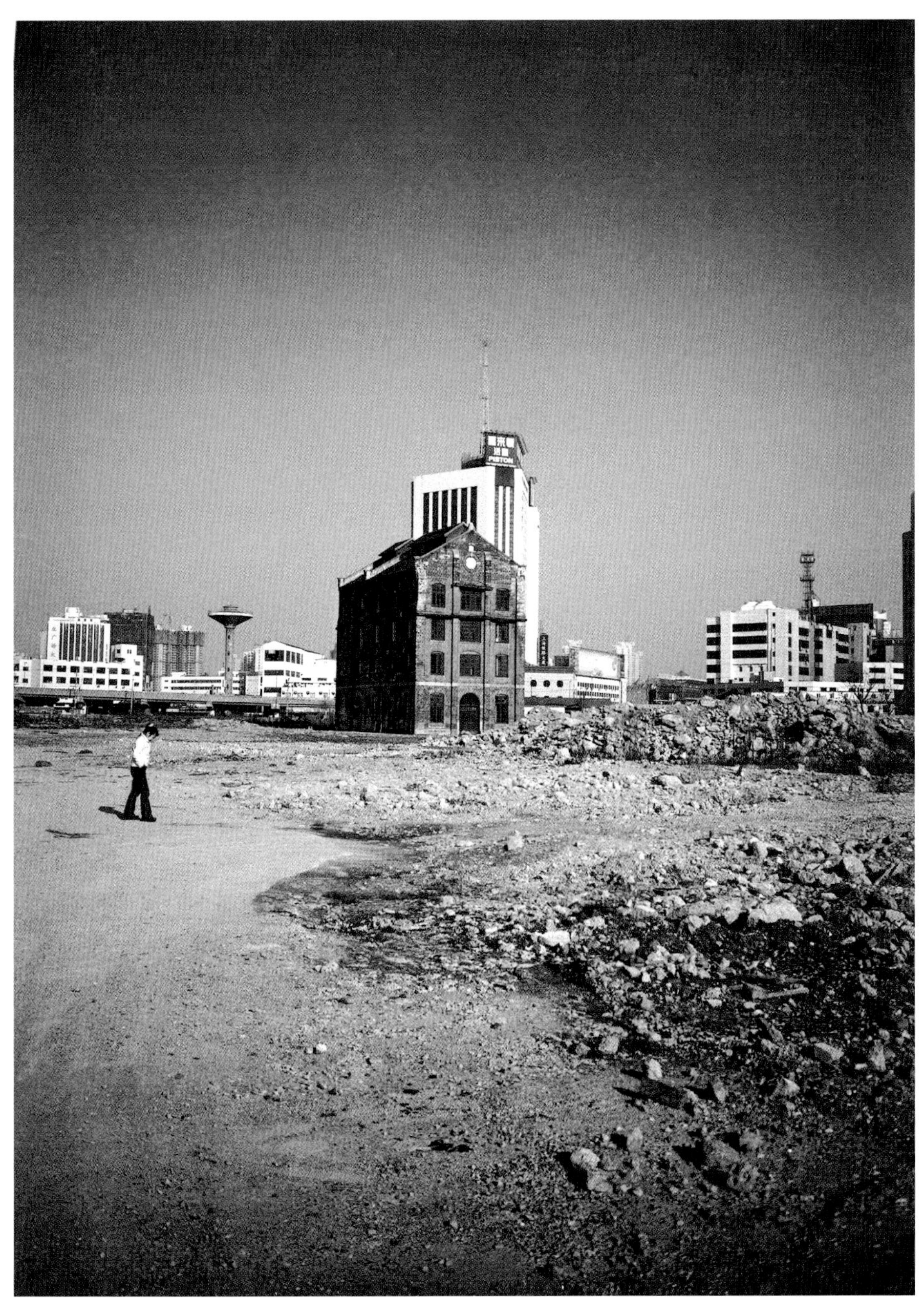

LIANG WEIPING 梁卫平 *Untitled (no. 3)*, 2006

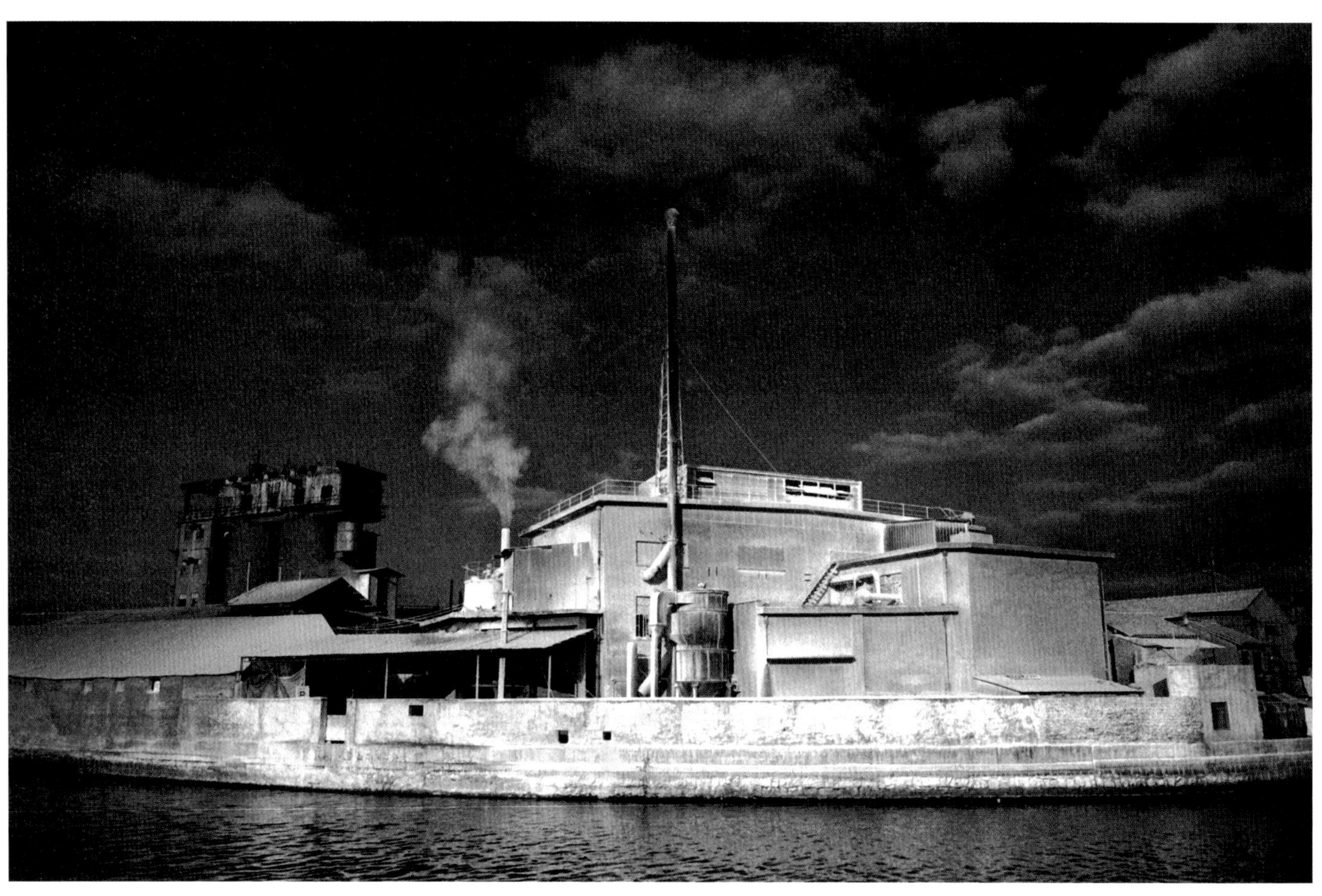

LIANG WEIPING 梁卫平 *Untitled (no. 1)*, 2006

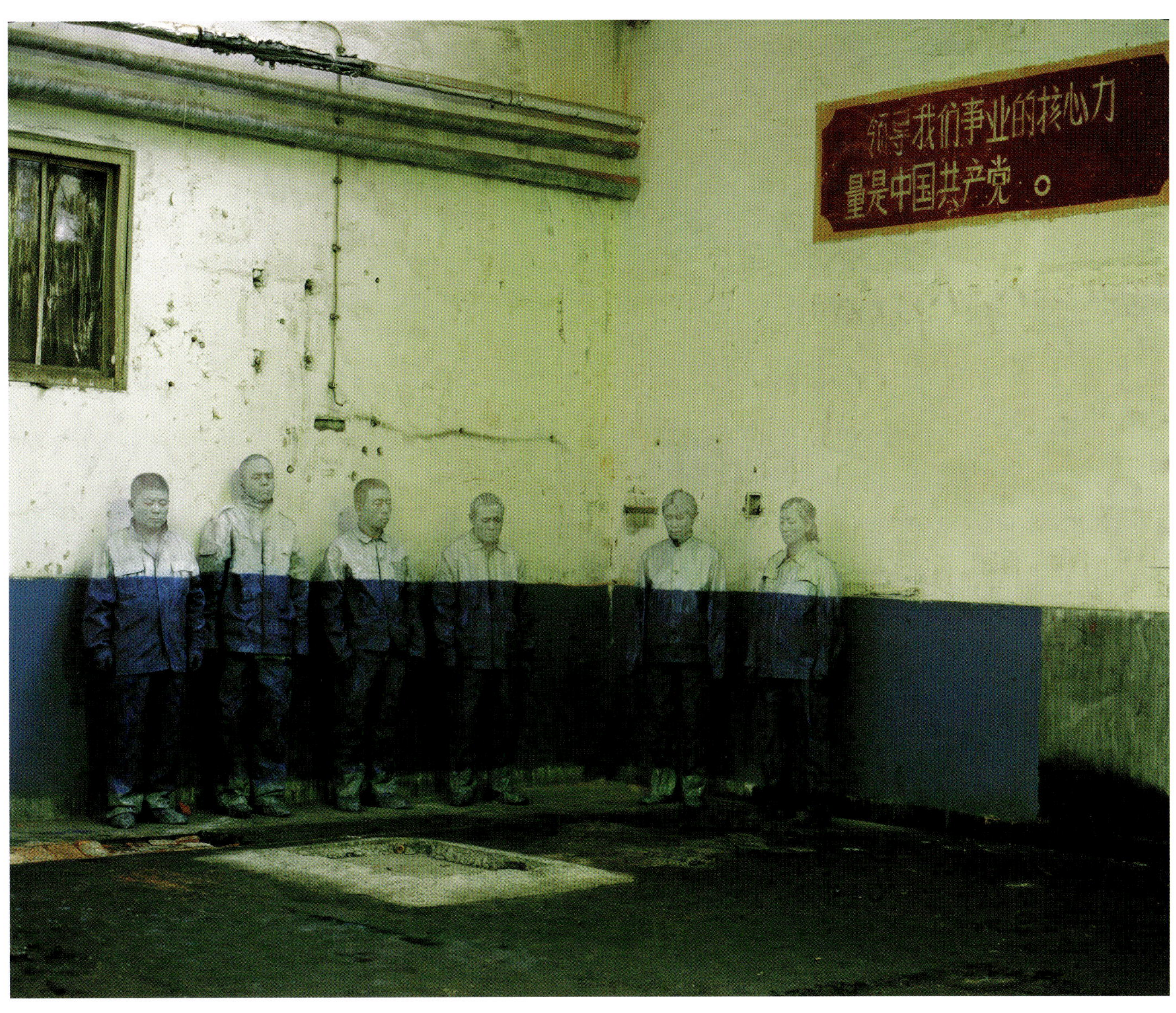

LIU BOLIN 刘勃麟 *Laid Off*, from the series *Hidden in the City*, 2006

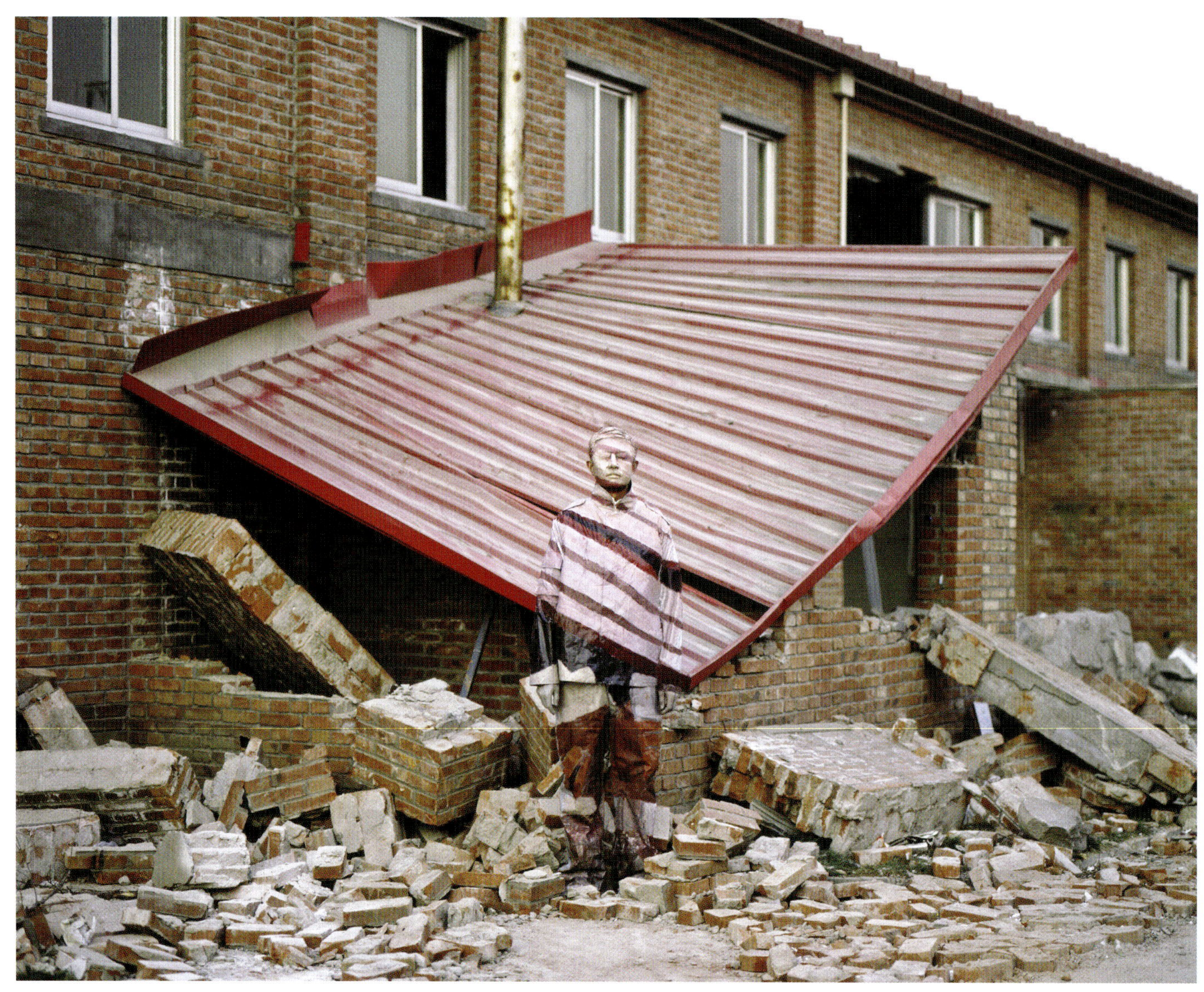

LIU BOLIN 刘勃麟 *Suo Jia*, from the series *Hidden in the City*, 2006

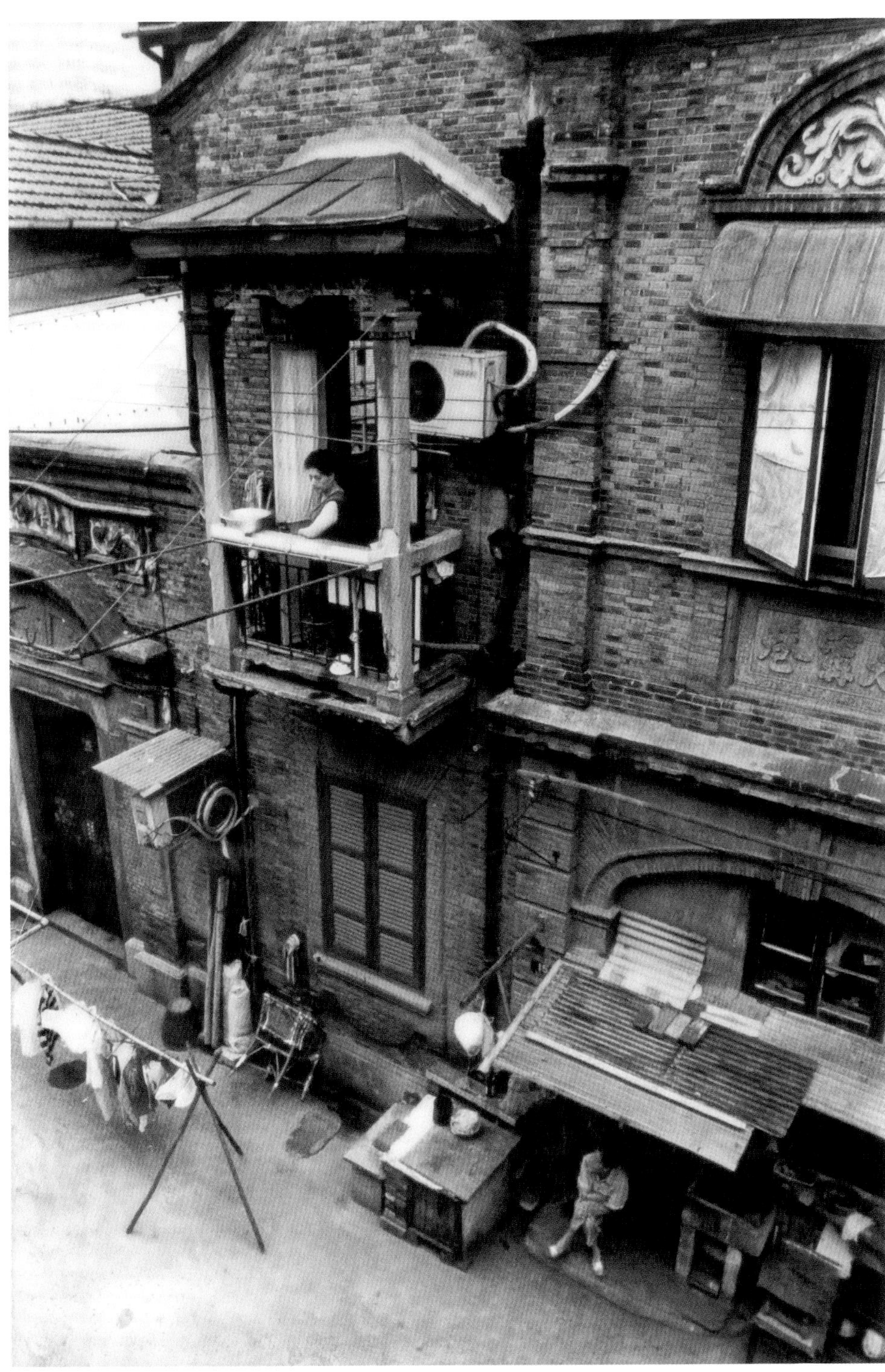

LU YUANMIN 陆元敏 *Untitled
(no. 2),* from the series
Shanghainese, 1990–2000

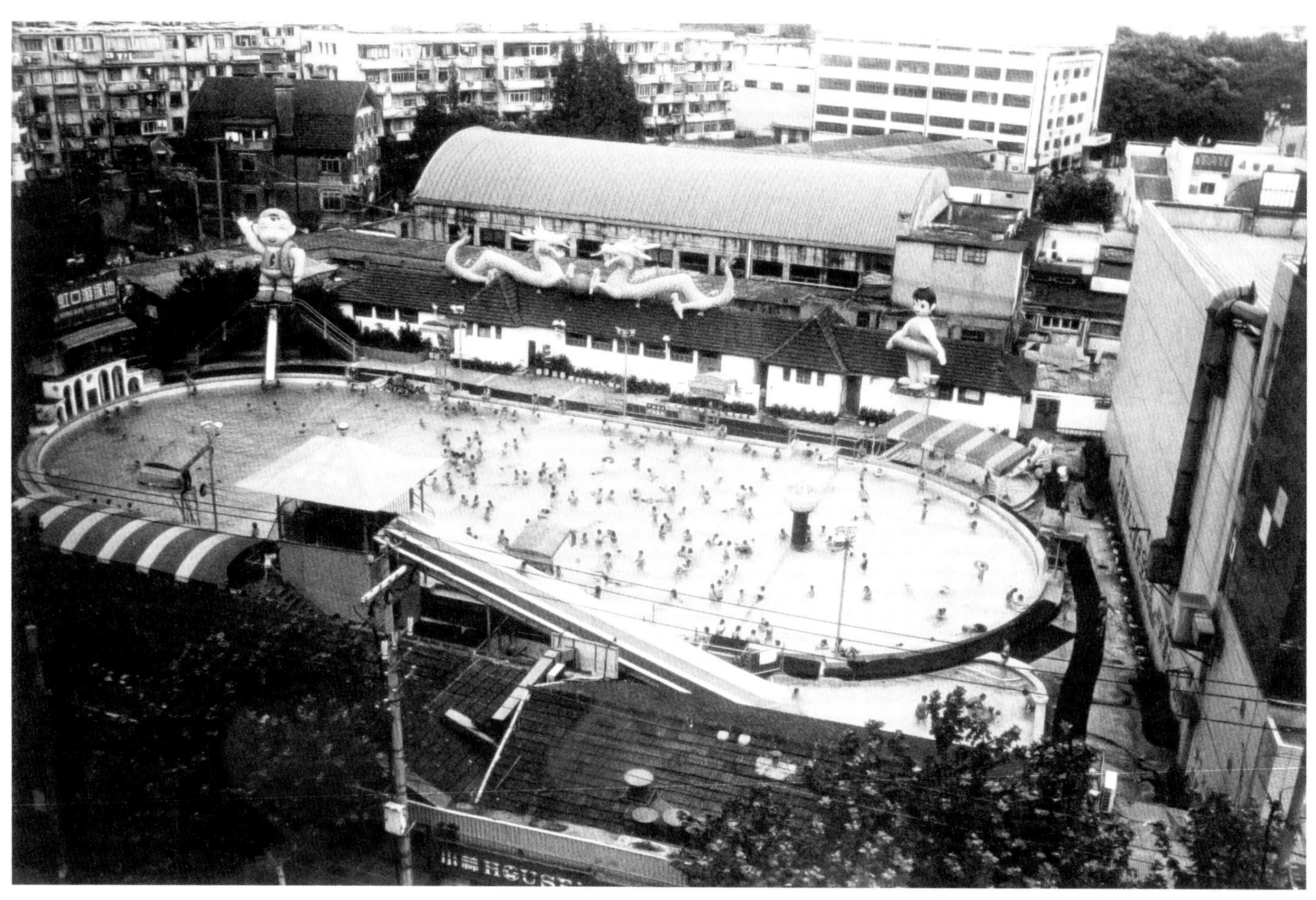

LU YUANMIN 陆元敏 *Untitled (no. 1)*, from the series *Shanghainese*, 1990–2000

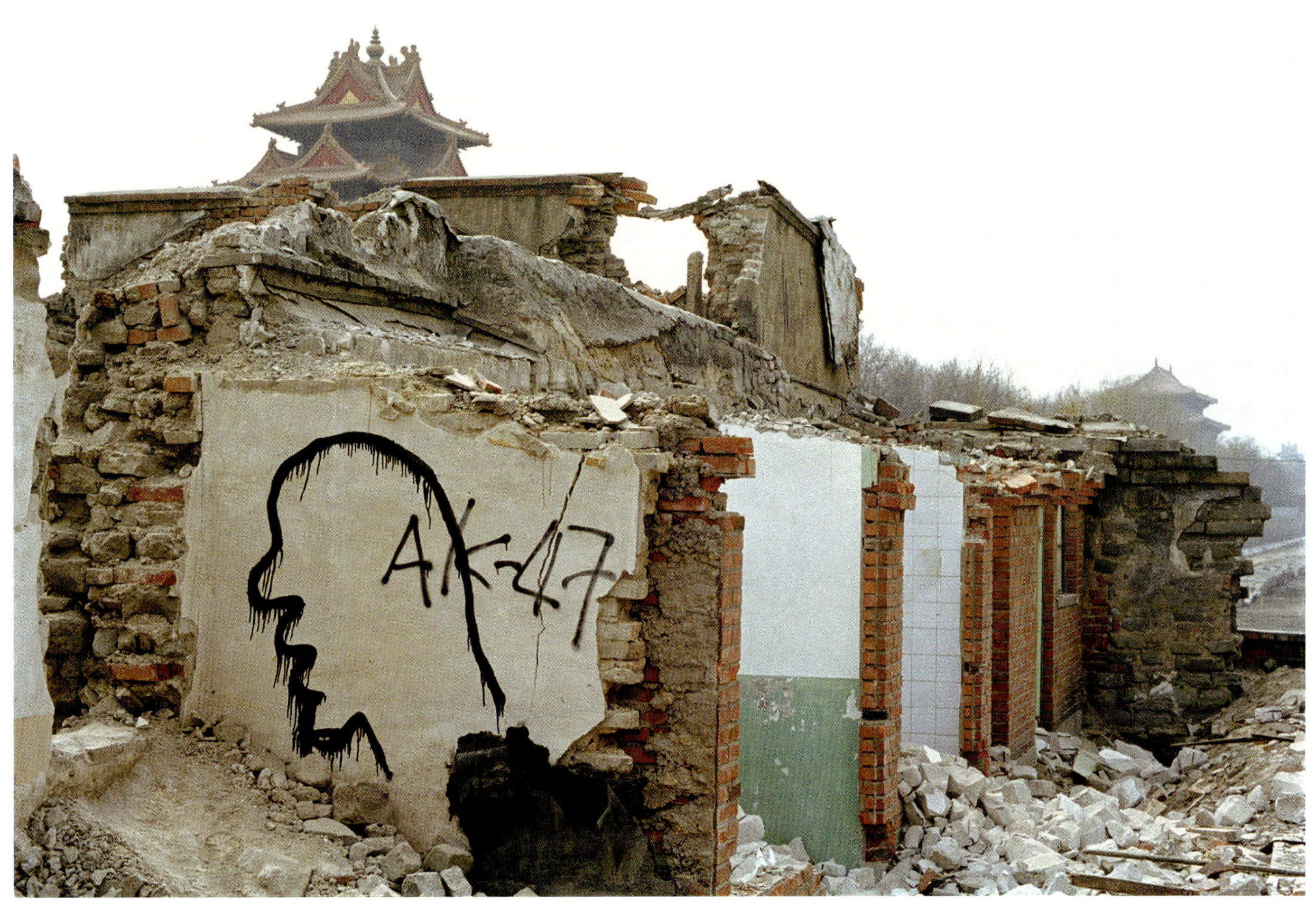

ZHANG DALI 张大力 *Dialogue Forbidden City*, 1999

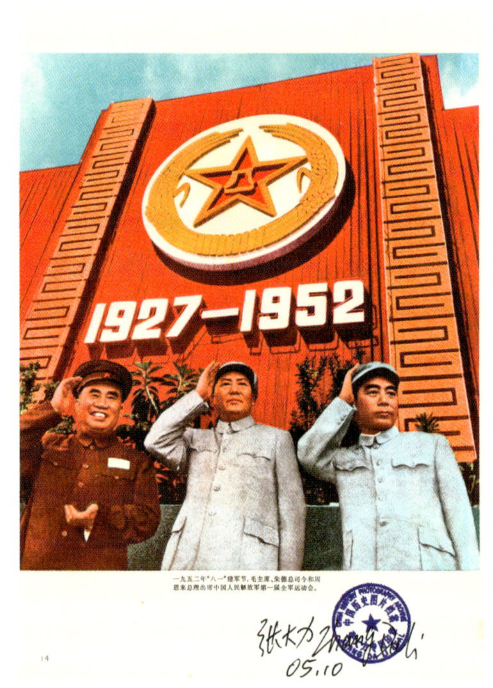

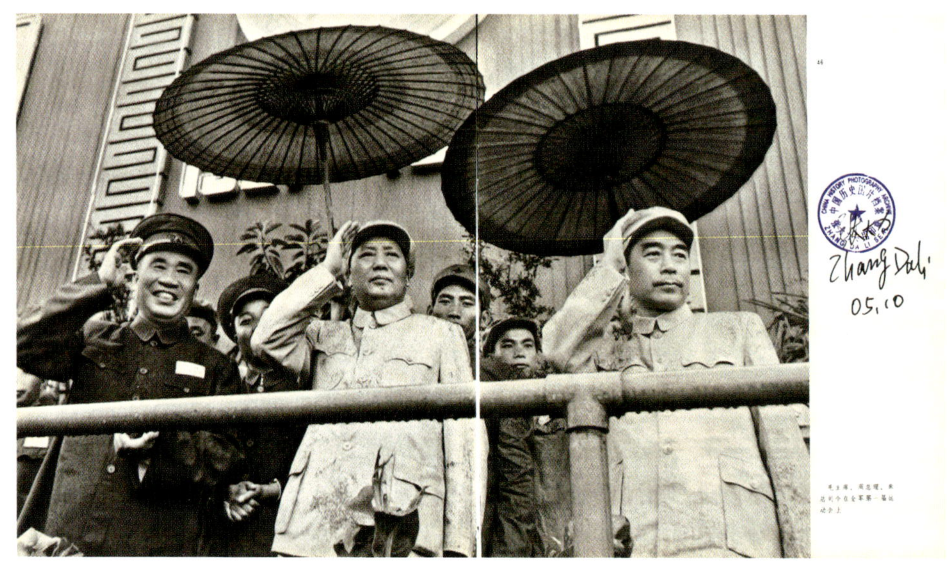

ZHANG DALI 张大力 *The First Sports Meeting of the National Army, 1952*, from the series *A Second History*, 2006

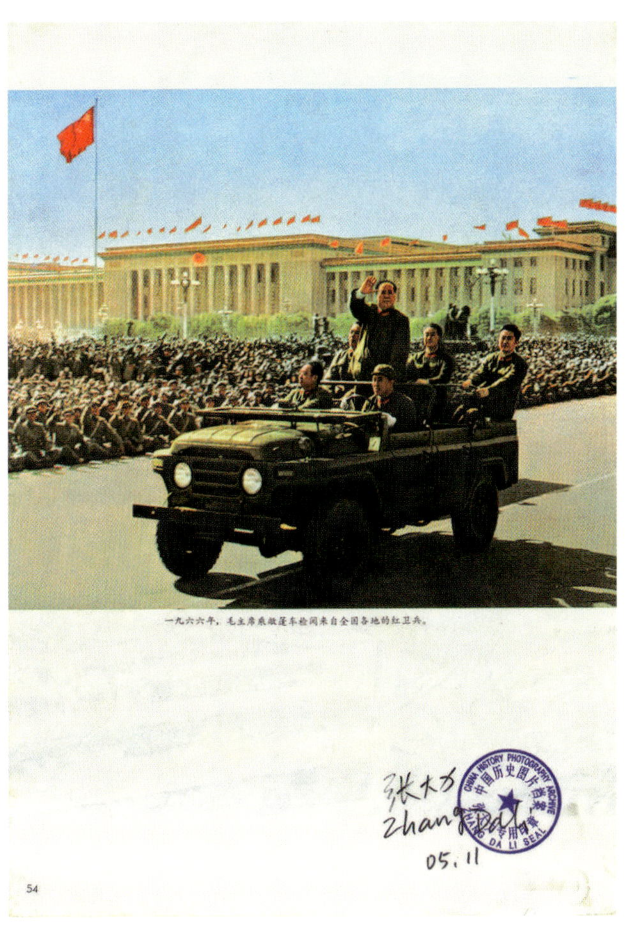

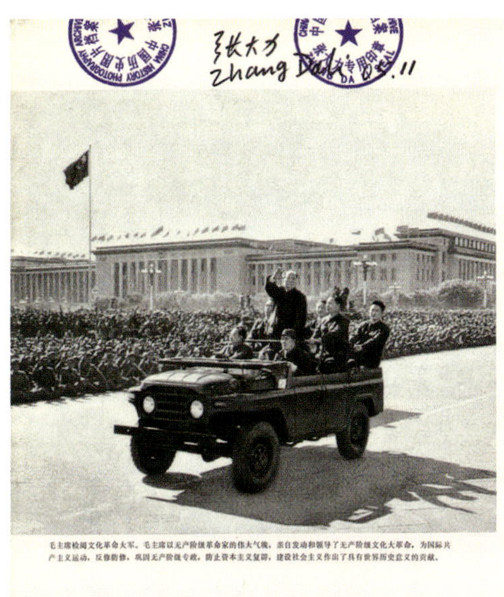

ZHANG DALI 张大力 *Chairman Mao Reviewing Red Guards, 1966,* from the series *A Second History,* 2006

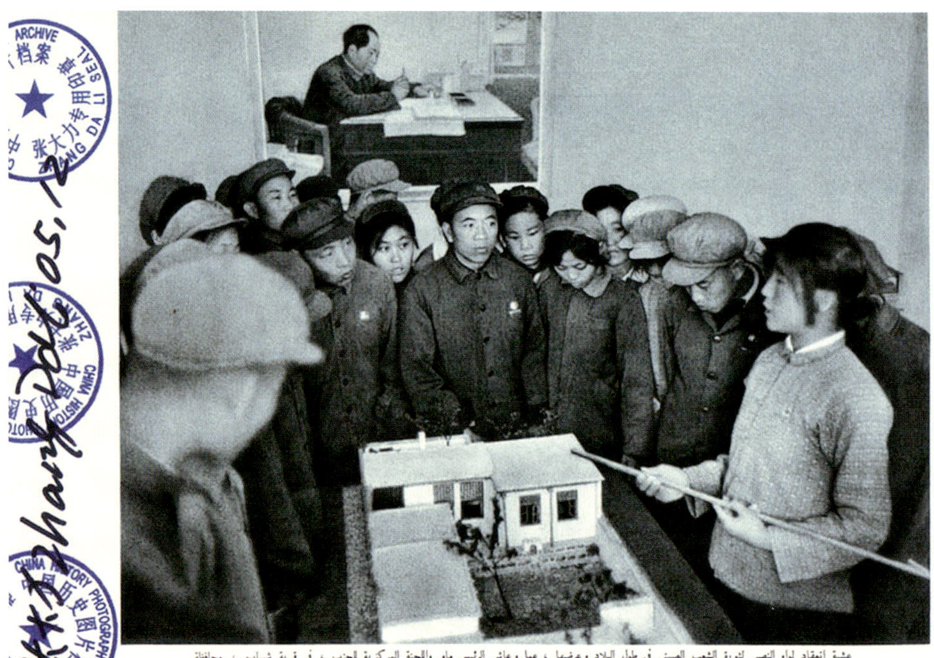

عشية انعقاد لواء النصر لثورة الشعب الصيني في طول البلاد وعرضها ، عمل ومعاش الرئيس ماو واللجنة المركزية للحزب ، في قرية شيبايبو ، محافظة
بينغشان ، مقاطعة خابابي لمدة قصيرة . وفي تلك القرية ألقى الرئيس ماو " تقرير الى الدورة العامة الثانية للجنة الحزب الشيوعي الصيني المركزية السابعة "
الذي هو تقرير ذو مغزى تاريخي عظيم . في هذا التقرير أشار الرئيس ماو بحصافة الى أنه "بعد القضاء على الأعداء المتبدلين سيبقى هناك أعداء غير متبدلين.
ولا مناص لهم من النضال المستميت ضدنا ، لذلك لايجب أن نفض الطرف عنهم ." الصورة : عمال المعمل رقم ٤ المشتركون في صف دراسي يقدمون
الى قرية شيبايبو حيث يدرسون هذا التوجيه العظيم بناء على أحوال الصراع الطبقي في العمل

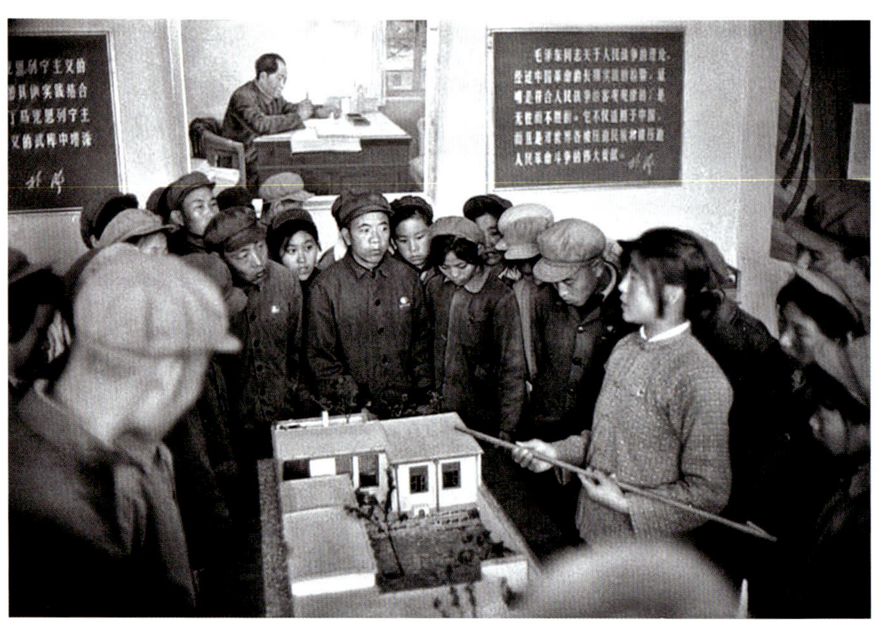

ZHANG DALI 张大力 *Organizing a Study Class Is a Good Method*, from the series *A Second History*, 2006

In contemporary Chinese urban photography images of the street and the skyscraper epitomize the current transitional phase of Chinese society. The artists in this exhibition are creating photographs that reflect and critique the evolving relationship between Chinese culture and the new culture of street and skyscraper.

Street life and its visual culture gained new ground due to the economic reforms of 1978 which encouraged and validated the surging economic activities of its citizens. A new private economy injected energy and life into the street allowing cities to embark on a journey of transformation, from industry-production centers to consumer-oriented cities. Average citizens began to participate in a nascent market economy and interact with a public space shaped more by commercial activities and advertising, realities that were previously banned under the state-controlled economy. Increasingly these new market forces formed the predominant elements and relationships that would redefine urban space. Commerce and vibrant economic activity were fresh elements inserted into public space and constituted a new spectacle, one that infiltrated private living space, prompting a different way of life and new set of values. The marketing of products, often through the use of photographic images, also visualized the expanded possibilities of a *modern* life that emphasized the value of the individual while promoting a new ideology of consumption.

The streets inevitably became the public space where the new ideology was market tested. The American urban critic Jane Jacobs has suggested:

> The trust of a city street is formed over time from many, many little public sidewalk contacts . . . Most of it [the contact] is ostensibly utterly trivial but the sum is not trivial at all. The sum of such casual, public contact at a local level—most of it fortuitous, most of it associated with errands, all of it metered by the person concerned and not thrust upon him by anyone—is a feeling for the public identity of people, a web of public respect and trust, and a resource in time of personal or neighborhood need. The absence of this trust is a disaster to a city street. Its cultivation cannot be institutionalized. And above all, *it implies no private commitments.*[1]

As people took to the streets as never before, a new trust emerged as urbanites put their personalities on view, displaying individual choices of fashion, hairstyle,

1. Jane Jacobs, *The Death and Life of Great American Cities* (New York: Random House, 1989), 56.

and accessories with confidence. They observed and competed with one another, comparing style, appearance, and new levels of consumption. Ironically, some fashion trends blurred the boundaries between the private and the public. For example, some Shanghai residents, both men and women, began wearing pajamas on the streets. The ownership of pajamas had become a symbol of prosperity and many wanted to show off their wealth and independence in public so they wore them in the streets. But more importantly, this awareness of street life encouraged and shaped new ideas about neighborhoods and the display of a new cultural identity.

Many photographers engaged the street as a stage. On this stage, people put on a performance of newly formed identities, and photographers activated a site where they could observe and document innovative cultural trends and the transformation of Chinese urban life. Inspired by robust street life, a new Chinese urban personality was manifested through the medium of photography, and this spirit was displayed through the media confirming the transformation of the new China to the world. The artists were fascinated and awakened by the people in the street creating a symbiotic relationship that accelerated the transformation. The dramatic and vivid street life exhibited itself and achieved a consensus through published photographs, which stimulated the possibilities of photographic expression.

Street photography in China came alive during the middle and late 1980s as a direct challenge to staged propaganda photography. Artists began to search for different ways of photographic expressions, such as the use of flashing light by Zhang Haier in Guanzhou, the super fish-eye photography I used in Shanghai, and the noncompositional photography of Mo Yi in Tianjing. These nondocumentary techniques enriched the language of Chinese photography, which had been dormant for years, and gave rise to the eventual shift from documentary to conceptual photography. To the photographers of the 1980s, the cameras in their hands were symbols of their own changing identities. Previously, photographers had been controlled and personal expression was negated because of political ideology. By bringing the reality of the street into photography, artists invested daily life with greater legitimacy, creating a vibrant visual culture.

To build the tallest skyscraper in the world is the mission of many cities such as Beijing, Shanghai, Hong Kong, Taibei, Kuala Lumpur, Dubai, and Seoul. Seen as a symbol of modernity in developed countries, skyscrapers are considered a sign of economic success and advanced technology; they are also an economic strategy to maximize the efficient use of capital and limited urban areas for urban development. Because skyscrapers symbolize modernity, many developing countries try to prove to the world that they are modern countries and have a valuable role to play in globalization by building them. In Shanghai, for example, a city with very limited land, building higher and higher was a strategic decision to parallel economic development and the increasing growth of a migratory work force.

The emergence of the skyscraper in China is changing the configuration of the city as well as people's concept of space. Traditional Chinese architecture is dominated by horizontal design even though some nonutilitarian architecture such as the pagoda exhibits the determination of upward movement, showing a desire to conquer the heavens. In a concentrated format, the skyscrapers in modern architecture reveal the collusion between capital and power as they pierce through the clouds in the sky, as in Zhu Feng's image of the Jin Mao tower in *Top* (2004). As they spring up, they block people's views and level the horizontality forcing people to look upward and orient themselves more vertically, as suggested in Yening's series *Dream in the Deserted Peking* (2006) and Xing Danwen's *Urban Fiction* series (2004–2008). A new vision emerges when the old view is blocked and a new concept of space is revealed. The threatening existence of skyscrapers forces us to ponder other new relationships between the city and its inhabitants, and concepts such as alienation, marginalization, and loss are explored by many of the artists in this exhibition. As the skyscrapers achieve greater and greater heights, they may promise to free people from the confinement of the earth while demonstrating the progress of humanity and modern technology, but their existence also creates cultural anxiety and adds new complexity to understanding urban space. A sense of competition has been instilled with the increasing presence of skyscrapers dominating the horizons of Chinese cities, evoking the ongoing search for an unattainable heaven.

Historically, skyscrapers were a subject of interest to artists as early as the 1930s when their presence emerged in the photography of Lang Jingshan, Ao Enhong, and in Su Jiemin's *The Façade of the Metropolis*. However, the hopeful embodiment of modernity as seen in those early images of Chinese skyscrapers and their relationship to the stylistic evolution of the photographic medium in China was interrupted by a series of foreign invasions, civil wars, and revolution. It was not until the 1980s that we saw the return of the skyscraper in Chinese photography through the images of Chen Lingyang, Chi Peng, Jiang Zhi, Liu Jianhua, Ma Liang, Miao Xiaochun, Shi Yong, Wang Yiaodong, Wong Fen, Yang Fudong, Yang Zhenzhong, Zhou Ming, and more recently in the conceptual work of Xing Danwen, Yang Yongliang, Yening, and Zhu Feng.

The present moment in China is characterized by the emergence of new perspectives. The height of the skyscraper is changing the horizon of Chinese cities, creating a critical understanding of urban space. The street and its visual culture are marking the profound changes that are impacting the physical and cultural cityscapes of China. In this new generation of photography, artists explore the realities they witness from varying perspectives—consumerism, sexuality, urbanization, globalization, and memory—and the works they create analyze and reflect upon the modern city and city life. They become a social essay, social evaluation, social critique, and social practice. These images constitute the formation of a new visual culture. The visual imagery of the contemporary Chinese city cannot be simply separated into the categories of street and skyscraper: they are reciprocal, complementary, and interdependent. Often the skyscraperization of the street parallels the streetification of the skyscraper. Frequently, they coexist with each other, and provide the space and site for contemporary photographic practice.

在当代中国的都市摄影中，街道与摩天楼这两个视觉形象在表现中国社会的转型时，扮演了重要的角色。参加本次展览的艺术家们创作的摄影作品反应并评价了正在形成的中国文化与街头和摩天楼文化之间的关系。

1978年的经济改革，激发了中国公民蓬勃兴起的经济活动并使之合法化，街头生活以及其视觉文化得以壮大发展。全新的私营经济给街头注入了新的活力，引发了城市从生产中心型向消费中心型的转变。普通市民开始参与新生的市场经济，他们接触的公共空间被商业活动和广告这些在计划经济时代曾被禁止的东西所改变。这些新的市场力量形成的主导因素和关系重新定义了城市空间。商业和充满活力的经济活动给公共空间增添了新的血液，也创造了一种新的景观，它渗入私人居住空间，催生出一种不同的生活方式和一系列新的价值观。现代生活在促成新的消费意识的同时强调了个人价值，而常常是通过使用摄影影像来实现的产品推销，使现代生活的种种可能性更加形象化。

街头不可避免地成为对新的意识形态进行市场测试的公共空间。美国城市批评家简·雅各布斯（Jane Jacobs）说过：

> 对城市街道的信任是多年来通过很多很多的大家共用的小人行道连接汇聚起来所形成的。这些连接表面看起来微不足道，但汇总起来却是举足轻重的。这种连接起来的道路起源于长期以来对日常生活的信任。……因此，道路的深层根源蕴涵着人们的公共认同、公共生活中相互尊敬和信任的网络、对个人和邻里需求的资源依托。对这种信任的缺失是城市道路的一种灾难。而对这一资源的开发是不能制度化的。尤为重要的是，这一切绝非意味着个体的努力[1]

城市居民充满信心地通过他们对时装、发型和装饰品的选择来展示他们的个性。当人们以前所未有的方式走上街头，一种新的信任悄然出现。他们互相欣赏与攀比，比较着彼此的风格、形象和新的消费水准。具有讽刺意味的是，有些着装潮流混淆了私人与公共空间的界限。比如说，有些上海人，包括男人和女人，开始穿着睡衣上街。拥有睡衣成为富有的象征。很多人以此来炫耀他们的财富和自由。然而更重要的是，对街头生活的意识激发和促成了人们对邻里关系的认识和对新的文化认同的展示。

很多摄影家把街头当作舞台，人们在这个舞台上展现他们刚刚形成的身份，摄影家们则开发了一个场地，他们据此观察和记录变革中的文化潮流以及中国城市生活的变化。在这种坚定的街头生活的感召下，一种全新的中国城市个性通过摄影这一媒介展现在我们面前，并向全世界肯定了新中国的变迁。街上的人群感染着艺术

从街道到摩天楼

— 关于城市空间与中国现代摄影之关系的笔记

顾铮

1. 简·雅各布斯《美国大城市的死与生》，纽约：兰登书屋，1989。

家，唤醒他们去创造一种共生关系，进而加速这种变迁。丰富多采、瞬息万变的街头生活自我展示着它的风情，并通过广泛发表的摄影作品得到认同，这进一步激发了摄影表达上更多的可能性。

中国的街头摄影在上个世纪八十年代中后期开始获得生机，它勇于挑战舞台式的宣传摄影。摄影家们也开始探索不同的表现手法，如广州张海儿对闪光灯的运用、我使用的超广角镜头和天津莫毅的非取景拍摄等。这些非记录式的技巧大大丰富了曾经沉寂多年的中国街头摄影语言，并促成了由记录式摄影向概念化摄影的必然转换。对于八十年代的摄影家来说，他们手中的相机标志着他们自身身份的转变。在那之前，摄影家受到操控，个人意愿的表达因政治意念而遭到否定。通过把街头现实带到照片中来，艺术家更加合法地介入日常生活，创造出一种震撼人心的视觉文化。

从北京、上海、香港、台北到吉隆坡、迪拜和汉城，所有这些城市都以建造最高的摩天楼为自己的使命。作为发达国家现代化的标志，摩天大楼被看作经济成功与科技发达的象征；它们也成为城市发展的一种策略，用以最大限度地有效使用资本和有限的城市空间。由于摩天楼象征了现代化，许多发展中国家通过建设摩天楼向世界证明它的现代化以及它们在全球化过程中所扮演的重要角色。例如在土地资源十分有限的上海，把楼建得越来越高是为了平衡经济发展与外来劳力增长而做出的决策。

摩天楼在中国城市的出现，改变了城市的构成，也改变了人们对于空间的认识。传统的中国建筑，以向水平方向扩展的建筑为多，但像宝塔这样的不具实用性的建筑，在体现了向上升华的宗教意志的同时，也展示了征服上天的欲望。象朱峰的《顶》系列中的影象金茂大厦（2004）所表现的那样，现代建筑中的摩天大楼高耸入云，它们以密集排列的形态，揭示了权力与资本的亲密无间的勾结。当摩天大楼拔地而起的时候，它们阻碍了人们的视线，改画了地平线，强迫人们向上看，并把自己纵向化，从也宁的《游园京梦》（2006）系列和邢丹文的《都市演绎》（2004－2008）系列中，　我们不难看出这一趋势。旧的景观被挡住，新的景色出现了，新的空间概念昭然若示。摩天楼的威胁性存在迫使我们认真思考城市与居民之间重新形成的其他种种关系，而诸如异化、边缘化和失落这些概念也在参展作品中得以阐释。越来越高的摩天楼在展示人类进化和技术进步的同时也向我们承诺，它们可以把人从地球的限制中解放出来。但它们的存在又造成文化焦虑，同时深化了我们对城市空间理解的复杂性。随着主导中国城市视线的摩天大楼越来越多地出现在人们的视野中，竞争意识也被灌输到我们的头脑中，刺激着人们不断去寻找那遥不可及的天堂。

回顾历史，早在上一世纪三十年代摩天大楼这一题材就为艺术家所感兴趣。从郎静山、敖恩洪的摄影作品和苏介民的《都市建筑外观》中可以看到它们的存在。不过，通过表现摩天大楼来体会现代性、并使之转化成摄影自身的现代性的过程，后来马上被一系列的外国入侵、战争和革命所中断。直到八十年代后期，摩天楼这一题材又回到中国摄影作品中，不断出现在陈羚羊、迟鹏、蒋志、刘建华、马良、缪晓春、施勇、王晓东、翁奋、杨福东、杨振中、周明的作品中，以及更近时期出现在邢丹文、杨泳梁、也宁和朱锋等人的概念摄影作品中。

今天的中国具有新观念层出不穷的特点。摩天大楼的高度改变着中国城市的地平线，也引发了我们对城市空间的独到见解。街道及其视觉文化标志着种种冲击着中国城市地理和文化空间的深刻变革。作为摄影界的新生一代，这些艺术家从不同视角探索他们所见证的现实情况 — 消费主义、性意识、城市化、全球化、回忆 — 他们的作品剖析并反思现代城市与现代生活，成为一篇社会论文，成为社会评价、社会批判和社会实践。这些作品构成了一种新的视觉文化。我们不能把现代中国城市视觉形象简单分类为街头影象与摩天楼影象：这两者互惠互补，并互相依赖。很多时候，街道的摩天楼化与摩天楼的街道化是并行不悖的。这两者往往是共同存在，并同时为现代摄影实践提供空间与场地。

Monuments 纪念碑

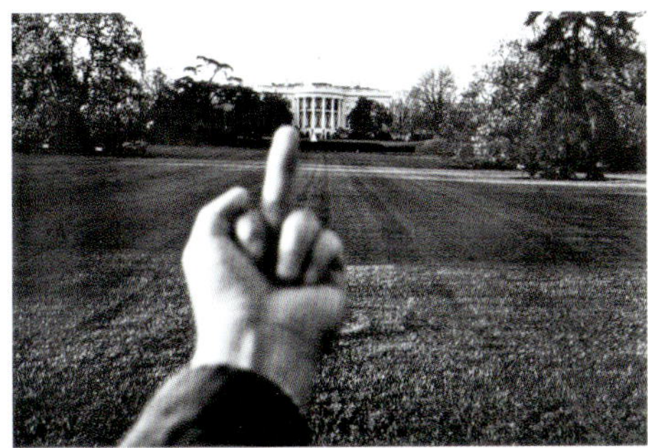
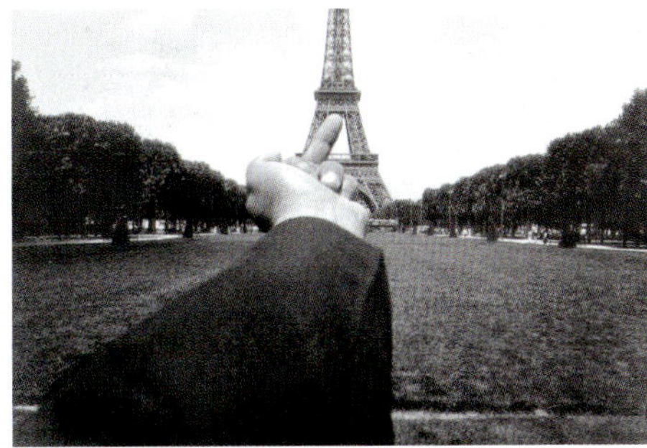

AI WEIWEI 艾未未

White House, from the series *Study of Perspective,* 1999–2003
Eiffel Tower, from the series *Study of Perspective,* 1999–2003

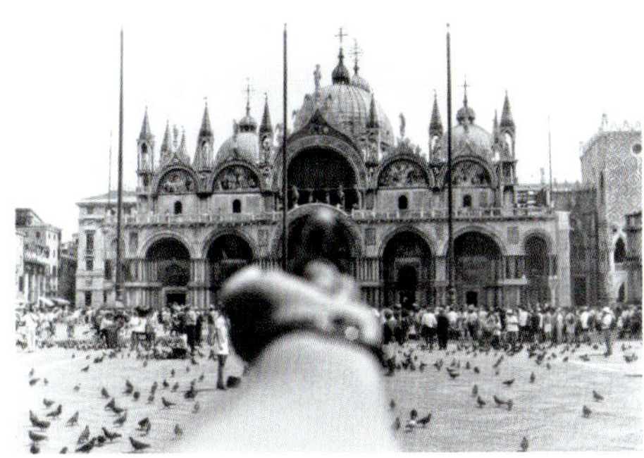
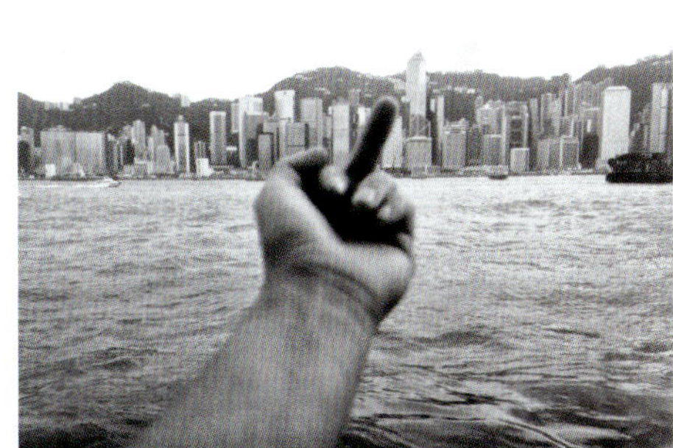

San Marco, from the series *Study of Perspective,* 1999–2003
Hong Kong, from the series *Study of Perspective,* 1999–2003

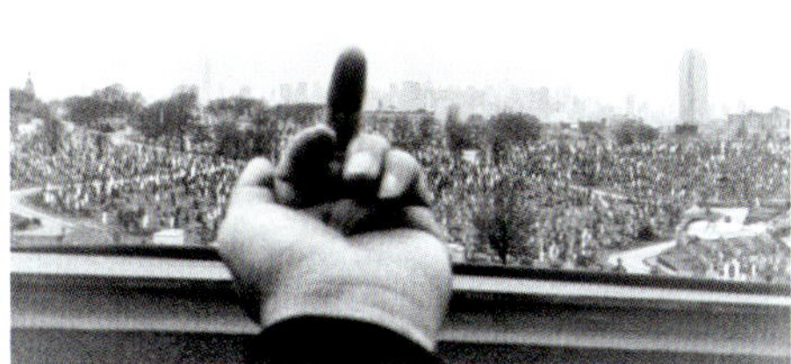
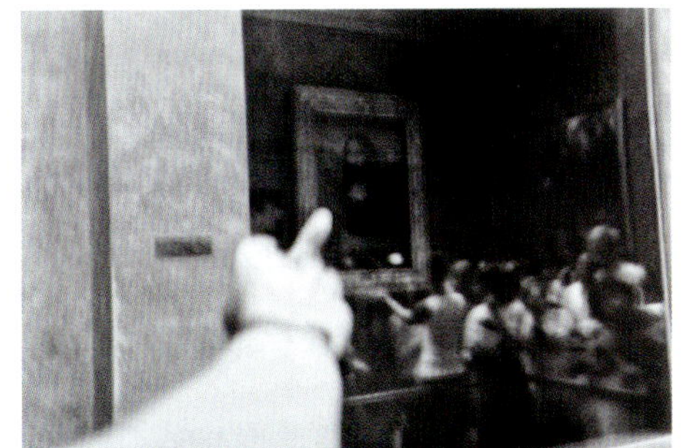

Long Island City, from the series *Study of Perspective,* 1999–2003
Mona Lisa, from the series *Study of Perspective,* 1999–2003

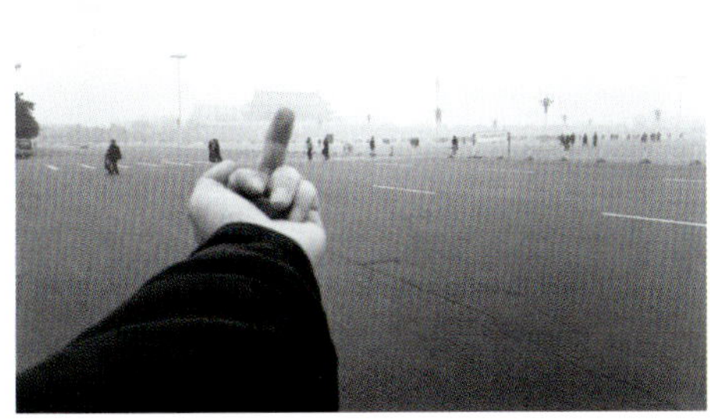
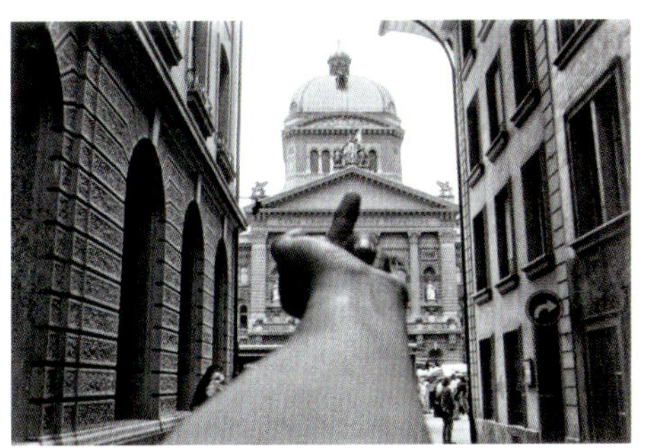

Tiananmen, from the series *Study of Perspective,* 1999–2003
Berne, from the series *Study of Perspective,* 1999–2003

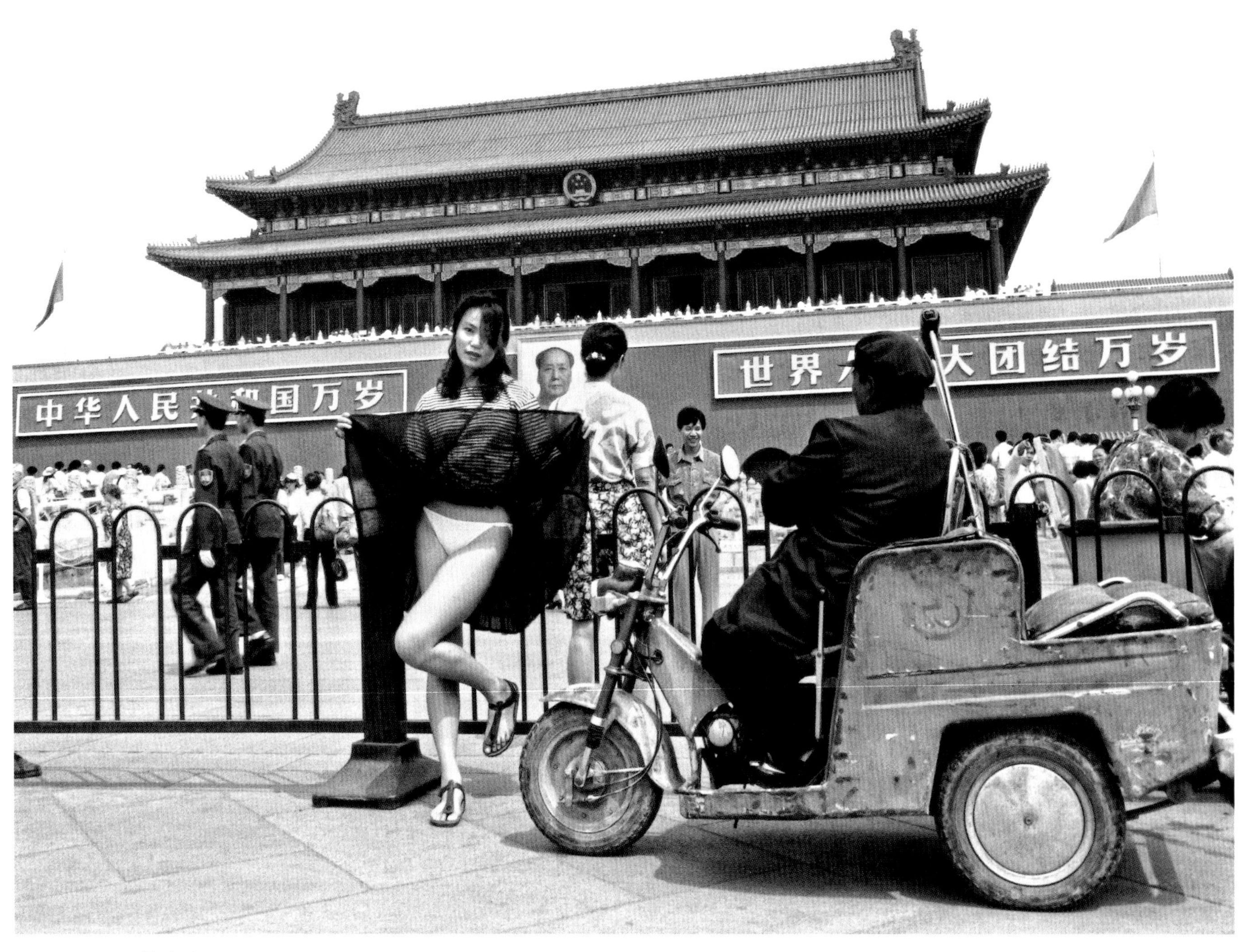

AI WEIWEI 艾未未 *"June 1994,"* 1994

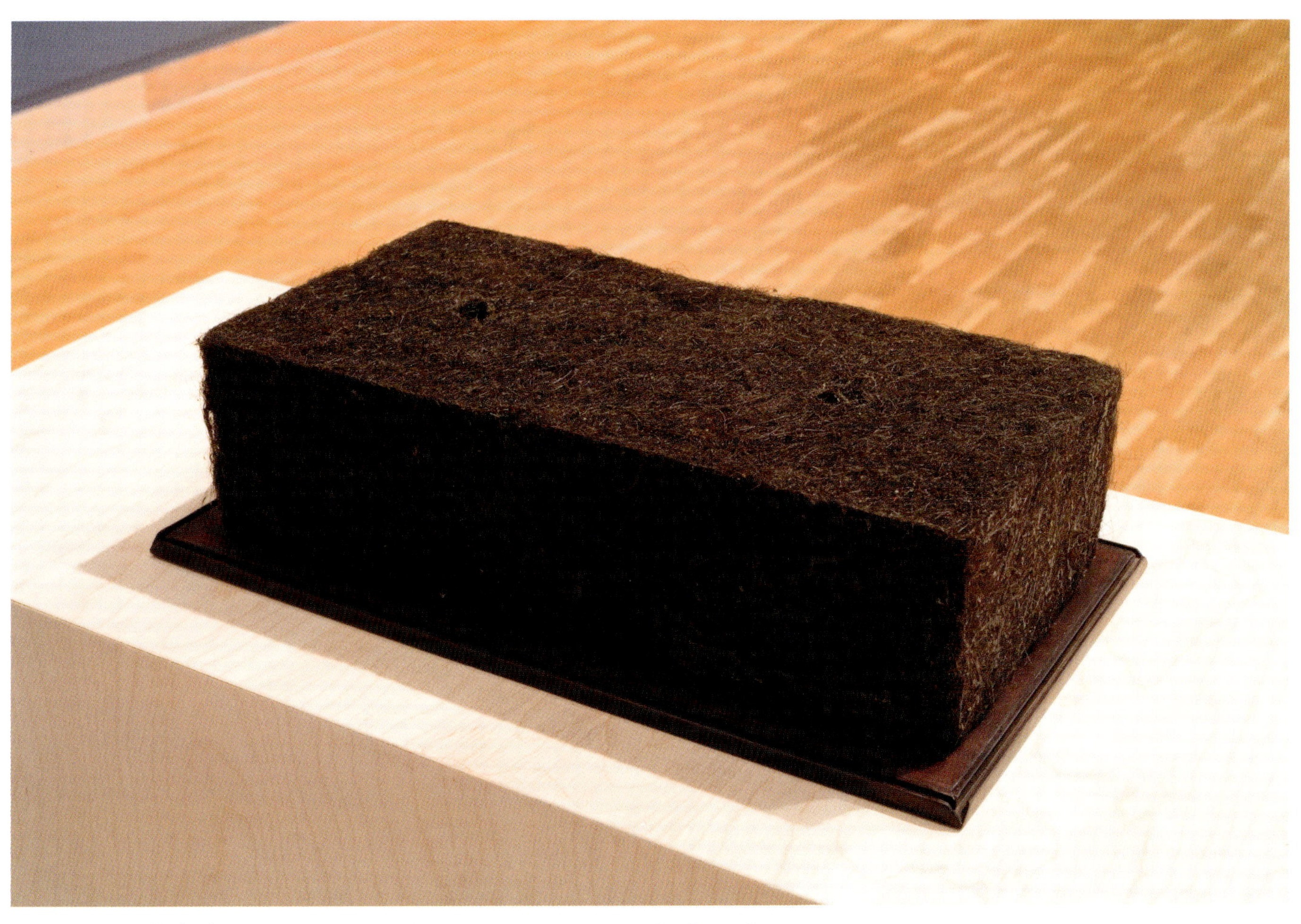

GU WENDA 谷文达 *Fragment (United Nations: The Great Wall of People)*, 2008

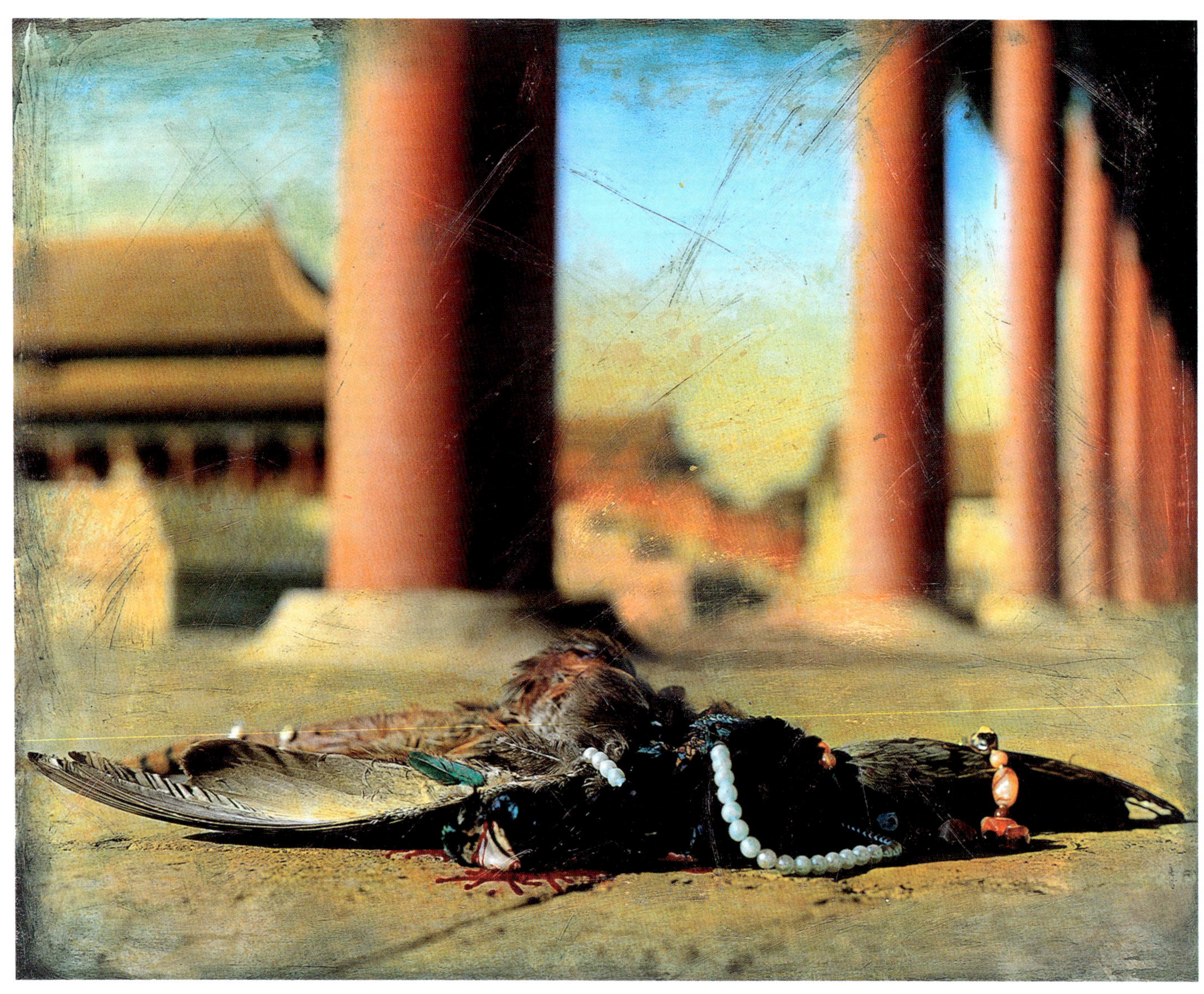

HONG LEI 洪磊 *Autumn in Forbidden City, East Veranda*, 1997

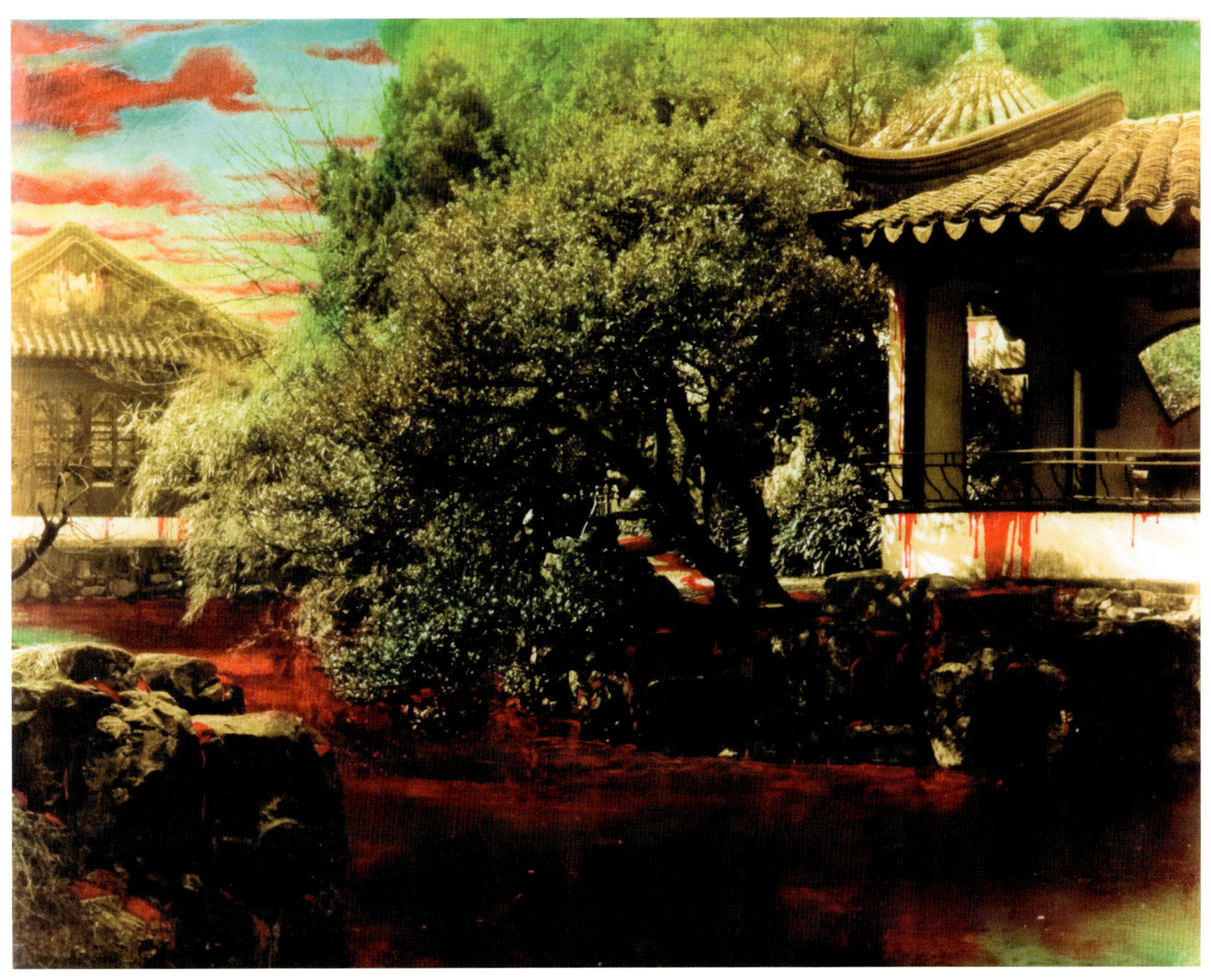

HONG LEI 洪磊 *Chinese Garden Landscape*, 1998

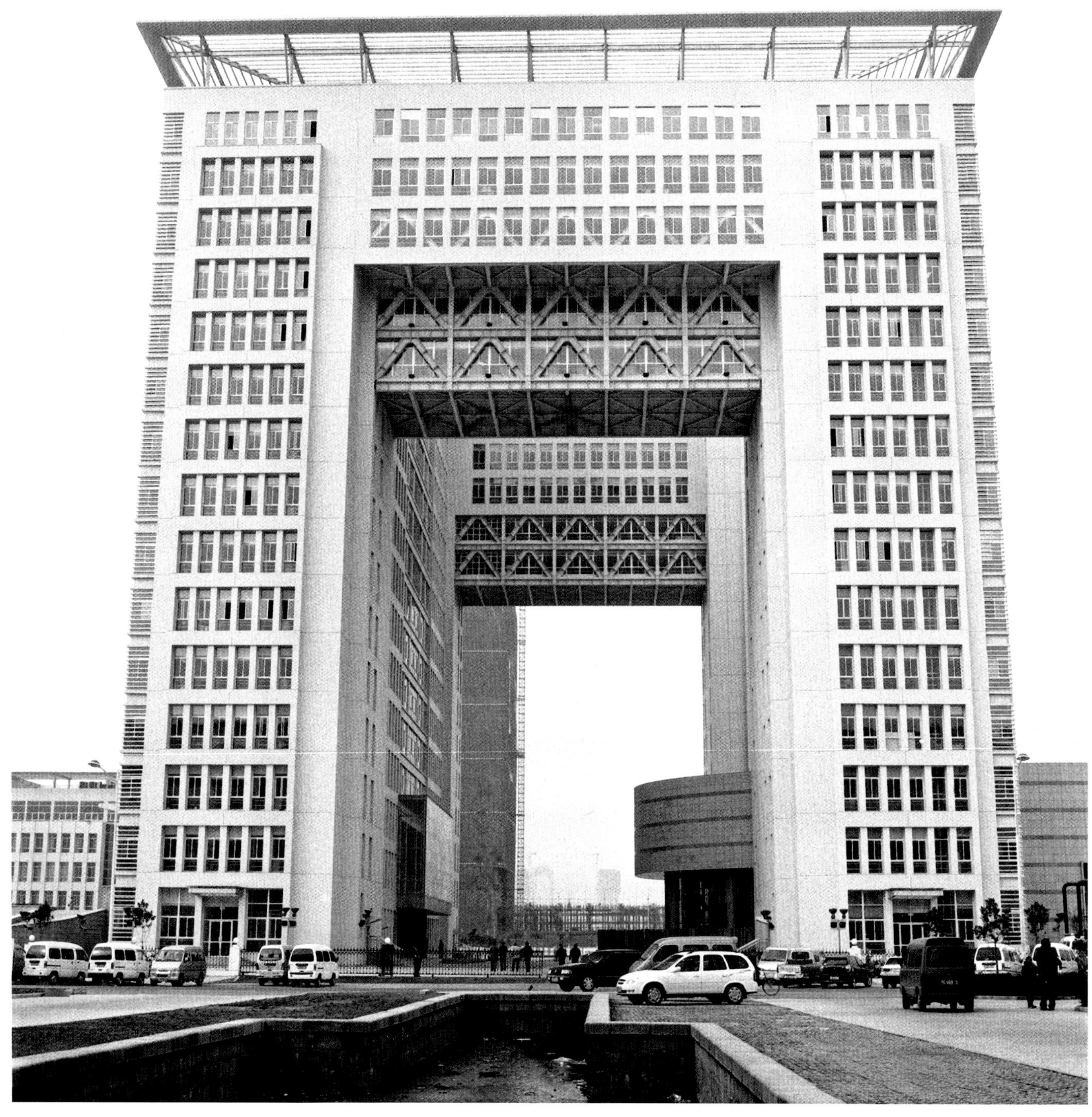

LUO YONGJIN 罗永进 *Luoyang (no. 2)*, from the series *Government Buildings*, 2005

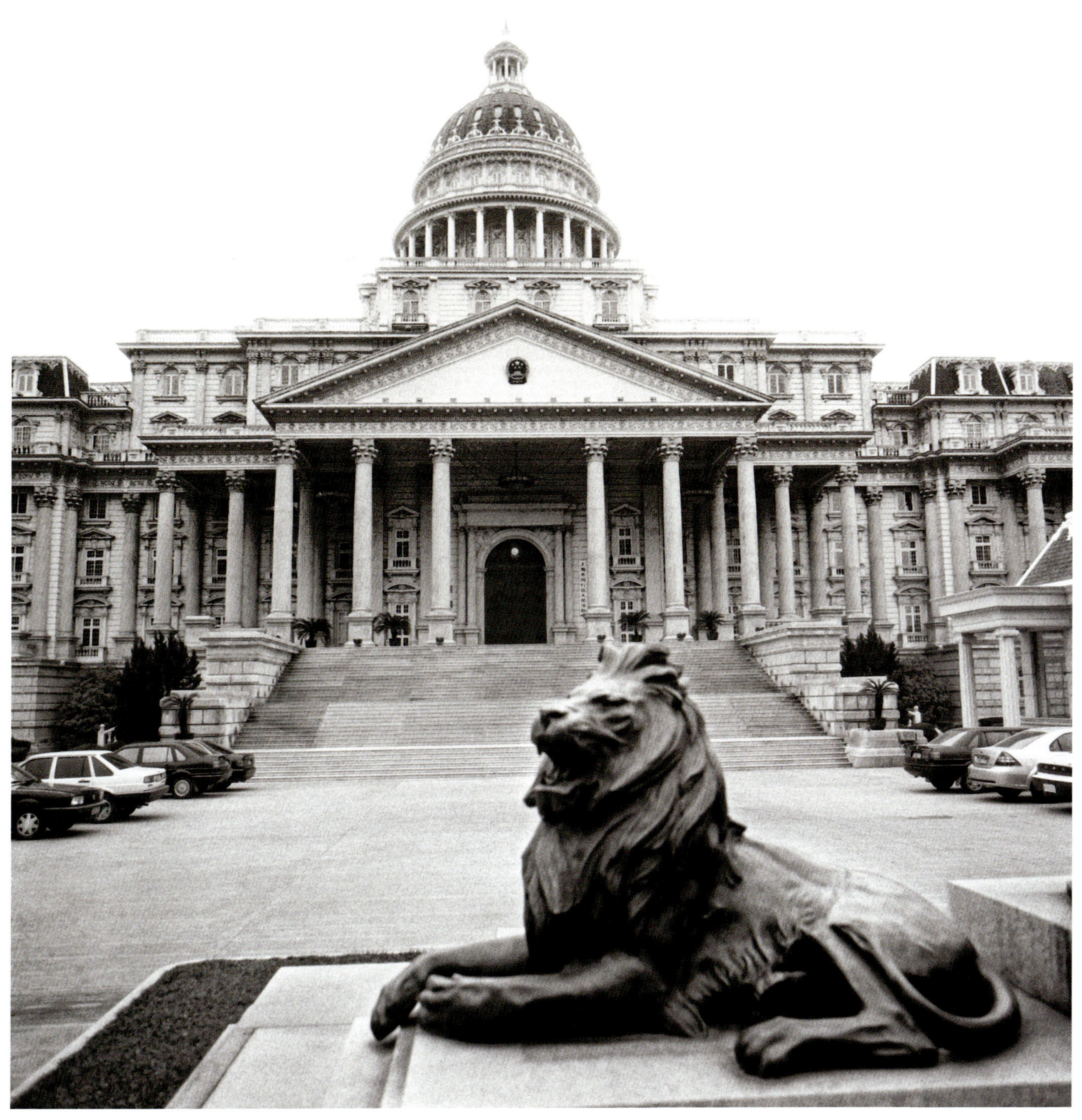

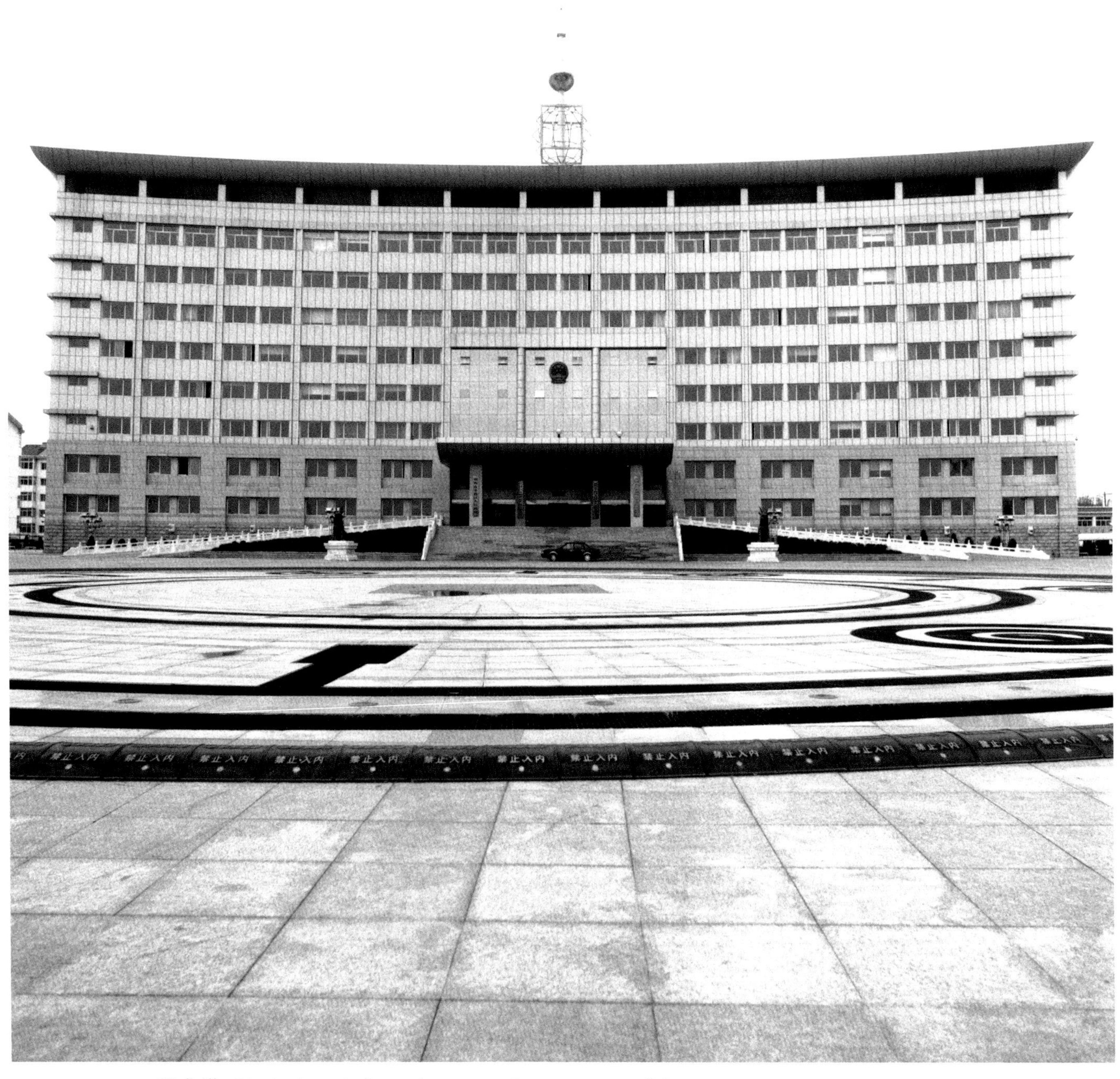

LUO YONGJIN 罗永进 *Pinglu (no. 7)*, from the series *Government Buildings*, 2005

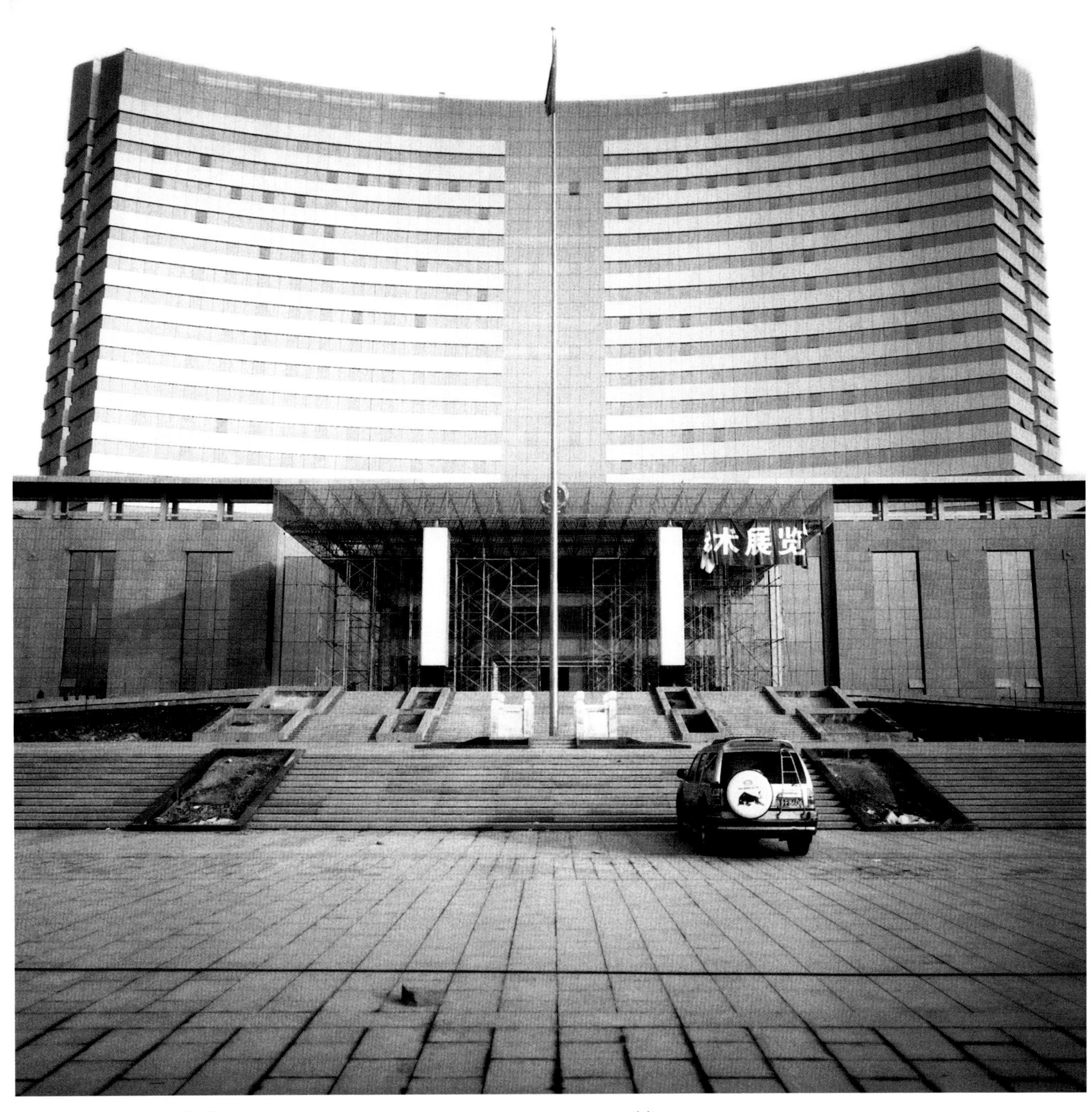

LUO YONGJIN 罗永进 *Lishui (no. 8)*, from the series *Government Buildings*, 2005

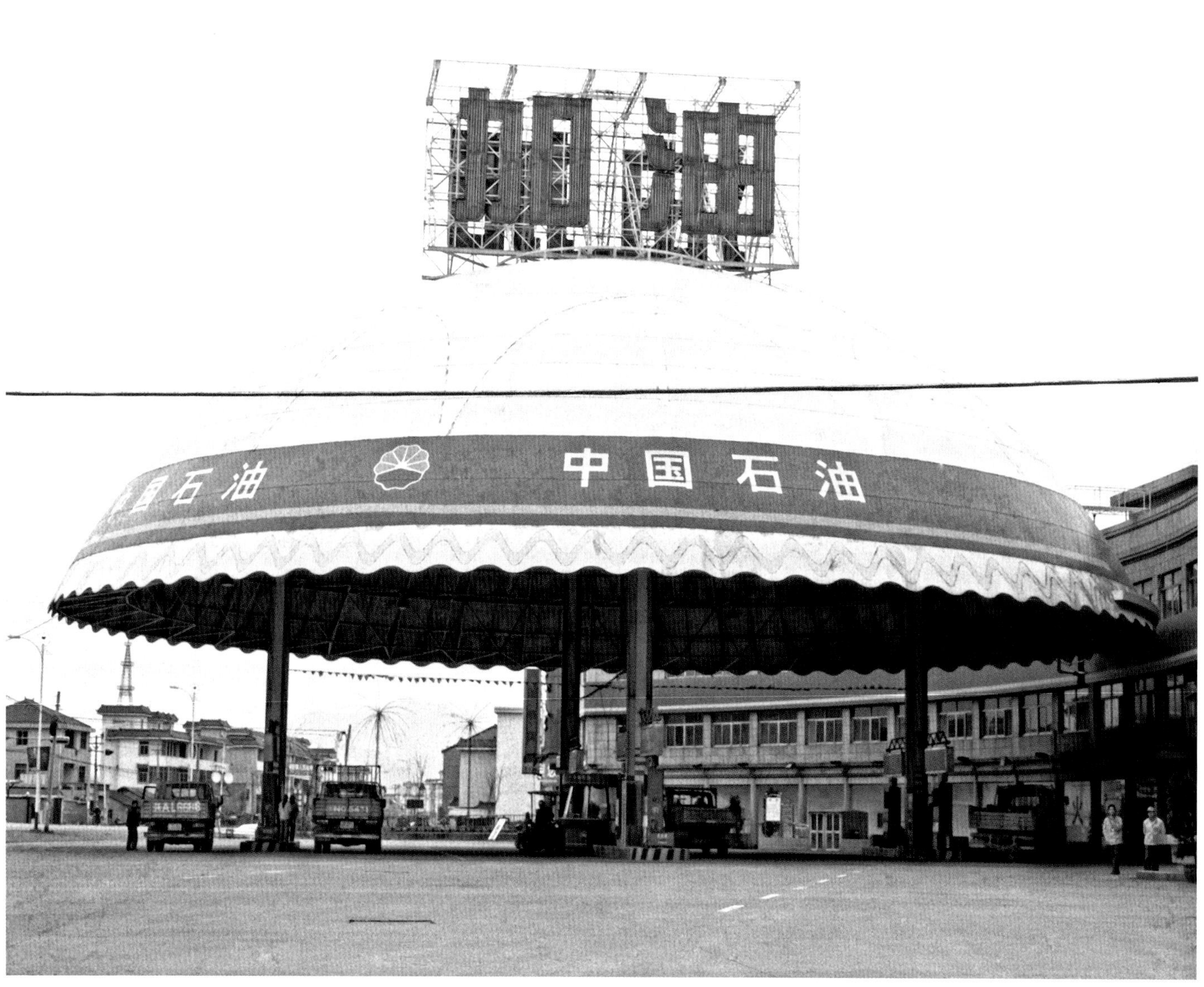

LUO YONGJIN 罗永进 *Hangzhou (no. 01)*, from the series *Gas Stations*, 2006

58

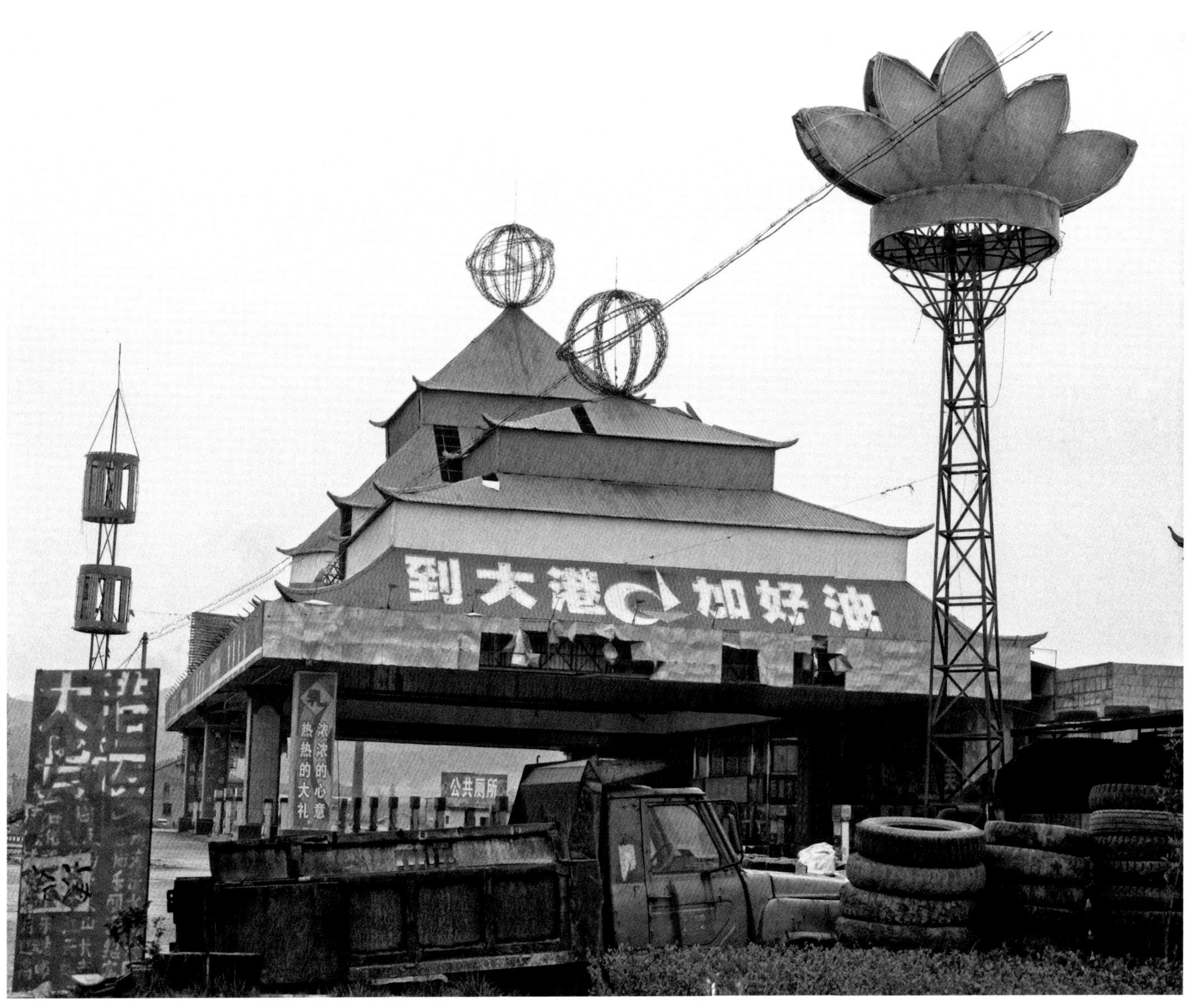

LUO YONGJIN 罗永进 *Yixing (no. 03)*, from the series *Gas Stations*, 2006

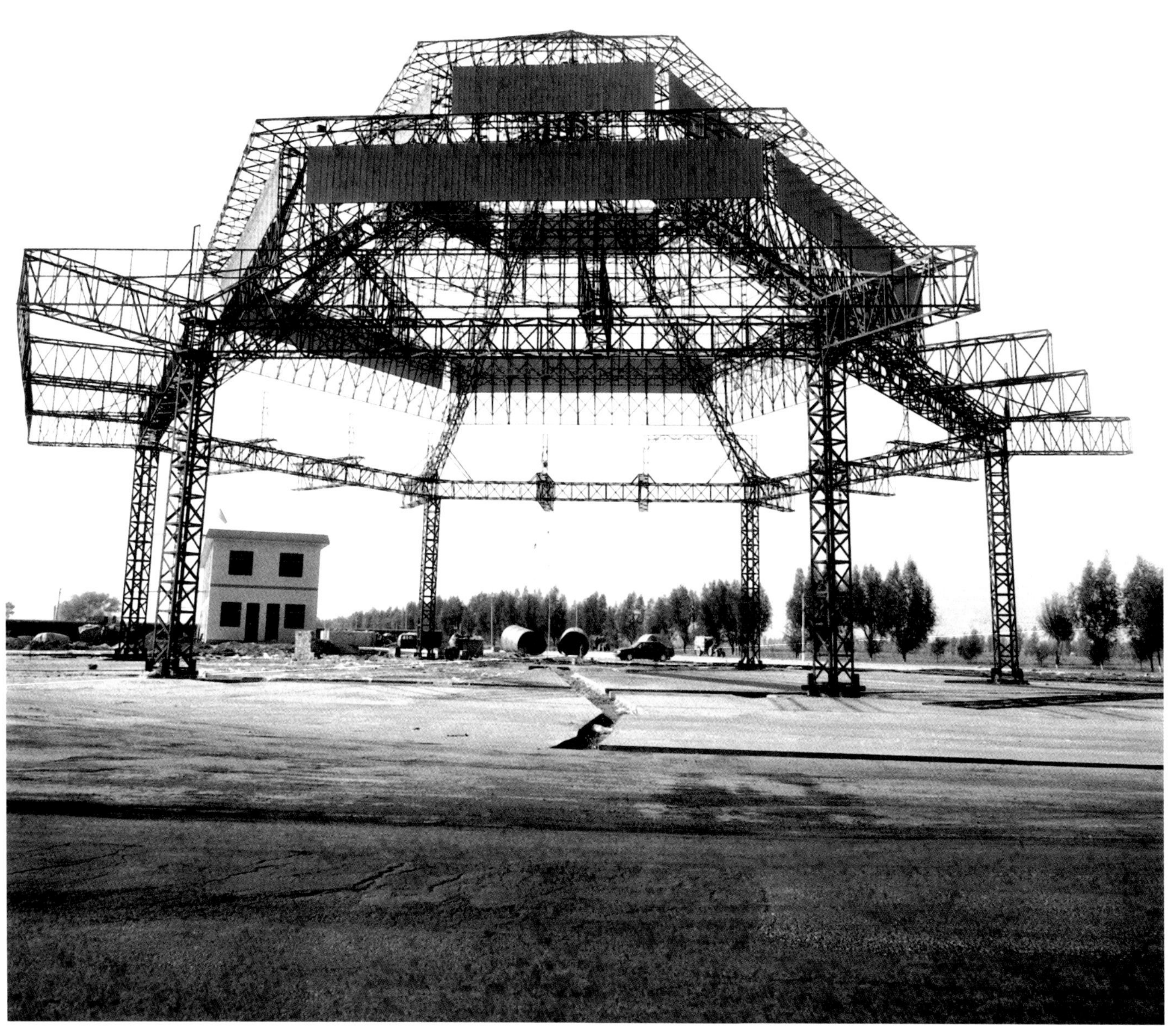

LUO YONGJIN 罗永进 *Xinzhou (no. 06)*, from the series *Gas Stations*, 2005

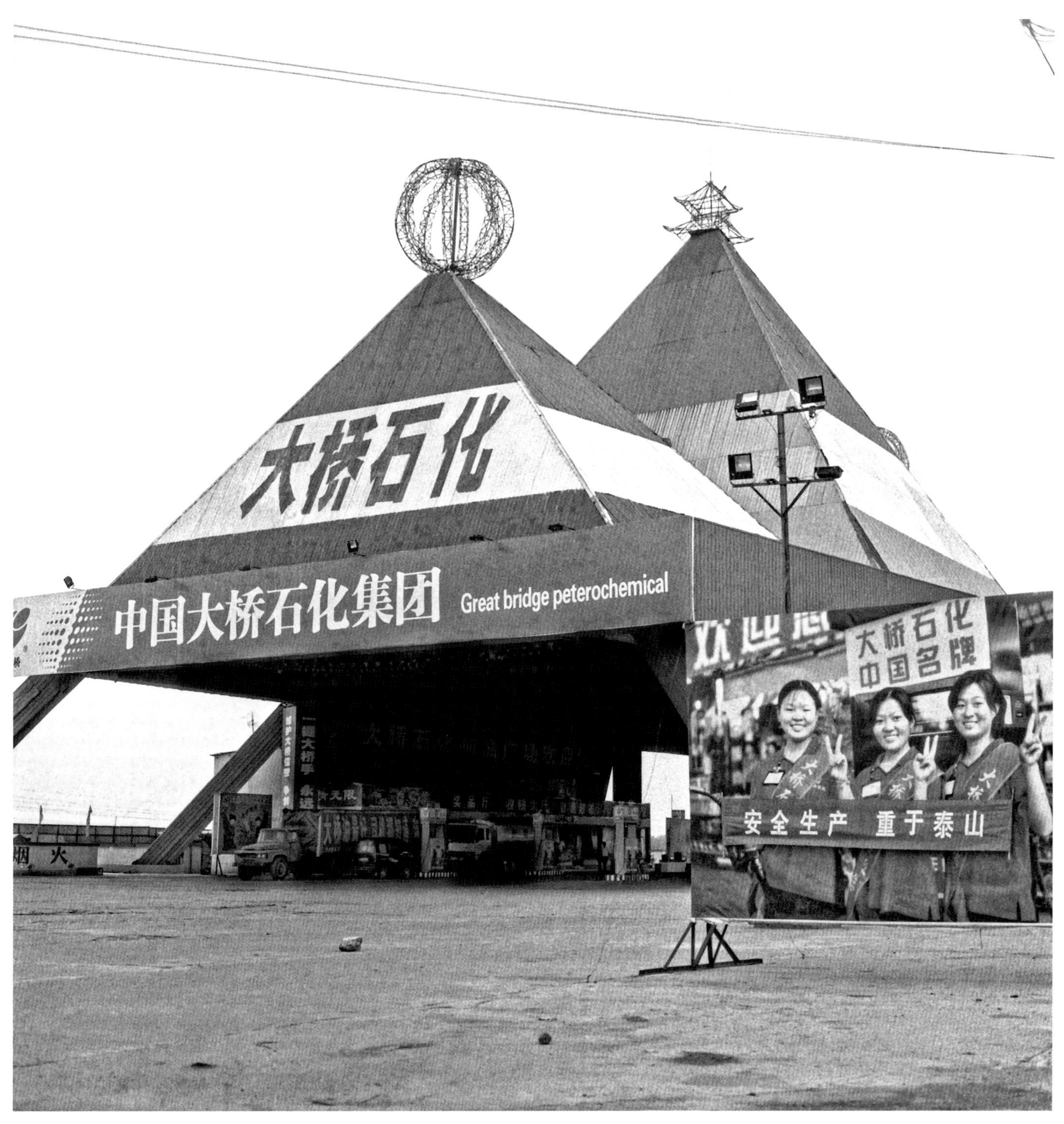

LUO YONGJIN 罗永进 *Zhengzhou (no. 08)*, from the series *Gas Stations*, 2004

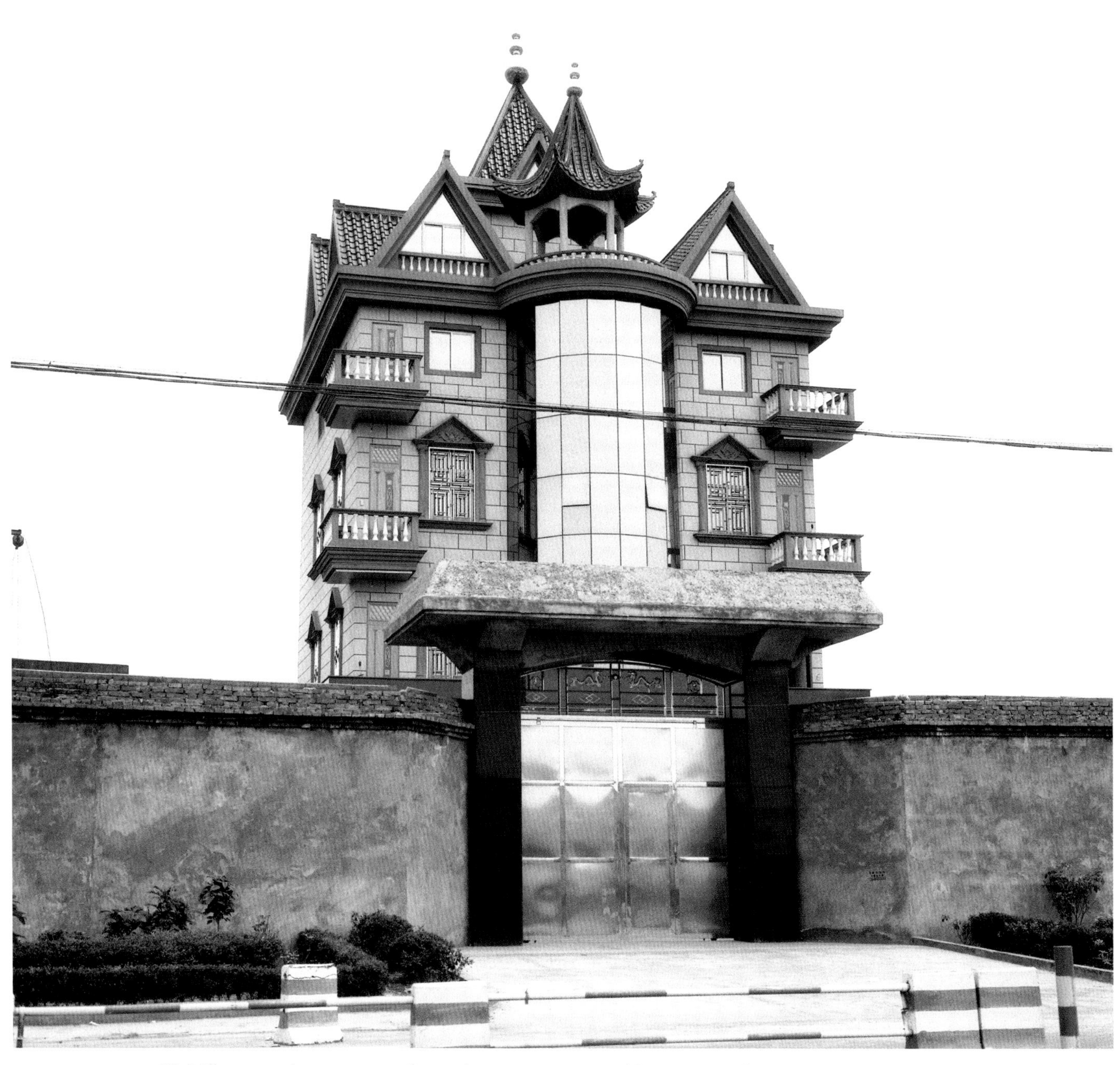

LUO YONGJIN 罗永进 *Hangzhou (no. 24)*, from the series *New Residence Hangzhou*, 2003

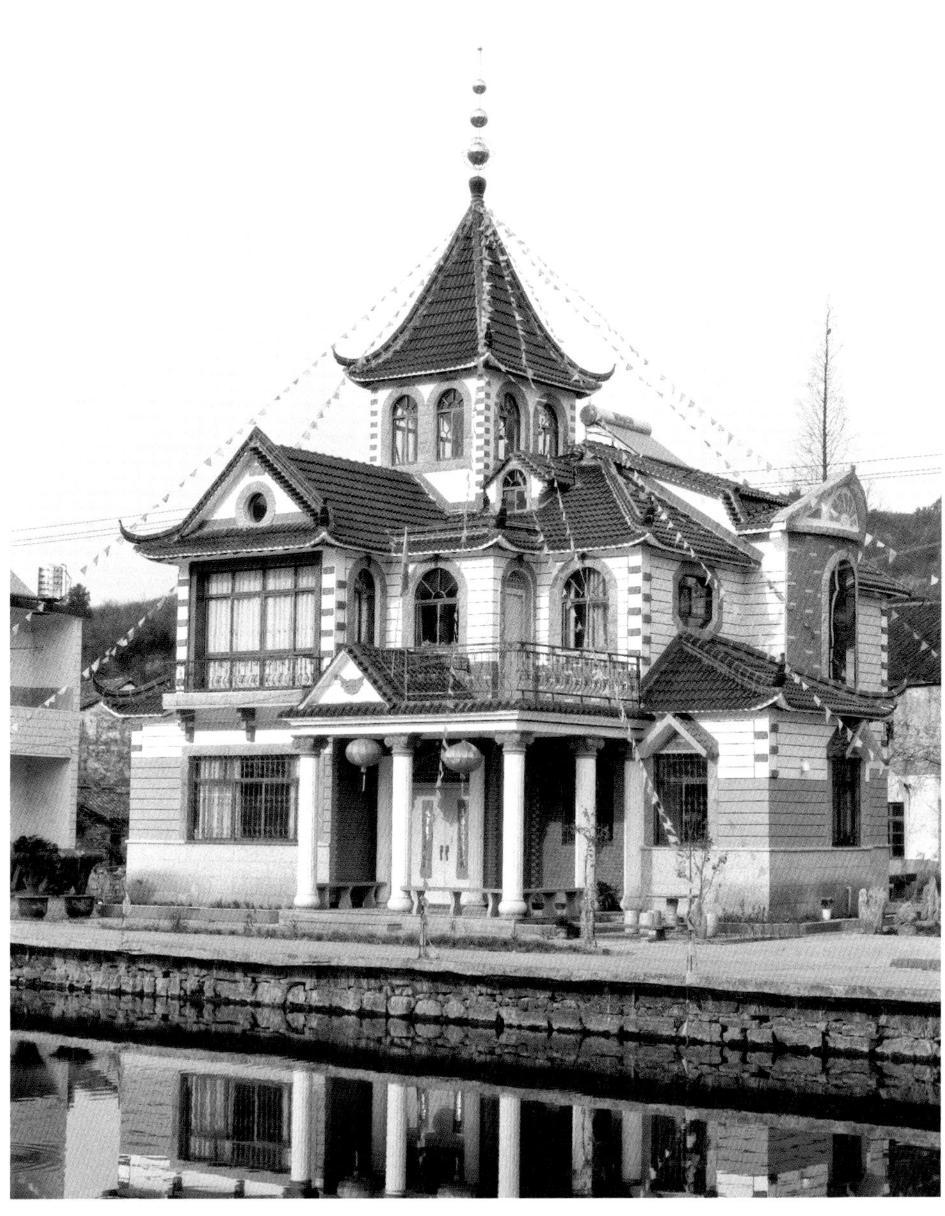

LUO YONGJIN 罗永进 *Hangzhou (no. 31)*, from the series *New Residence Hangzhou*, 2003

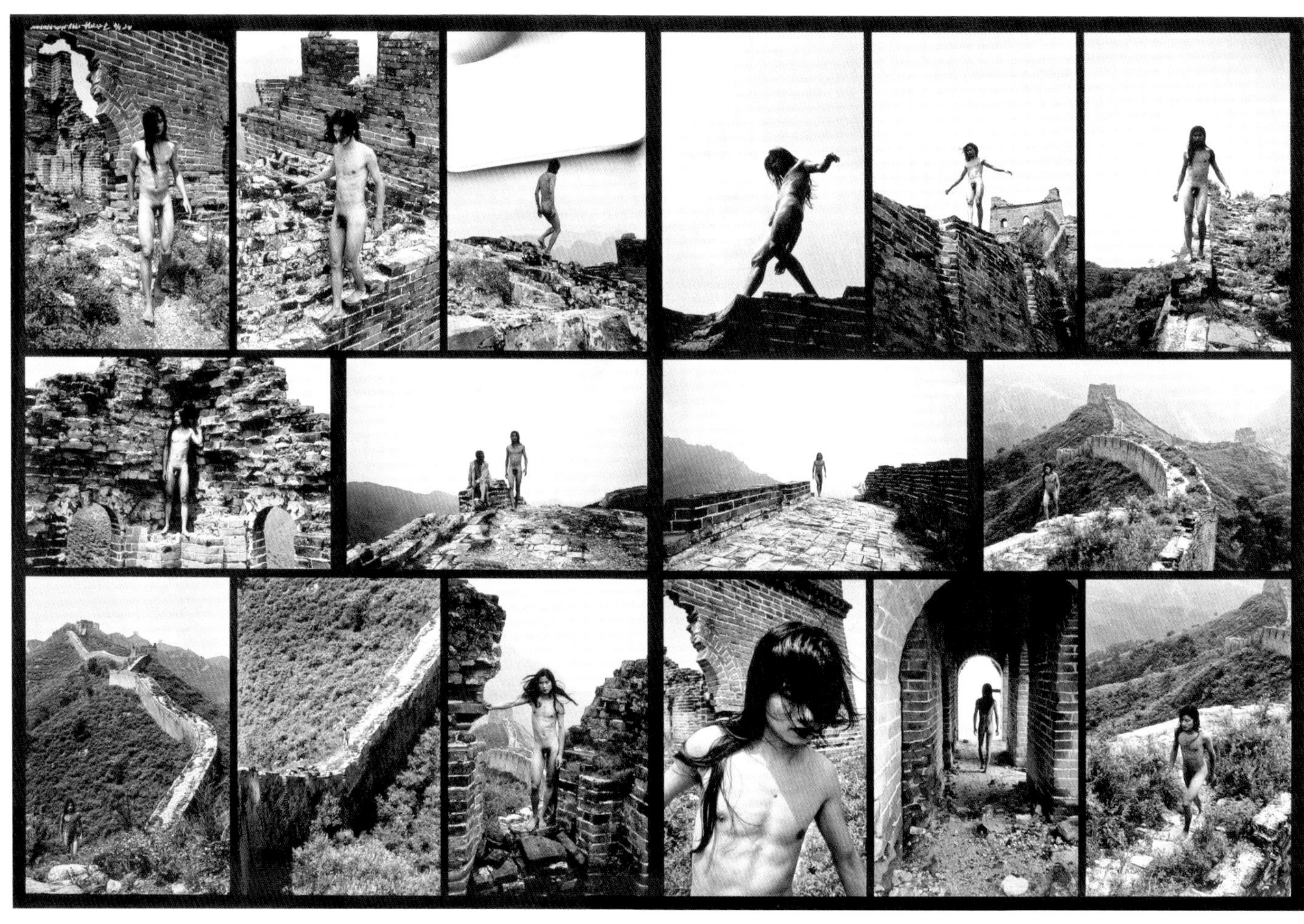

MA LIUMING 马六明 *Fen-Ma Liuming Walks the Great Wall*, 1998

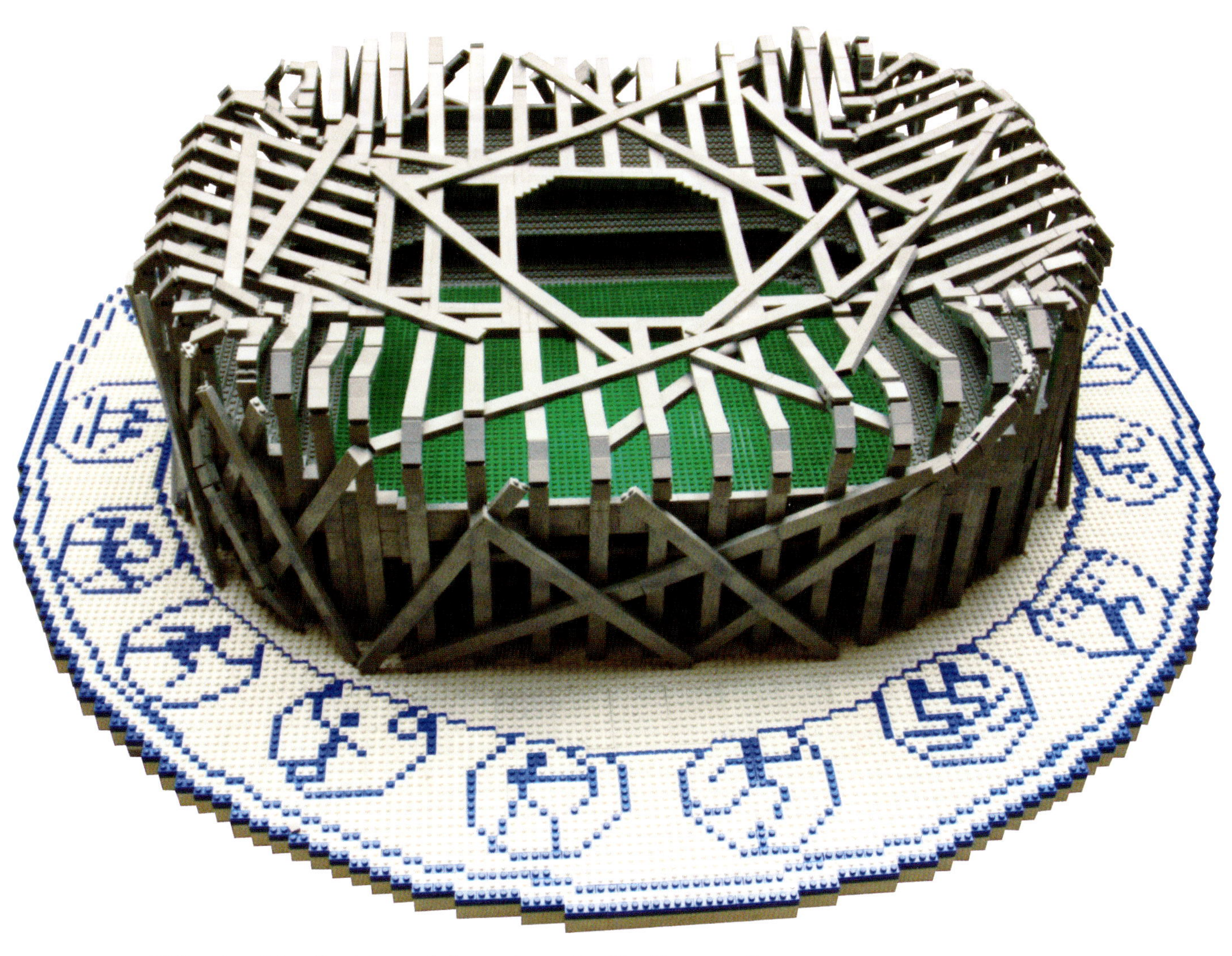

WANG JING 王净 *The China Food in 2008*, from the series *Toy Piece*, 2008

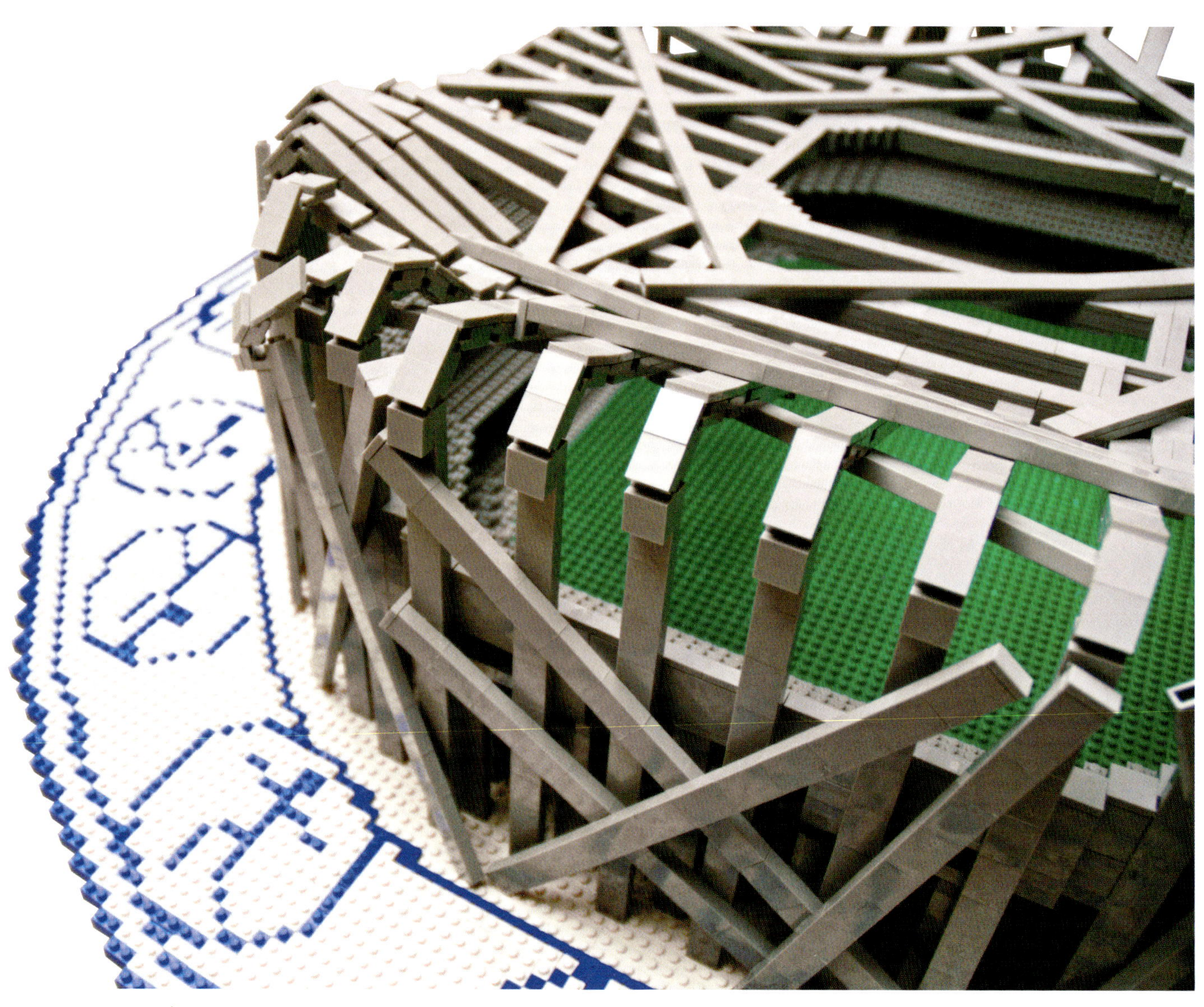

WANG JING 王净 *The China Food in 2008*, from the series *Toy Piece*, 2008

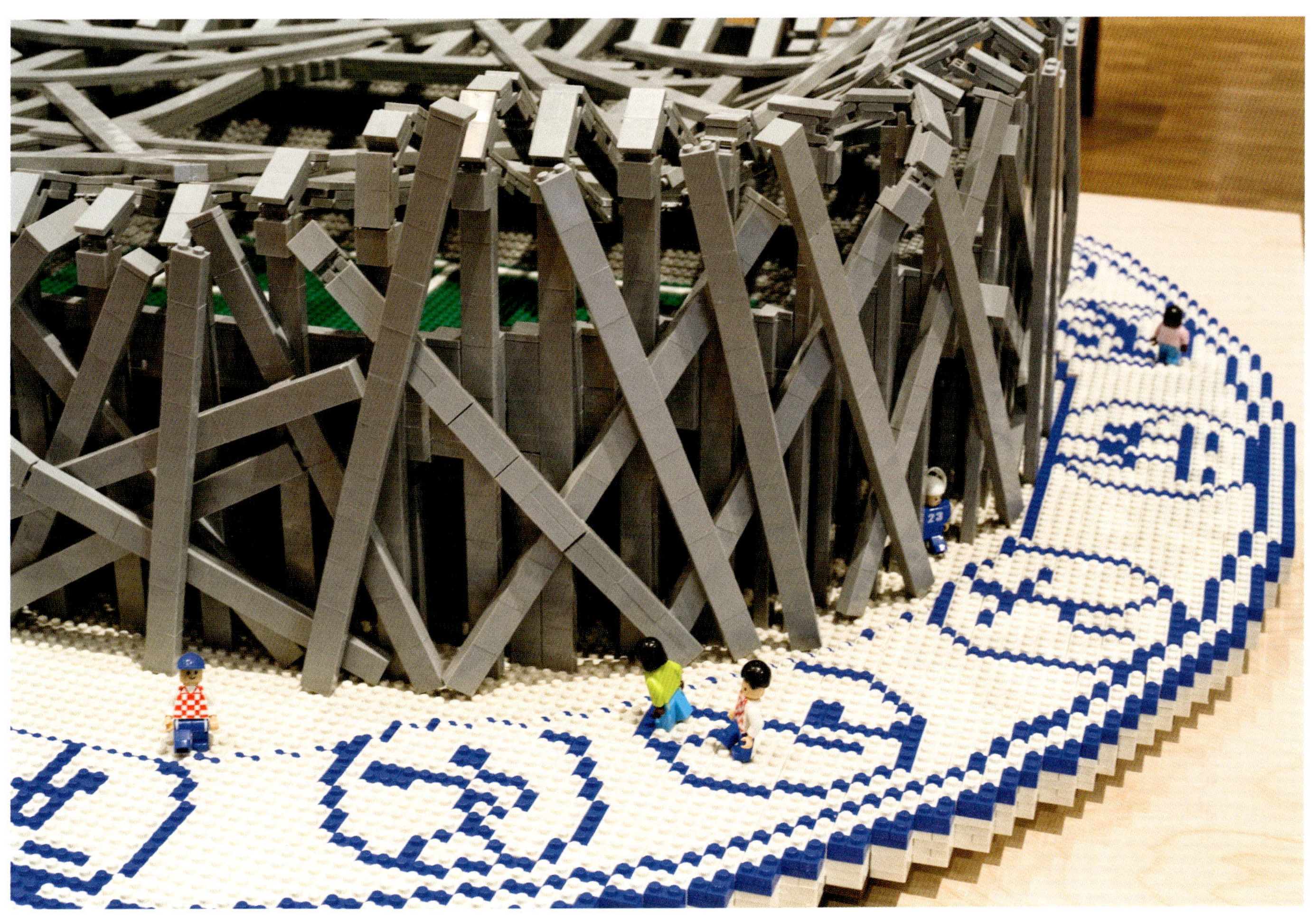

WANG JING 王净 *The China Food in 2008*, from the series *Toy Piece*, 2008

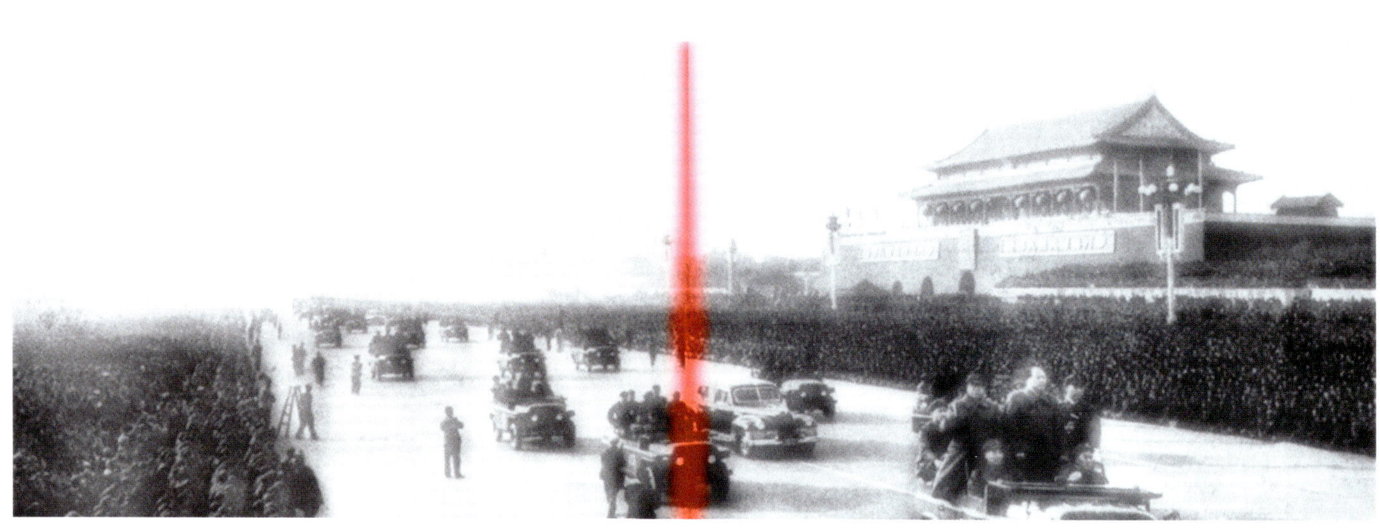

ZHU FENG 朱锋 *The Old and New: The Red Guard Parade at Tiananmen Square and Chang'an Street on November 11, 1966, 2007*

GAN XU

With the 2008 Beijing Olympics as its window display, China is now eager to show the world its dramatically transformed cities. To the outside world, China's unprecedented change is manifestly visible in the mushrooming skyscrapers of her urban environments. We are undergoing what some would call China's "Architectural Great Leap Forward." And indeed, skyscrapers are the most direct and powerful sign of a "Second Cultural Revolution," characterized by a hurried rush toward westernization. However, the images of skyscrapers in this exhibition are not monuments to the Communist Party's illustrious achievements or material efforts to reinforce its authority. These artists aren't running to join a parade of celebration; instead, they seek to reveal what is happening behind the buildings and in the contradistinctive urban environments, which can be seen as the other side of the China miracle.

Half a century ago, at the birth of the People's Republic of China in 1949, the distant golden rays of the Soviet Union shone like a heavenly paradise to the Chinese. Since architecture was hardly the focus of the Great Leap Forward in the late 1950s, or in any of the subsequent political struggles, the proletariat's idea of "heaven" during the Cultural Revolution in the 1960s was often a simple, earthen, whitewashed shed built to demonstrate one's revolutionary spirit. Thus, the Park Hotel in Shanghai, built before the Revolution, would remain the tallest skyscraper until Mao's death in 1976. The living conditions of urban residents at the end of the Cultural Revolution were impoverished, and most families were packed into single rooms without a toilet or kitchen. Peeping through the "Open Door" policies of the late 1970s, Chinese people had their first glimpse of western cities, and they truly seemed like an unreachable heaven. Today, just as the notion of a nice home with a white picket fence is the symbol of the "American Dream," ownership of a house has become the new "Chinese Dream." And it is a dream with a long pedigree: the utopian vision described by fifth-century Chinese poet Tao Yuanming included rows and rows of houses, while similarly, grandiose architecture is a standard motif in the Western Paradise, the Buddhist heaven, of the Pure Land Buddhist tradition.[1] Thus, the question is, are skyscrapers the new symbol of heaven for most Chinese? It certainly could be if you, as I, had witnessed one of your classmates living with his father and brother in a single room with ceilings only four feet high.

While the recent economic miracle has transformed China in drastic ways, the need for building monumental celebrations to Communist achievements seems to

1. In simplified Chinese: 净土宗, *Jingtuzong*. It is a branch of Mahāyāna Buddhism.

persist. Skyscrapers are the ideal illustrations of the post-Mao era, simultaneously reflecting both the increasingly materialistic and autocratic ideology of contemporary China. Chinese skyscrapers produce a sense of hyper-reality: decontextualized postmodern architecture, most of them inoculating copies of western designs. And the virus spreads. Skyscrapers require a vast mobilization of workers migrating from poor rural areas in order to build on a scale not seen since the days of the pyramids. The artists' images of untold numbers of skyscrapers silently remind us of the unseen faces of the cheap labor that constructed the buildings. As we see here in this exhibition, Ai Weiwei, who participated in the design of the Beijing Olympic Gymnasium, shows his middle finger to demonstrate his attitude of negation. Architecture as propaganda, custom built for the 2008 Beijing Olympics, is incompatible with the reality of most Chinese people. "How related are these Olympic Games to the true state of the country, the city, and the people? It is far away from the reality. Therefore, it is something fake and hypocritical."[2] Nevertheless, the city of Beijing will be an open-air museum for three of the world's top ten architectural marvels of 2007, as designated by *Time* magazine.[3] The eye-catching and astonishing "Bird's Nest" and "Water Cube" of the 2008 Olympic park together with China Central Television's breathtaking, twisted triumph gate and the "Floating Pearl," as the National Center for the Performing Arts is known, are truly phenomenal structures. Shanghai, especially the Bund, is the showcase of China as spectacle.[4] Its extravagance has made it a mecca for visitors both from all over China and the West hoping to get a taste of a changing China. Shanghai was named the "Most Happening City in the World" by *Time* magazine in 2006. Meanwhile, some photographers took it upon themselves to reconnoiter and archive what was, is, and will be happening in Shanghai with their cameras. The audience may look on with mixed feelings of admiration and regret, not unlike one's response to the almost religious grandiosity seen in American painter Charles Demuth's *My Egypt* (1929), where factories become modern shrines. While fighting liver cancer, Liang Weiping chronicles the doomed factories along Suzhou Creek, a river that meanders through the city of Shanghai, which served as an important waterway for some of the earliest and most important factories in China. To Weiping, these factories were monuments to the heroic struggle of the Chinese people to shake off the image of the shuffling "Chinaman" throughout the world.

Not all Chinese look at skyscrapers as stairways to heaven. To Yang Yongliang, the skyscrapers aren't towering monuments to nationalist pride but steles built atop the remnants of China's 5,000-year-old civilization. In an odd juxtaposition, his images of skyscrapers and cranes evoke traditional Chinese ink paintings. Allegori-

2. From a video made in 2007, http://www.youtube.com/watch?v=R-CdWcszb_8.

3. http://www.time.com/time/magazine/article/0,9171,1694467,00.html.

4. The former international settlement and economic center of China before the establishment of the People's Republic of China in 1949, known for the many historical buildings lining the banks of the Huangpu River in Shanghai.

cally, those skyscrapers are heavenly and beautiful from a distance but ugly and horrifying upon closer inspection: you see nothing but a forest of reinforced concrete. Metaphysically, these conceptual images of skyscrapers advocate an invalidation born in a new Cultural Revolution: the buildings have caused more destruction of traditional architectural treasures and historical sites than Mao's Cultural Revolution. It reminds us of Mao's suggestion that only on a clean sheet of paper can the newest and most beautiful picture be drawn. One of the most beautiful pictures drawn in the landscape of China today is "Orange County, China"; a housing development an hour's drive North of Beijing where all the designs, major building materials, hardware, and furniture were imported from the United States.[5] In contrast, the work of Ma Liuming displays the neglected and tumbledown nontourist sections of the Great Wall, the architectural icon of Chinese history. It provides a shocking paradigm of the degree to which skyscrapers now overshadow the historical monuments of China.

Like Yang Yongliang, Yening adopts a similar approach manifesting her negation of such concrete nightmares. The melting together of skyscrapers leaves no space for life to intercede, with the "reflection-like" mirror images of the same suffocating buildings under a band of repeated images of Tiananmen, the gate of the former Forbidden City. Even more dramatic and emotional, almost invisible, tiny faces of the artist appear in the countless windows of the skyscrapers: the desperate howl of a prisoner in an inhuman environment. The photo has thus become personal and compelling. To represent the mourning associated with the loss of historical architecture in Beijing, she uses repeated images of the celebrated National Opera House, the "Floating Pearl," as the axis, in striking contrast with the ghost-like shadowed courtyard houses of old Beijing.

Xing Danwen has created utopian-like imageries of people who live in and around the skyscrapers. The sense of alienation is intensified by enlarging building models and scaling down human images inside them. The artificial shots of apartment building models like you'd find in real estate offices act as stages for Xing to present the human drama of the urban landscape. Aloofness born of isolation, alienation due to uprootedness, the estrangement and abandonment of this caged-bird existence, are all performed by the artist. In a variety of costumes, Xing Danwen, plays out the scenes: adultery, bloody murder, a horrible car accident, and a housewife filled with a sense of ennui. Her performance-based photography is a visual sociology of contemporary China, autopsying the impact of the alienating urban environment. Wang Jing, another female artist and a college professor, produced a similarly cinematic display (this time with children's toys) of a Surrealist nightmare

5. Mike Anton, "Welcome to Orange County, China," *Los Angels Times*, 9 March 2002.

with soldiers and tanks flooding the Shanghai Television Tower, which has been proudly nicknamed "The Pearl of the East." In another nightmare vision staged with children's toys, millions of dinosaurs flood the skyscrapers, reminding one of the disaster movies produced by Hollywood. The artist's work is a warning against the uncontrolled expansion of cities in China that is destroying the natural environment. These artists demonstrate that skyscrapers are fundamentally commercial entities, soliciting and stimulating conspicuous consumption, construction advocating for the limitless production of the economy. The spread of skyscrapers also produces homogenized cities. Standing on any urban street in China today, it is all too easy to forget which city you're in. These new urban landscapes create homogenized culture where stimulation and dizzying variations are needed to save city residents from their own irredeemable boredom, and in a vicious circle, all of this meaningless effort leads to more building and greater homogeneity. The endless reproduction of skyscrapers not only serves to exasperate the phenomenon but also comes to represent it. Fighting a doomed battle, like some modern-day Don Quixote, to save the visual archives of disappearing "Old Shanghai," Lu Yuanmin's photos are mourning the very death of "Shanghainess."

Sometimes, illusion can make people happy. Thus, the courtiers of Russia's Catherine the Great constructed false façades to hide the peasants' hovels just to keep her ignorant and happy. In the *Shanghai Zero Degree* series Zhu Feng photographed a construction site papered over with the image of a charming landscape of mountains, woods and streams, and water-reflections. Everybody knows it's a fake, an impossible illusion in modern Shanghai. The illusionary landscape serves to dramatize the artificiality of the newly built urban environment. It reveals the stark contrast between nature and the concrete skyscrapers and reveals how alienated people have become from their surroundings. Zhu Feng has reproduced the collective consciousness of the urban inhabitant. The work echoes the desire to return to nature as described by Guo Xi in his treatise on landscape painting, *Linquan Gaozhi* ("Lofty Record of Forests and Streams") in the Song Dynasty, some 1,000 years ago.

Luo Yongjin's series *Government Buildings* expands formally and conceptually on his earlier *Castle* project. The so called "castles" from both the pre-Mao and post-Mao era in Luo's work refers to the elevated buildings in villages that displayed the owners' wealth and superiority. In other words, they were village skyscrapers. Though a nearly century-wide gap exists between these two types of buildings—both high-rise buildings towering over others—they share the same postmodern Chinese characteristics: grafting architectural components from the West. These "castles" replace the traditional Chinese houses in villages all along the Yangtze River Delta. Has the globalization of architecture already spread to rural Chinese villages? An author once visited a village in a remote mountainous area in southeast China where the architectural attractions were unique: wood-framed, slate-roofed, and slate-floored village houses of a type that had existed for centuries. The author tried in vain to persuade the peasants to refrain from tearing down their beautiful traditional houses, but they were sadly replaced with concrete buildings. Houses with cement façades were the realization of their "Chinese Dreams." They could never have dreamed of building a house with cement during the era of Chairman Mao. This kind of architectural transformation in remote mountainous villages is unlikely to be seen as part of the spectacle of a new China, though the peasants living in newly built concrete buildings must think they're in heaven.

However, living in a beautiful apartment in a skyscraper-congested downtown is not always a realization of the "Chinese Dream"—at least according to the artists in this exhibition. Sometimes, Chinese dreams-gone-wrong crop up. For example, the privatization of state-owned factories was a nightmare for those who lost their jobs as is the case when the 798 factory was shut down and the new owner replaced the old Soviet-made machines with works of contemporary Chinese art. The unemployed workers were eager models for Liu Bolin's photo shoot, which took place in the very building where they had once proudly worked. The unemployed workers wanted people to witness the tragedy of their dream gone sour. Hong Lei shows the Chinese dream-gone-bad in his allegories of ancient Chinese palaces and Ming dynasty gardens. Xing Danwen stages her nightmare visions as a rose-colored "Chinese Dream": loneliness, alienation, confusion, bleakness, and absurdity all combined. Wang Jing has nightmares of the total destruction of the natural environment and the doomed future of mankind. Yening chokes on her dreams-gone-bad as revealed in the "concrete prisons" crammed into high-rise buildings. Yang Yongliang's nightmare was discovering that China had turned into a landscape of hell: all the trees and grass had been replaced by skyscrapers.

The skyscraper is an American invention. Early on, skyscrapers were built as giant, visually appealing, commercials for corporations. In the troublesome 1960s and 1970s, skyscrapers often became a symbol of modernity and nations. Most recently, the felled towers of the World Trade Center in New York have come to represent American resilience and courage. Today, amidst the global competition for commercial visibility and market domination, skyscrapers have become monumental advertisements to China's success and, according to government bureaucrats, symbols of their administrative achievements. However, artists in this show do not work for the propaganda department of the Central Committee of the Communist Party of China, nor the provincial and city propaganda departments of the Party. Thus, they do not have to take picture-postcard landscapes of Chinese cities. Their visions go beyond the monumental façade of the China spectacle. Inspired by the hot market for Chinese contemporary oil paintings that began in the 1990s, these Chinese photographers have been experimenting with a variety of photographic techniques such as digital manipulation, abstract use of colors, photographic metamorphosis, illusion of the artificial, the detachment of human images from their environment, and surrealist treatments of subject matter. With a richness of variety, a depth of conceptual investigation, and an intriguing combination of traditional and modern Chinese motifs, a growing number of avant-garde photographers have brought photography into major biennials and art exhibitions throughout the world. The twenty-first century has been deemed "China's Century."[6] The artists in this exhibition are not simply pessimistic and gloomy, but raise a serious and thought-provoking question: What will China sacrifice in order to catch up with the West?

6. Laurence J. Brahm, *China's Century: The Awakening of the Next Economic Powerhouse* (New Jersey: John Wiley and Sons, 2001).

徐淦

以2008 年北京奥林匹克运动会作为展窗，现在中国比以往更热切地向世界展示它正在戏剧般变化中的城市。对世界上其他国家而言，中国史无前例的变化本身，最为明显地体现在都市里象蘑菇一样蔓延的摩天大楼上。呈现在人们眼前的是人们所说的中国的"建筑大跃进"。摩天大楼是"第二次文化革命"最直接和最强烈的标志。这场"文化革命"是迫不及待的"西化"洪流。但是， 就如在这次展览中所见，摩天大楼的图象，不是展示党的伟大成就，也不是物化党的权威。这些摄影师没有急不可待地加入欢庆的游行；而是把他们探索的镜头，对准在高楼大厦背后和在贫富悬殊的大都市里的事物，而这一切都以感知的形式，被界定为中国奇迹的另一面。

半个世纪以前， 1949年中华人民共和国诞生， 对于中国人来说，遥望苏联的金色光芒，象是人间天堂景象。但是， 在五十年代后期的"大跃进"中，以及在以后一系列的政治斗争中，建筑被忽视。六十年代文化大革命期间的无产阶级"天堂" ，是显示革命精神的刷白灰的干打垒。这也解释了为什么国民革命前建造的上海国际饭店，直至1976年毛泽东逝世，一直保持中国最高摩天大楼的记录。文化大革命后期城市居民的居住条件窘迫得令人难以想象，多数家庭全家人挤在没有洗手间和厨房的单间里。七十年代末，由于"开放"政策，中国人民第一次瞥见西方城市的真容，那些高楼大厦象是可望不可及的天堂。今天，就象一座白色篱笆环绕的漂亮房子是"美国之梦"的象征一样，拥有一处住房是新的"中国之梦"。事实上，居者有其屋是中国人自古以来的梦想。五世纪中国诗人陶渊明所描述的乌托邦天堂里屋舍俨然。同样，在中国佛教净土宗[1]对西方乐土的刻画里，必有楼阁巍峨壮丽。所以，问题是，对于大多数中国人来说，这些摩天大楼是天堂景观吗？答案可能是肯定的，如果你见过作者的同学与他的父亲、哥哥曾经挤住在一间天花板只有四英尺高的屋子里。

当前的经济奇迹使中国产生了前所未有的变化，但为了欢庆共产主义神话，对纪念碑式表述的需要仍然存在。摩天大楼是后毛泽东时代的最佳例证，它们不仅反映了当代中国越来越物质主义至上的思想观念，也体现了当代中国的集权主义意识。中国的摩天大楼产生了一种虚幻的现实：脱离自身文化背景的后现代建筑，其中大多数是西方建筑设计的变种，并象病毒一样蔓延。这是自从金字塔时代以来人类所进行的最大规模的建设，使得浩浩荡荡的农民工，离乡背井。 摄影中成片的摩天大楼，无声地提醒观众去关注那些人们视而不见的廉价劳力的面孔。在这次展览中，曾参加北京奥林匹克体育馆设计的美术家、建筑师艾未未，伸出中指来表示他的抗议。为2008年北京奥林匹克运动会量身定制的建筑仅是一种宣传，与多数中国人民的现实相距甚远。 "这次奥林匹克运动会与我们国家、与城市和人民的真

1. 净土宗是中国佛教宗派，属大乘佛教。

实状态有什么联系？它与现实的差距太大了。因此它就是虚假的和虚伪的。"[2]，北京以其拥有《时代杂志》选出的2007世界十大建筑奇迹中的三座，必将成为建筑奇迹的露天博物馆[3]。令人眼睛一亮、精彩绝伦的"鸟巢"、"水立方"、中央电视台大楼叫人喘不过气来的凌空折转的凯旋门和"水上珍珠"国家大剧院，确确实实是些让人叹为观止的建筑。上海，特别是外滩，是中国景观的对外展示[4]。上海奇迹成为中国各地游客以及对巨变后中国一探究竟的西方游客必到之处。2006年，美国《时代周刊》的一期封面上，上海被誉为"世界上最活跃的城市"。 一些摄影师在上海用他们的摄影机记录了上海的过去和现在，在图像中审视未来。观众会在这些摄影中看到象美国画家查尔斯·迪姆斯的《我的埃及》(1929)所表现出来的宗教般的宏伟，产生敬仰和追思的复杂感情，因为在这幅画作中，工厂成为圣地。十多年来，梁卫平一面与肝癌做斗争，一面为许多苏州河边注定要消亡的工厂建立图像档案。在蜿蜒流经上海城区的苏州河这条重要的水道旁，曾聚集了一批中国最早和最重要的工厂。对梁卫平来说，这些工厂是中国人民英勇奋斗、在世界上摆脱落后"中国佬"形象的纪念碑。

　　并非所有的中国人都把摩天大楼看作是通往天堂的阶梯。对杨泳梁来说，摩天大楼不是高耸入云、展示民族主义自豪感的纪念碑。摩天大楼湮没了中国五千年的文明痕迹。他作品中数不清的摩天大楼和图像，按照中国传统墨水绘画形式构图紧密排列，同那些起重机图像一起，创造出意想不到的墨水绘画的感觉。从寓意的层次来看，远看这些摩天大楼象天堂般美丽；但走近细看，却丑陋不堪、让人恐惧：除了密不透风的钢筋混凝土大厦组成的森林，什么都看不见。从更隐晦、更抽象的层次看来，这些摩天大楼的概念性图象，显示了"新文化大革命"的破坏性：摩天大楼对传统建筑珍迹和历史遗迹的破坏，比毛泽东的文化大革命有过之而无不及。这使我们想起毛泽东的语录， "一张白纸好画最新最美的图画。" 今天在中国大地上画出的最新最美的图画之一，可能要算中国的"美国加州橙县"[5]。这个住宅区座落于京城北面开车一小时之远的地方，它的设计、主要的建筑装修材料、五金配件及家具等都从美国直接进口。与之形成鲜明对比，在马六明的作品中，中国建筑的撼世之作长城，那些游客罕至的区段，一片断壁残垣、破败不堪。他以触目惊心的长城图象，揭示了中国不少纪念碑性的历史建筑，已经消失在摩天大楼的阴影之中。

　　象杨泳梁一样， 也宁也用类似的方法表现她的摩天大楼恶梦。重叠拥挤的摩天大楼窒息了生命的空间，昔日的紫禁城皇家城门天安门图象，重复组成下方镜象的隔离带，象水中倒影一样的是同样拥挤的大楼。更加戏剧化和情感化的是，艺术家小得几乎看不出的面孔，重复出现在那些摩天大楼不计其数的窗口里：这是身困冷漠环境中的人，在可怜地哀叹。这张作品因而变得富有个人色彩，更加震撼人的心灵。为了哀悼老北京历史建筑的陨失， 她用国家大剧院 — "水上珍珠" 重复的图象为轴，与鬼魂阴影般的老北京四合院，构成强烈对比。

　　以一种女性特有的敏感和细腻，以女权主义的姿态，邢丹文的图象刻画了生活

2. 摘自艾未未2007年的一段录像。

3. 见网址：http://www.time.com/time/magazine/article/0,9171,1694467,00.html。

4. 中华人民共和国建国前的国际租界和经济中心，以黄浦江沿岸的历史性建筑著称。

5. 麦克·安通， "欢迎来到中国橙县"，《洛杉矶时报》，2002年3月9日。

在摩天大楼以及现代都市里人们理想国般美丽的天堂。但是，放大的建筑模型和其中微缩人物的怪异比例，赋予都市人异化这一社会现象以可视的具象。以房屋开发商售楼处展售楼房模型为舞台，邢丹文用伪写实的手法，演示了在都市中时时发生的人间戏剧。摄影作品中的女主角因为孤独而神情恍惚、因为离乡背井而缺乏归属感，象笼中的金丝鸟一样被抛弃和疏远。而作品中这些人间戏剧的女主角扮演者就是艺术家自己。在荒谬的通奸、血腥的谋杀、恐怖的交通事故或百无聊赖的家庭妇女等场景中，邢丹文穿上不同的服装，扮演了一个个不同的角色。她的摄影既是舞台设计又是表演艺术。它们是可视的当代中国社会学，深刻解剖了使人异化的中国当代都市环境。王净，另一位女性艺术家和理性的大学教授，以儿童玩具为道具，创作了相似的电影场景，极似超现实主义的恶梦。骄傲地被称为"东方明珠"的上海电视塔，被潮水一般的坦克和士兵包围，在她用儿童玩具搭出的另一恶梦里，成千上万只恐龙在摩天大楼之间横冲直撞。这些作品使我们想起好莱坞制作的灾难片。中国城市的无限扩展，破坏了生态环境，对此，王净发出了强烈的警告。这些摄影家警示我们，摩天大楼就是消费广告，它们刺激和诱导无节制的消费，它们是招摇炫富的建筑，意在为经济的过度增长推波助澜。摩天大楼的蔓延也导致了中国城市的单一化。站在许多中国城市的街道上，人们失去了地域感。单调划一的城市，产生单调肤浅的文化，人们将不得不更加依赖更为强烈的刺激和令人目眩的花样来逃避单调和沉闷。这构成了一个糟糕的社会怪圈，这些徒劳无益的努力，又把人们引向缺乏变化的同一化。无休止地复制摩天大楼，更放大了这种枯燥乏味。就像唐·吉柯德在一场注定要失败的战斗中奋斗一样，陆元敏在为消失的"老上海"建立视觉档案，他的摄影叹息那些正在消失的可以称为"上海特性"的一切。

有时，幻像也能给人以欢愉。所以才会有俄国沙皇的大臣们为了蒙蔽和讨好卡特琳娜女皇，在她巡视的路旁建造布景式豪宅来遮掩后面的破旧农舍。朱峰在他的《上海零度》中给我们展示了用来遮掩建筑工地的美丽风景布景：高山、森林、溪流和水中倒影。人人皆知，这些都是假的，是自欺欺人的幻觉，在当代上海是绝无可能的。这些虚幻的美景把新建的都市生存环境里的人为矫饰，进行了戏剧化的表现。他的摄影揭示了钢筋水泥摩天大楼和真实大自然之间的触目惊心的对比，同时还显示了生存环境对人的异化。朱峰再现了都市居民向往大自然的集体意识。一千多年前北宋画家郭熙在他的《林泉高致》中就流露出了他对远离都市、回归自然的渴望，朱峰的摄影，宛如古人之回音。

罗永进的《政府办公楼系列》也是他的《城堡系列》的继续。这些被称为"城堡"的住宅分别是毛泽东掌权前和毛泽东逝世后修建的高楼，它们鹤立鸡群地矗立在乡村农居之中，展示主人的富裕和傲视独立，它们是乡村版"摩天大楼"。以上两类高楼相距百年，这些高楼与中国后现代主义建筑有一共通之处，那就是嫁接西建筑元素。在长江三角洲，这类不伦不类的"城堡"大有取代中国传统农舍的趋势。难道建筑的全球化已经扩展到了中国乡村？一次有位西方的作家参观中国西南边远地区的一个村子，那里有特有的，具有几个世纪历史的石板墙、石板屋顶、石板地面的木屋。他竭力说服村民们不要拆毁那些美丽的石板房，用丑陋的水泥房取而代之。水泥修建的房屋有可能是他们的"中国梦"。在毛泽东时代，农民做梦也不敢想用水泥修建住宅。虽然在边远山村里发生的建筑演变不会被认为是中国景观的一部分。但是，农民住在新建的水泥房屋里，他们认定那里就是他们的天堂。

然而，住在摩天大楼林立的市中心公寓里并不意味着"中国梦"的实现 —— 至少参加这次摄影展的艺术家们不这样认为。有时"中国梦"会突然变成"中国梦魇"。例如，象798厂那些原国有工厂企业的私有化对失业的工人来说，就是一场噩梦。他们引以为自豪的苏联制造机器被当代中国艺术前卫画廊所取代。那些不幸的失业工人非常急切地要在他们曾经工作过的车间里，为刘勃麟的摄影做模特儿。他们希望人们能见证他们的噩梦和痛苦。洪磊在中国古代宫殿和明代花园的象征图像中，显示了"中国梦"式的噩梦。邢丹文用舞台剧的形式，把她自己的梦魇演绎为蒙上一层玫瑰色的"中国梦"：难解难分的孤寂、迷茫、悲哀和荒谬。王净的梦魇是自然生态环境的彻底崩溃和人类劫数难逃的未来。就象置身她所展示的被摩天大楼重重包围的"水泥监狱"一样，也宁被她自己的梦魇所窒息。在杨泳梁的梦魇中，中国的自然风光变成了地狱的风景：所有的树木花草都被摩天大楼所取代。

摩天大楼是美国的创造。早期的摩天大楼是大公司修建的巨大的、吸引人们视线的摩天广告。在充满动荡的六十年代和七十年代，摩天大楼往往成为国家的象征。前几年纽约轰然倒塌的世界贸易大楼，成为表现美国人民勇气和重建的象征。当今，在全球竞争中，为了经济形象和市场占领，摩天大楼成为中国经济成就的超级广告。然而，这次展览中的摄影家并不为中国共产党宣传部工作，也不为省委宣传部和市委宣传部服务。所以，他们无须把中国城市拍摄得象明信片那样壮美。他们的镜头穿透了中国景观的宏伟表象。由于受到中国当代美术九十年代以来价格暴涨的影响，中国摄影家也开始尝试各种摄影手段，例如计算机图像处理、色彩抽象、影象异变、人造幻像、脱离生存环境的人物以及对物象的超现实处理。他们的创造形态丰富多样，具有深邃的观念内涵，饶有意味地融合传统和现代的中国元素。队伍逐渐壮大的前卫摄影师把中国摄影带进了国内和国际的重要双年展和大展。二十一世纪被认为是"中国世纪"[6]。这次展览展出的摄影不能简单地看作是悲观消极，它们提出了一个严肃的、令人深思的问题：为了赶超西方，中国到底准备付出什么样的代价？

6. 劳伦斯·布然，《属于中国的世纪：
觉醒的下一个经济发电站》，新泽西：
John Wiley and Sons，2001。

Skyscrapers 摩天楼

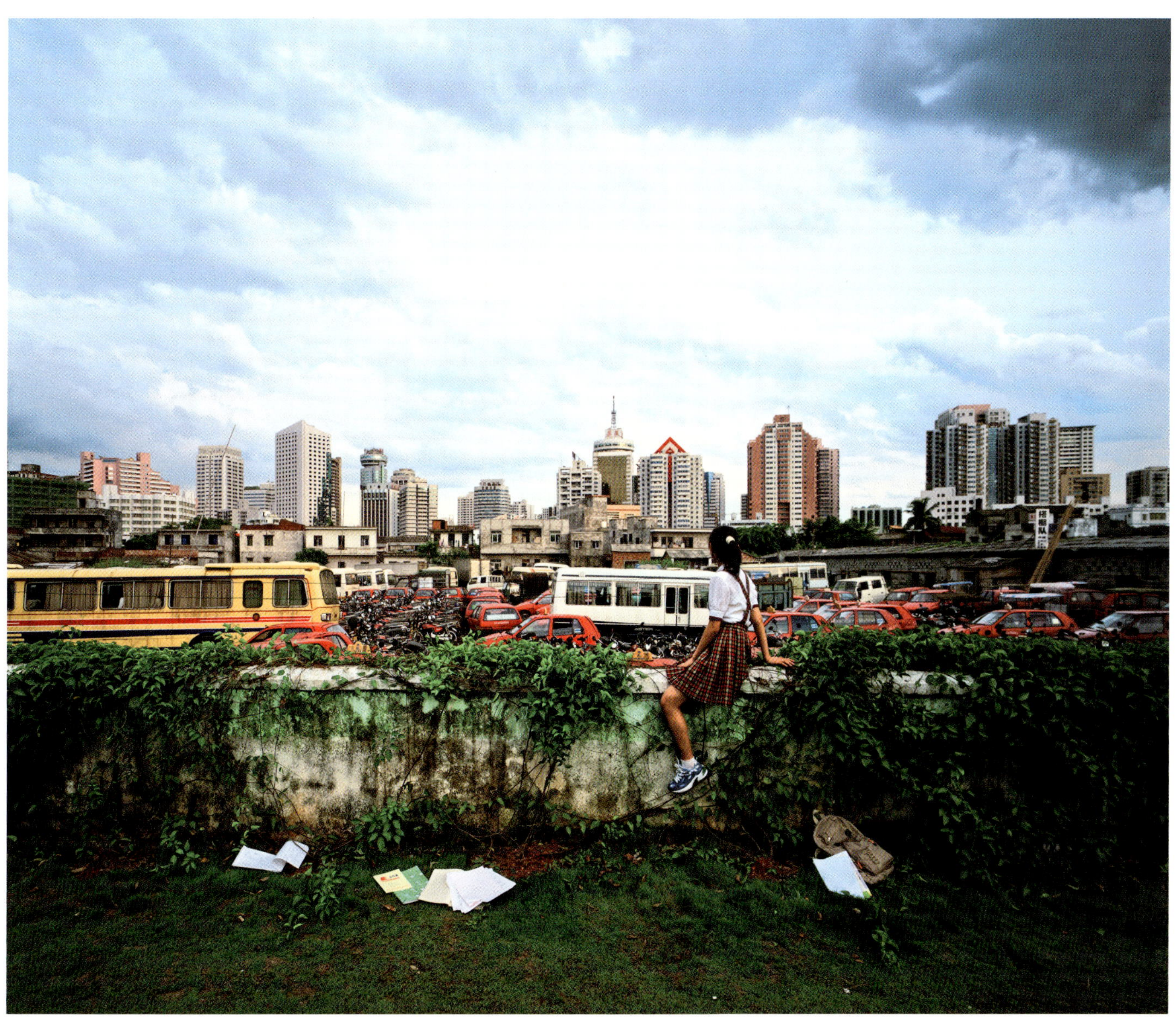

WENG FEN 翁奋 *On the Wall, Haikou 6, 2003*

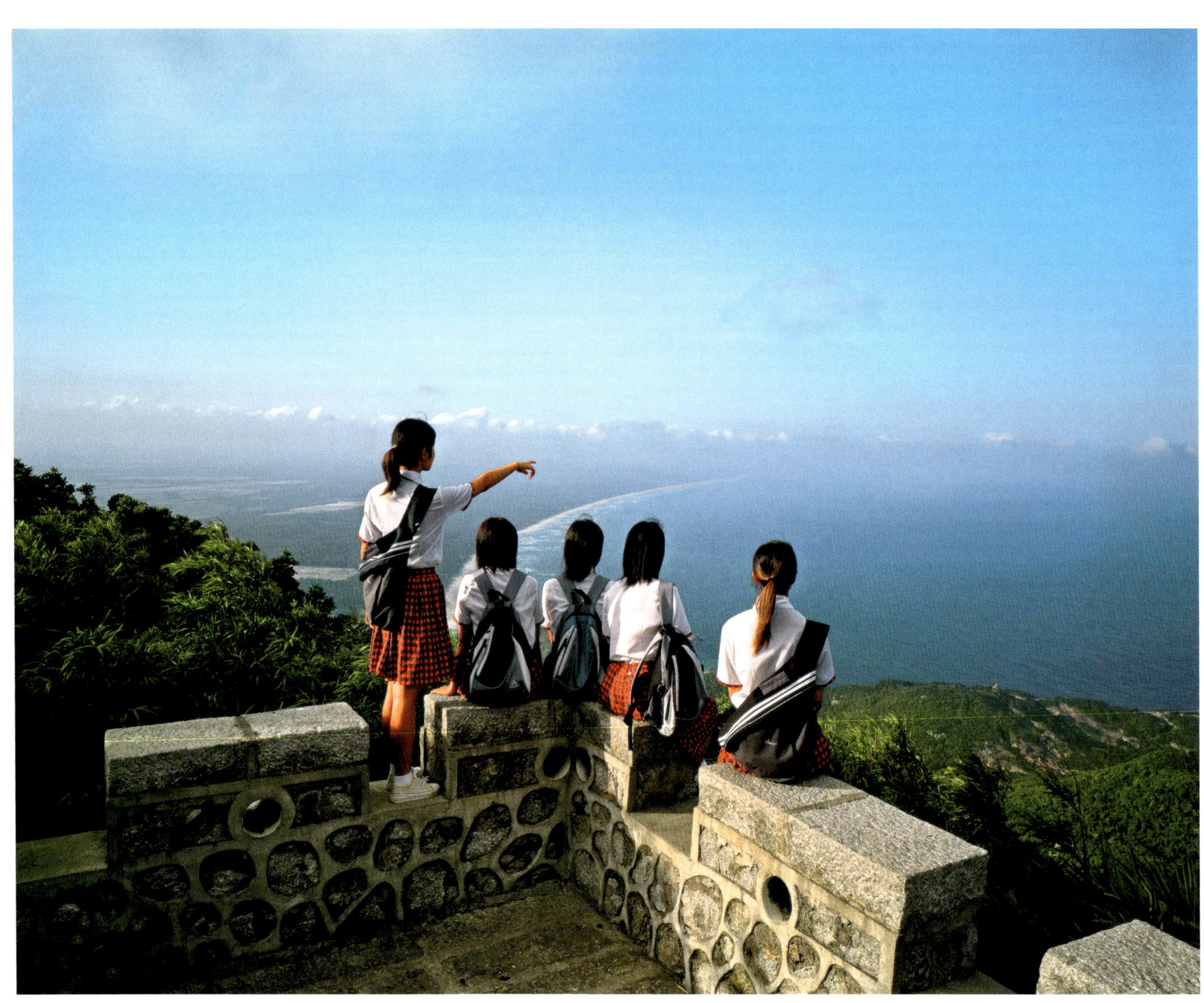

WENG FEN 翁奋 *Staring at the Sea, No. 6, 2003*

80

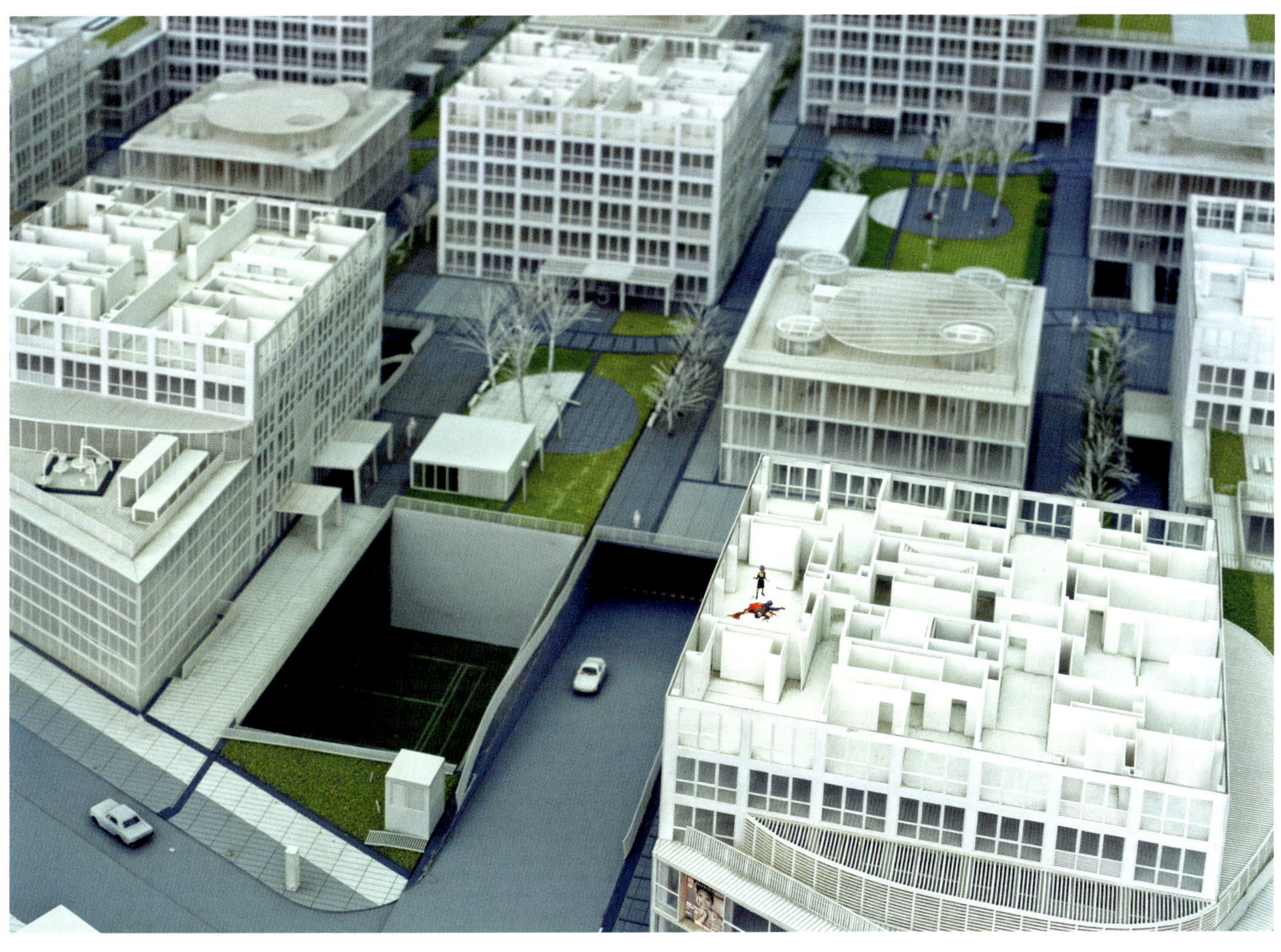

XING DANWEN 邢丹文 *Image 0*, from the series *Urban Fiction*, 2004

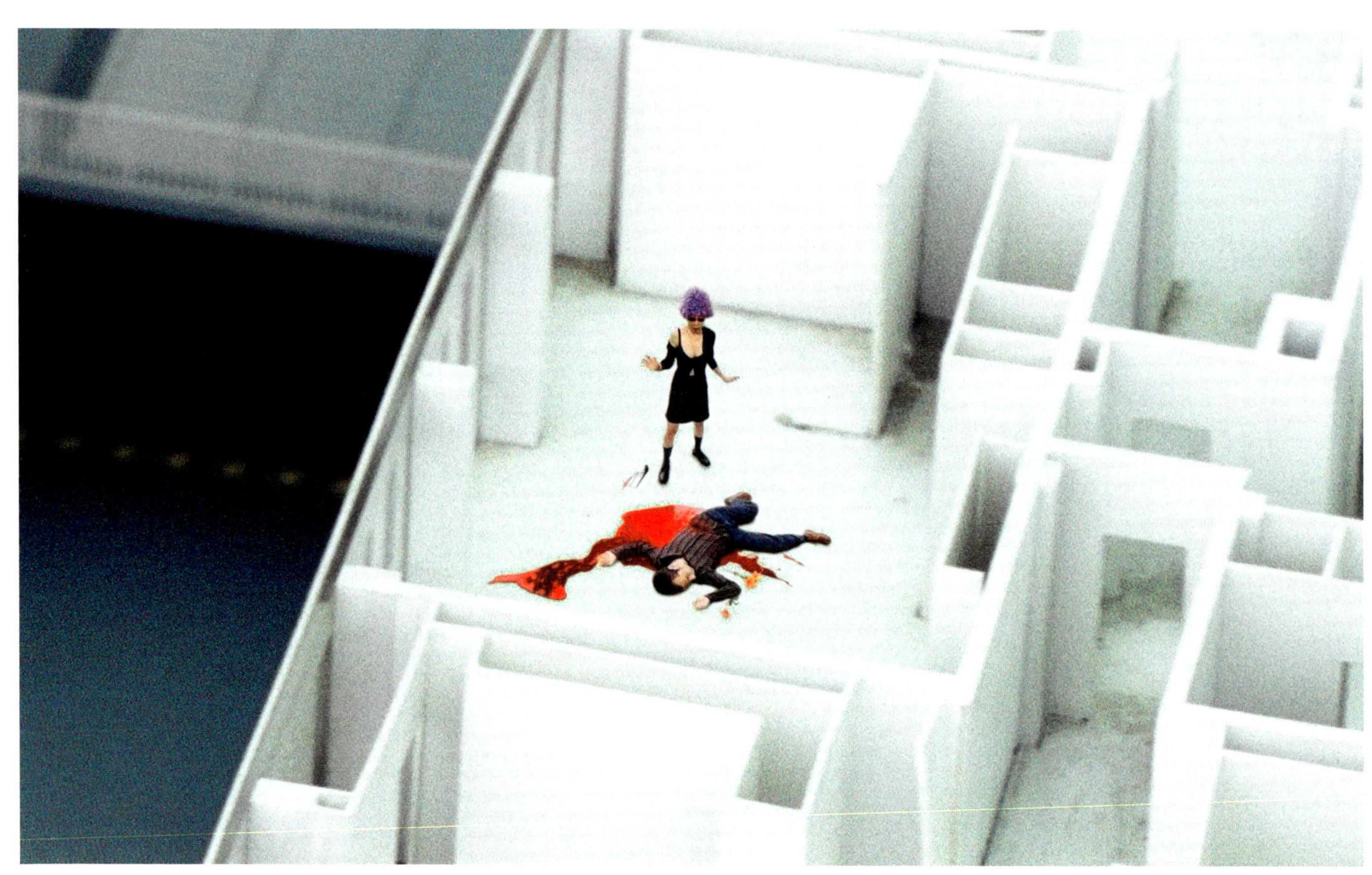

XING DANWEN 邢丹文 Detail

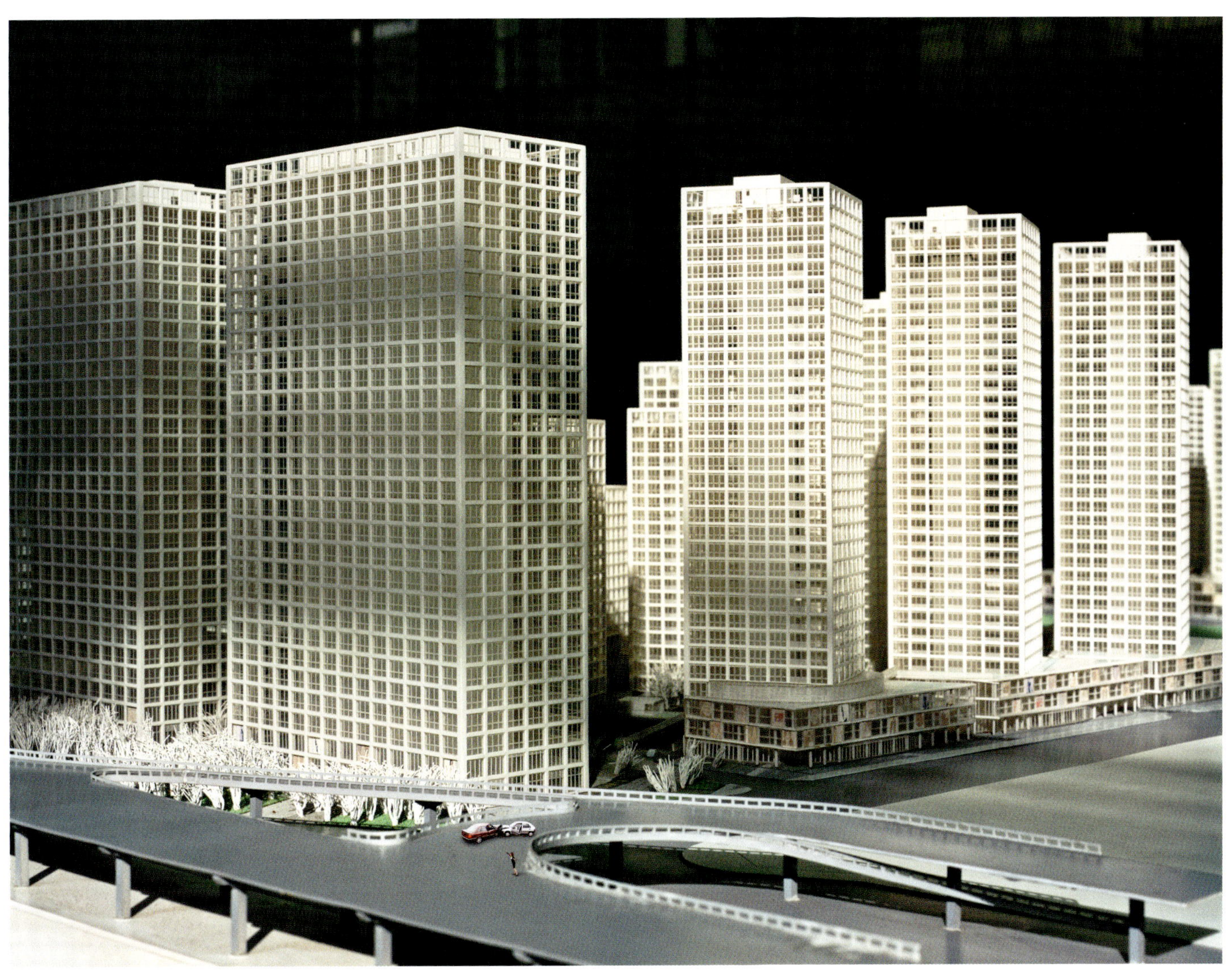

XING DANWEN 邢丹文 *Image 3*, from the series *Urban Fiction*, 2005

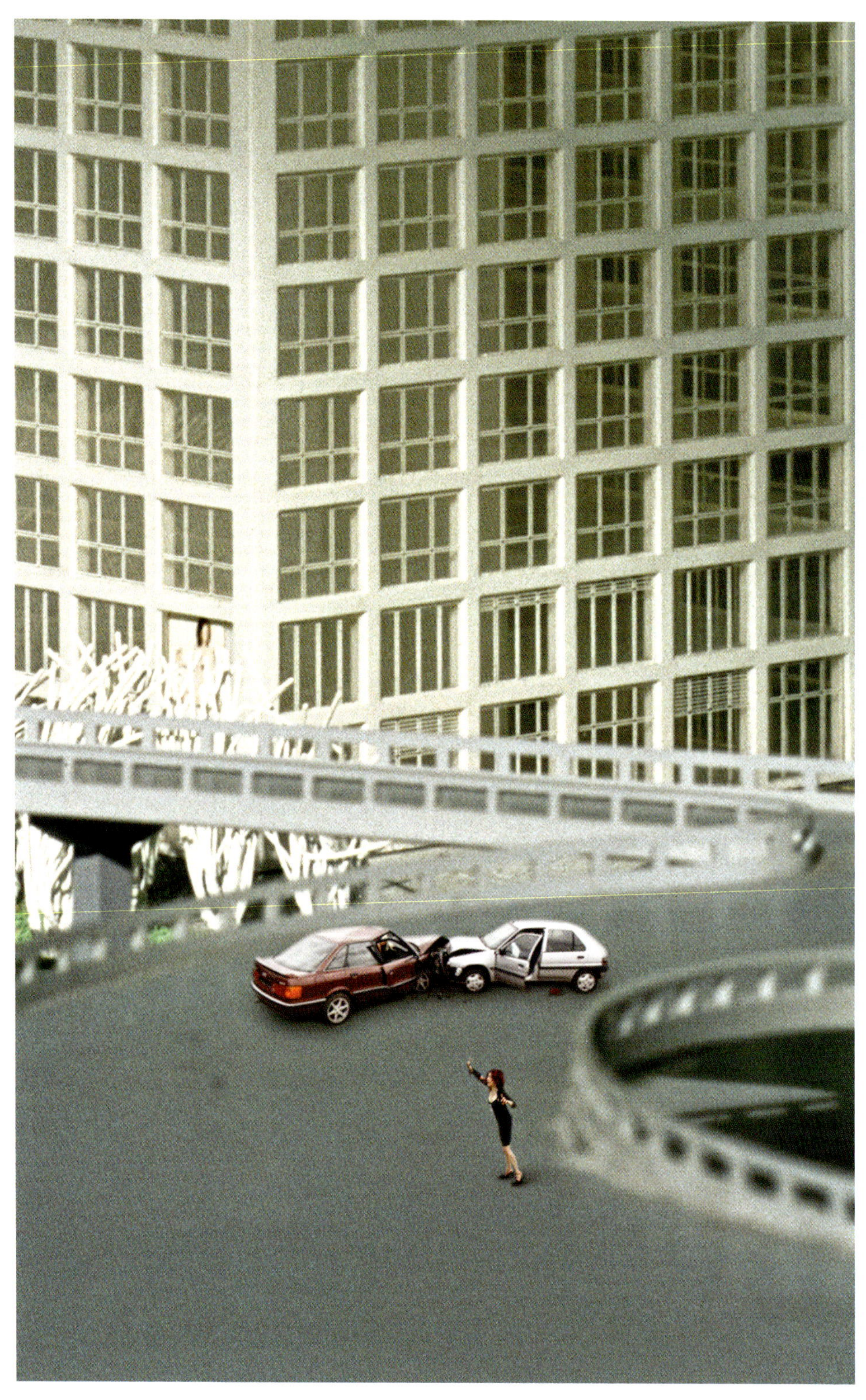

XING DANWEN 邢丹文 Detail

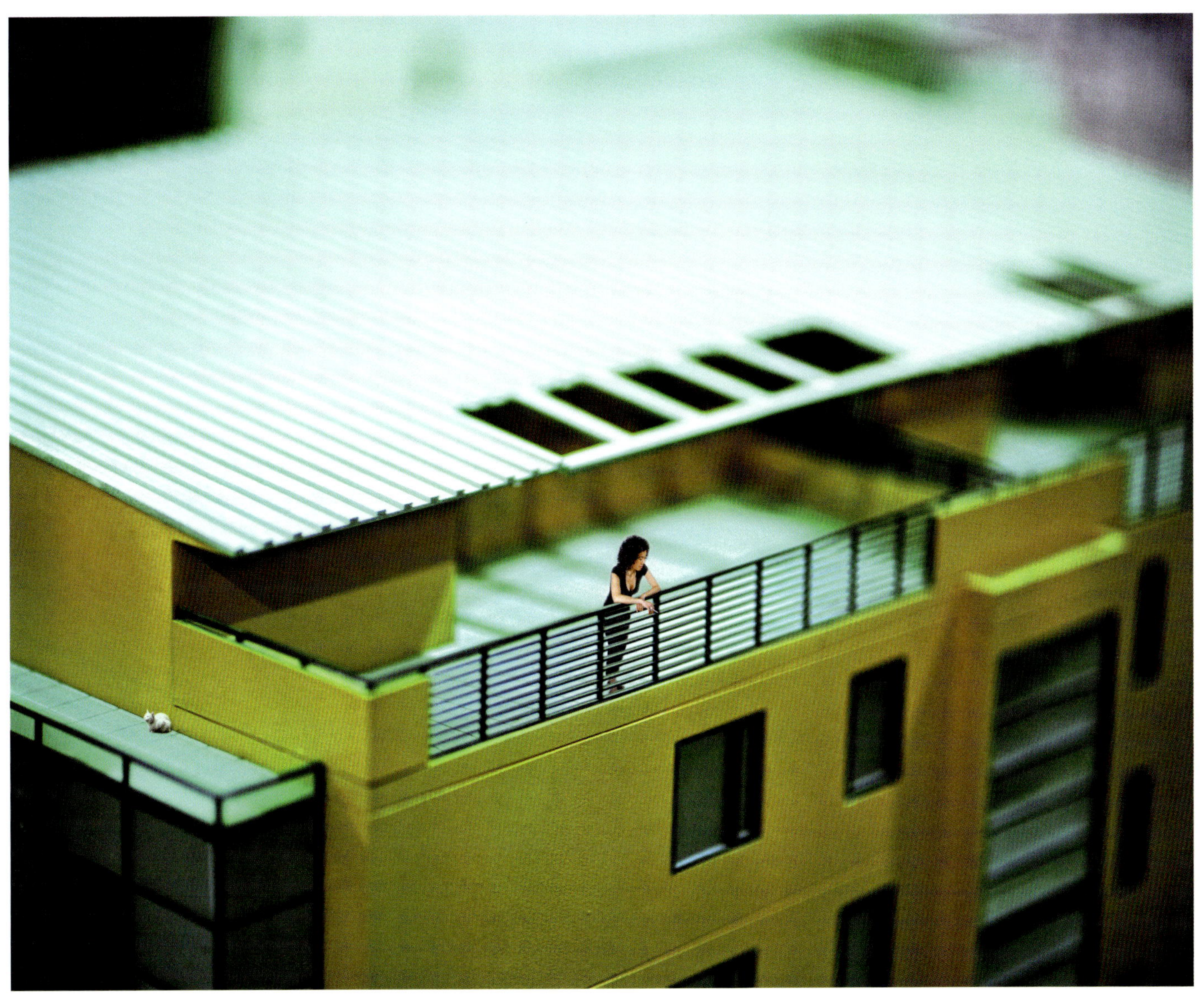

XING DANWEN 邢丹文 *Image 9*, from the series *Urban Fiction*, 2004

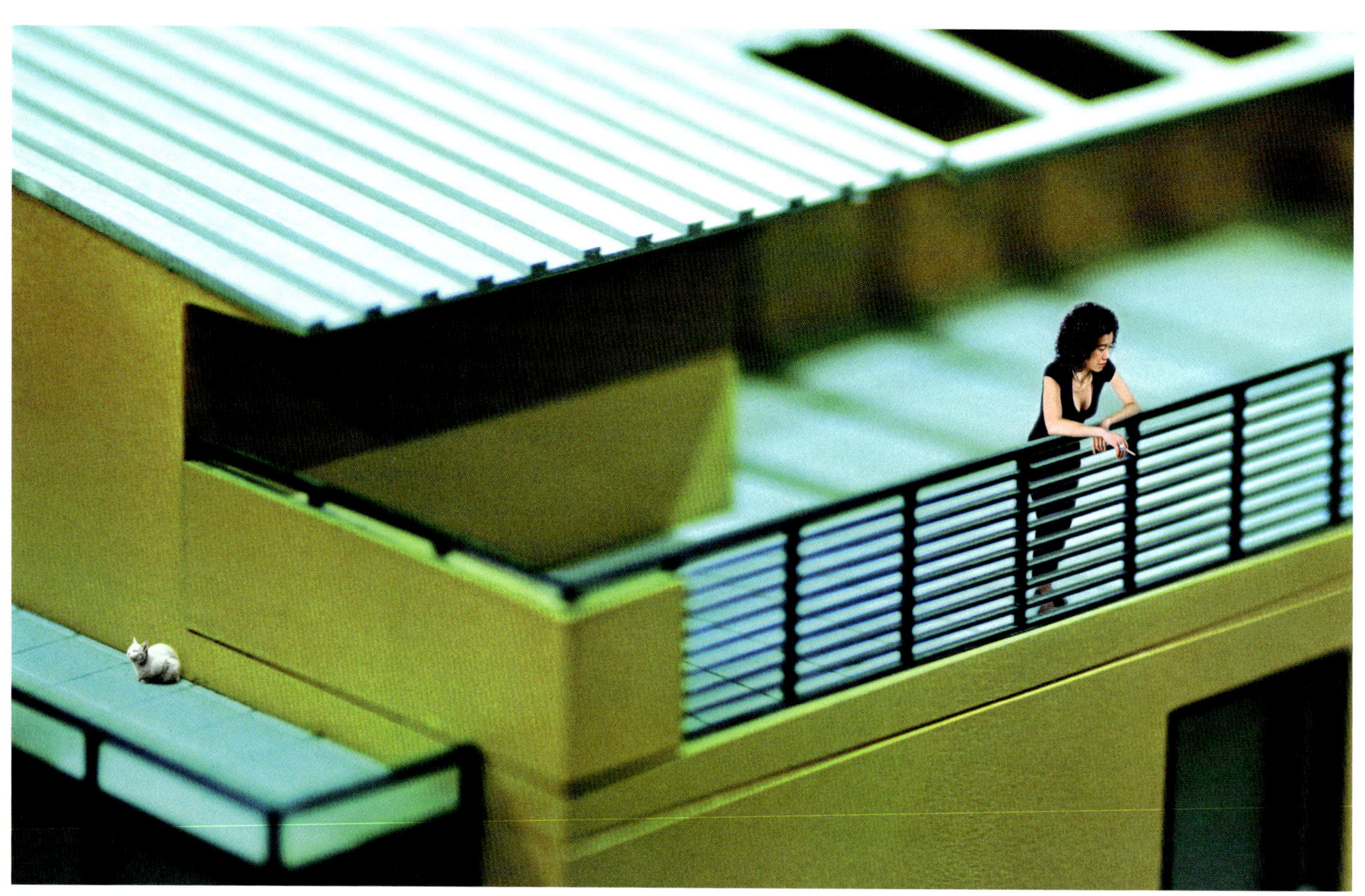

XING DANWEN 邢丹文 Detail

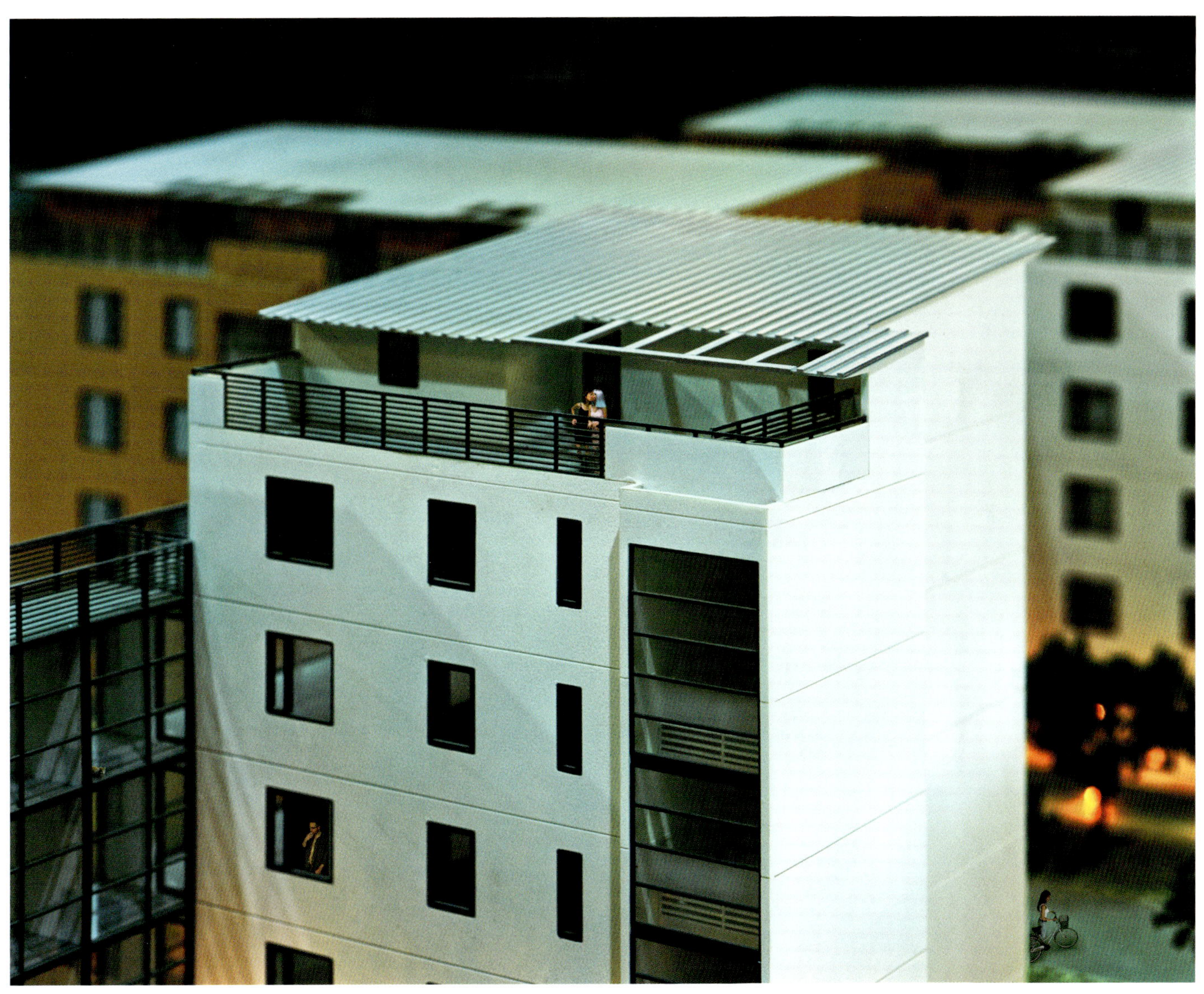

XING DANWEN 邢丹文 *Image 14*, from the series *Urban Fiction*, 2006

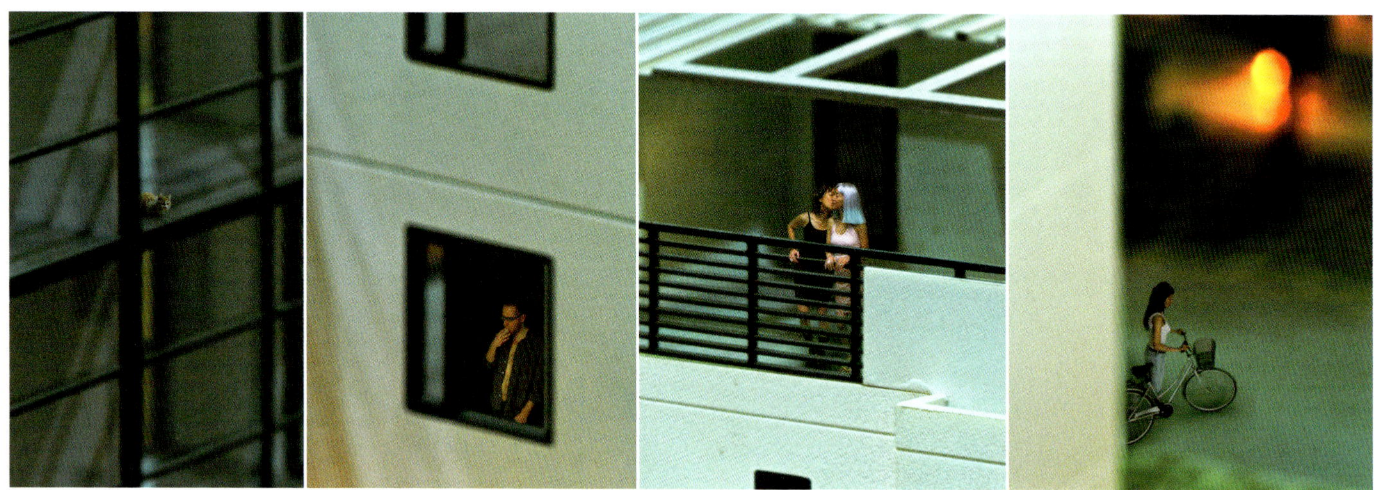

XING DANWEN 邢丹文 Detail

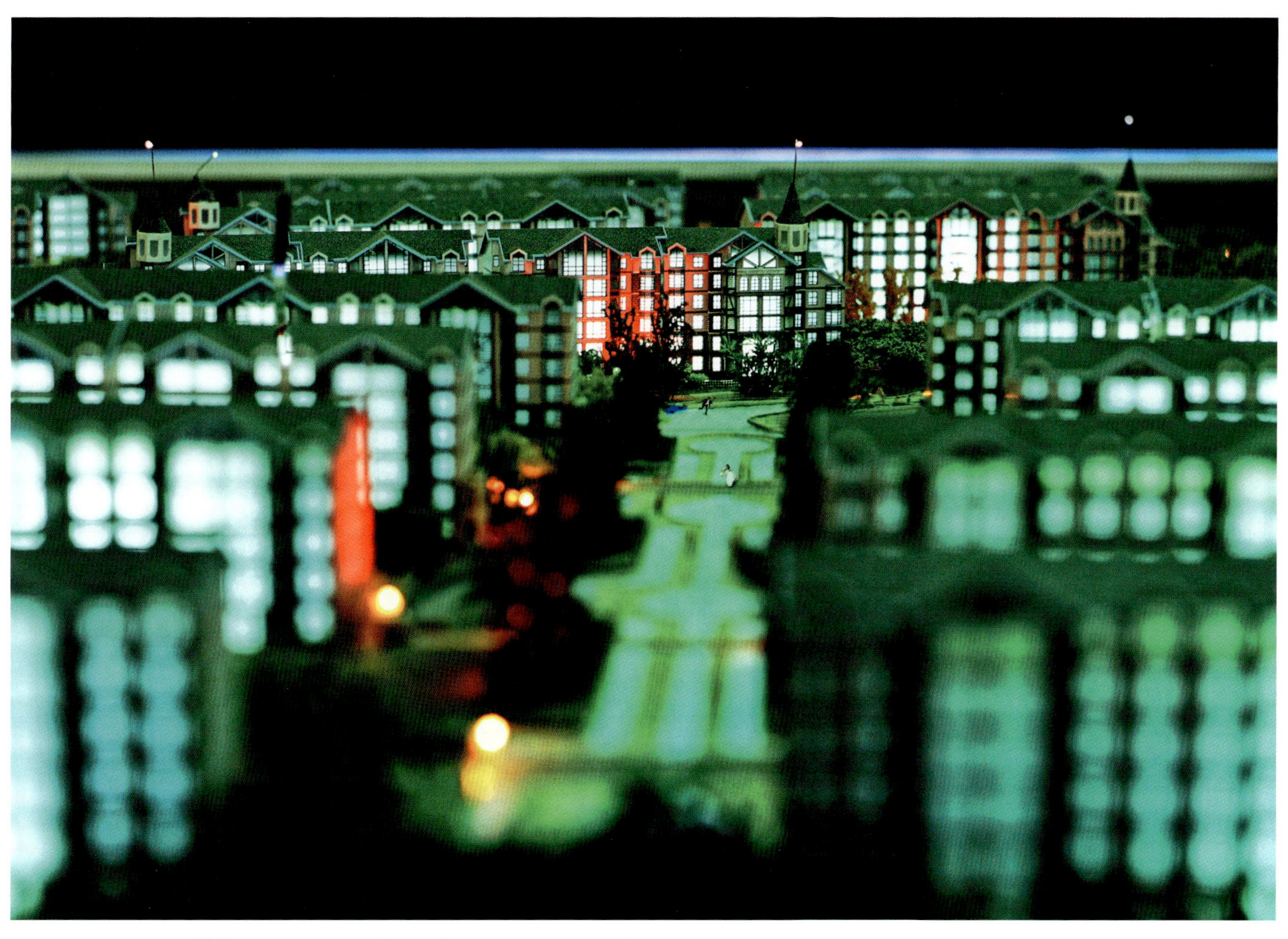

XING DANWEN 邢丹文 *Image 21*, from the series *Urban Fiction*, 2004

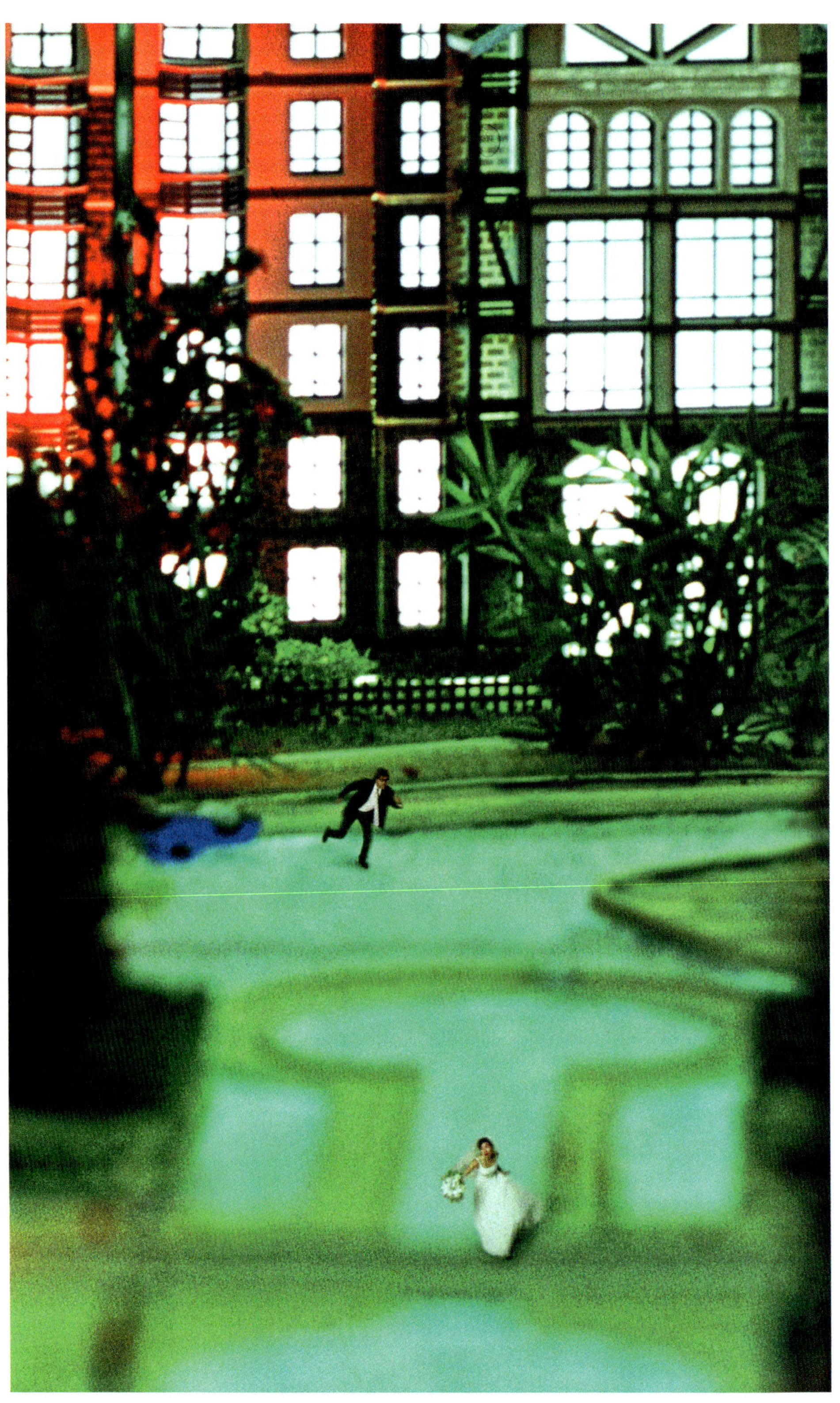

XING DANWEN 邢丹文 Detail

90

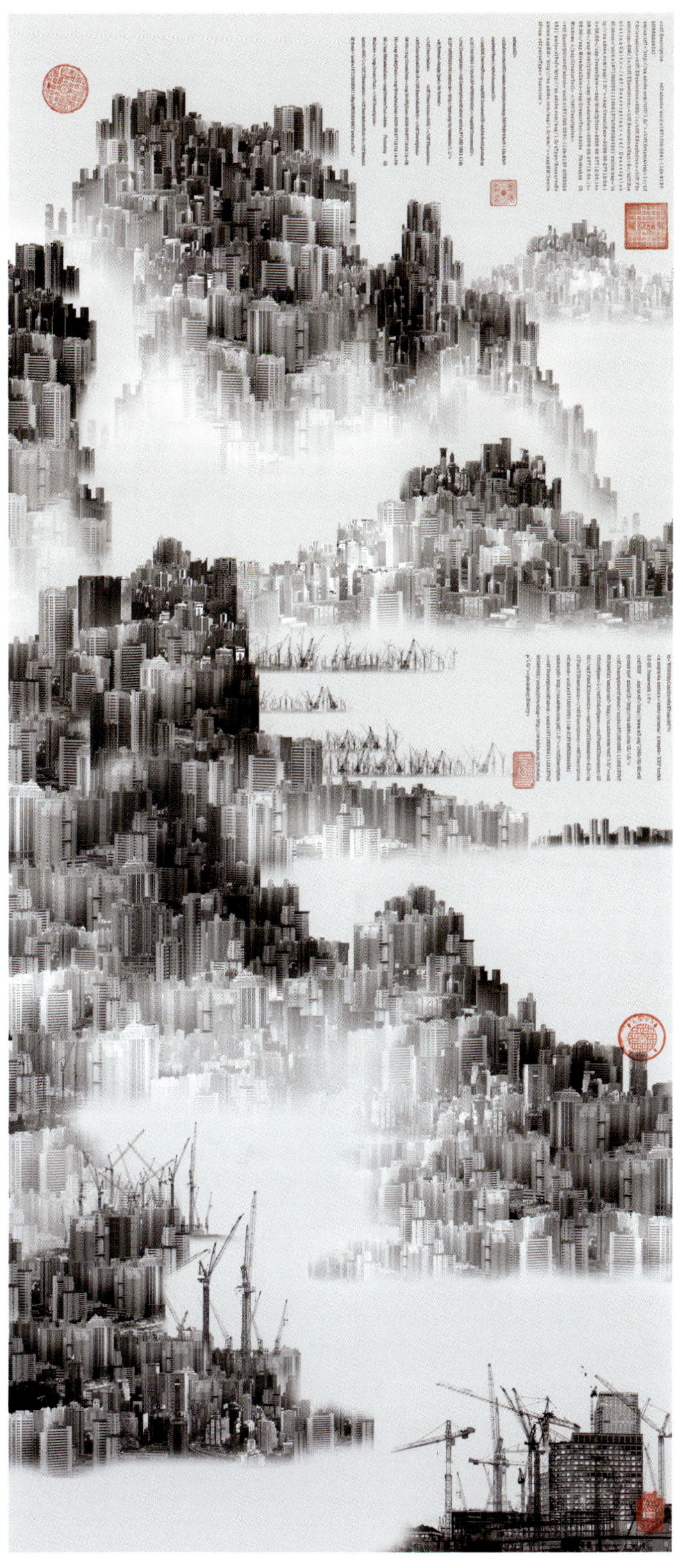

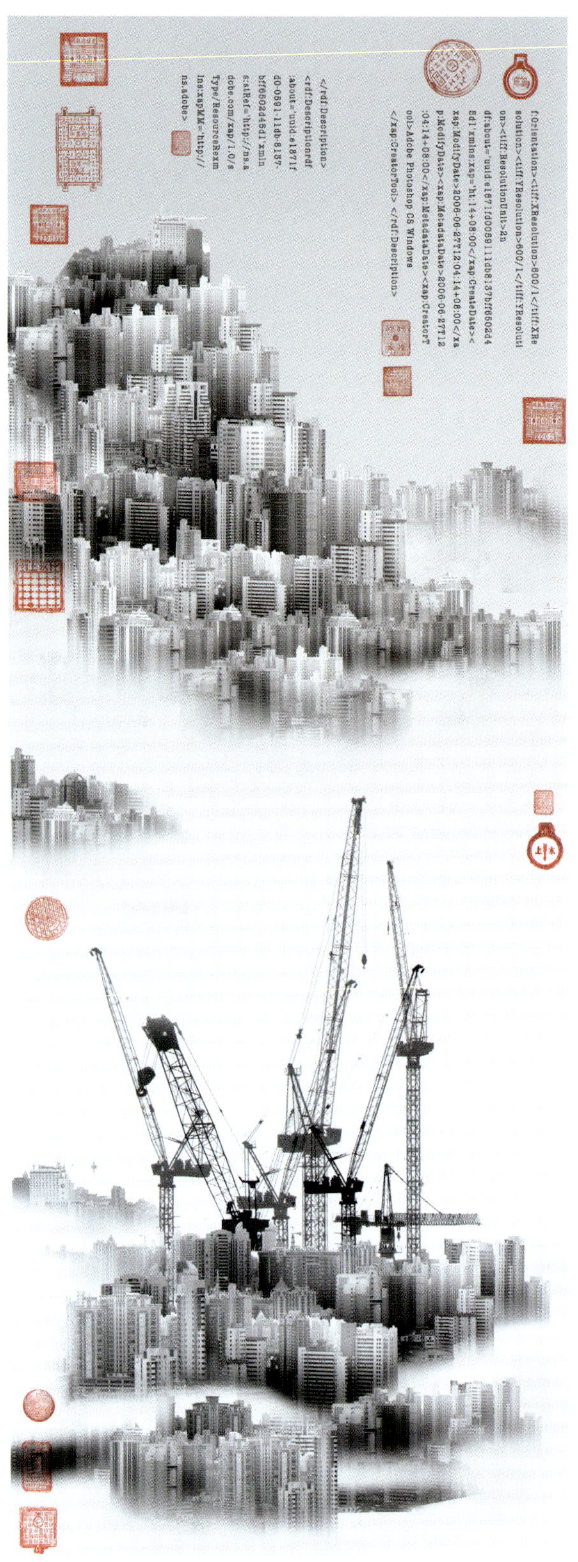

YANG YONGLIANG 杨泳梁
Untitled (no. 3), from the series
Phantom Landscape I, 2006

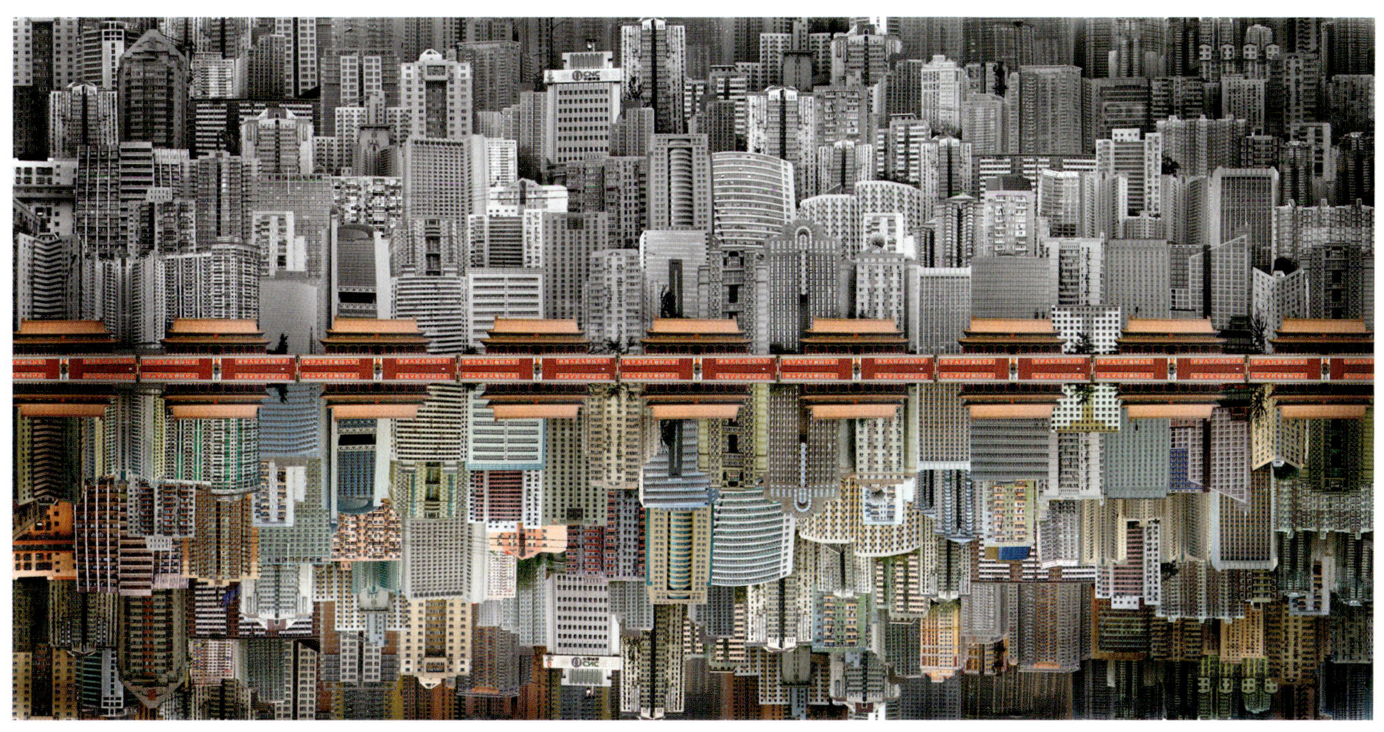

YENING 也宁 *Untitled (no. 1)*, from the series *Dream in the Deserted Peking*, 2006

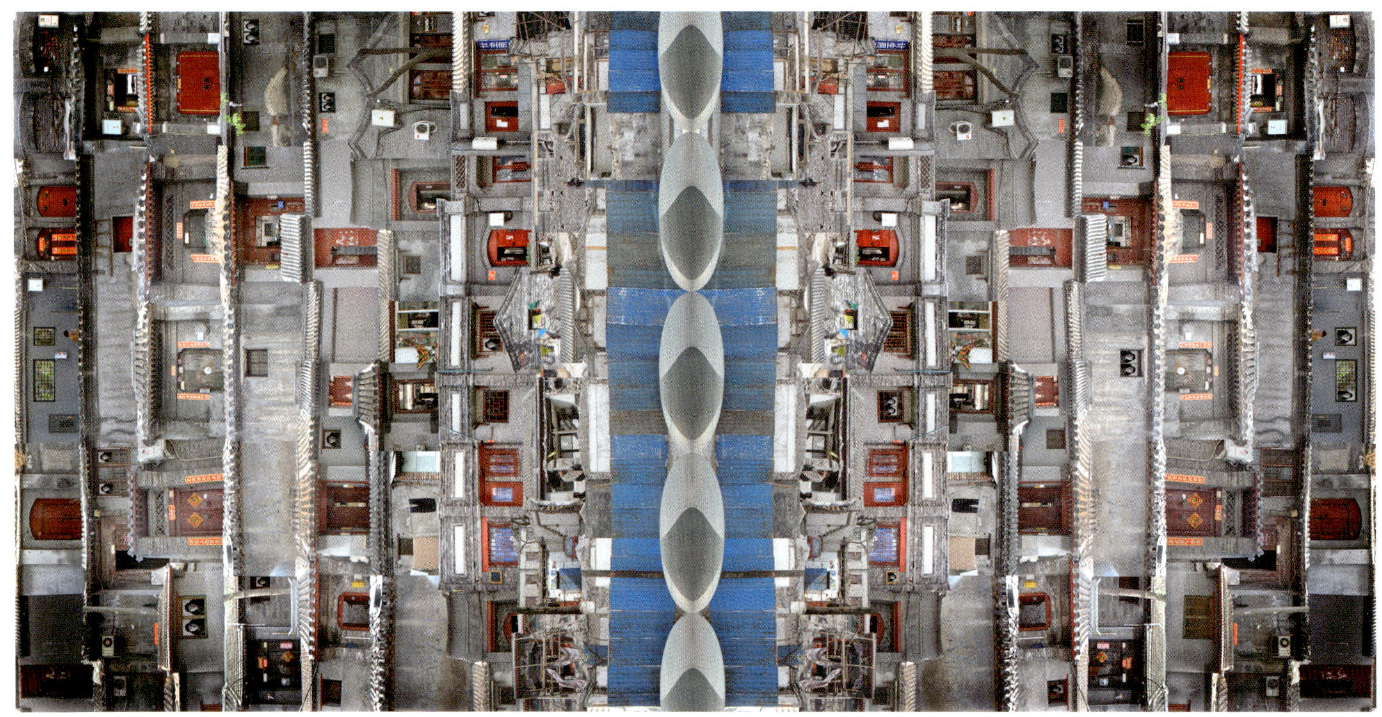

YENING 也宁 Untitled (no. 2), from the series Dream in the Deserted Peking, 2006

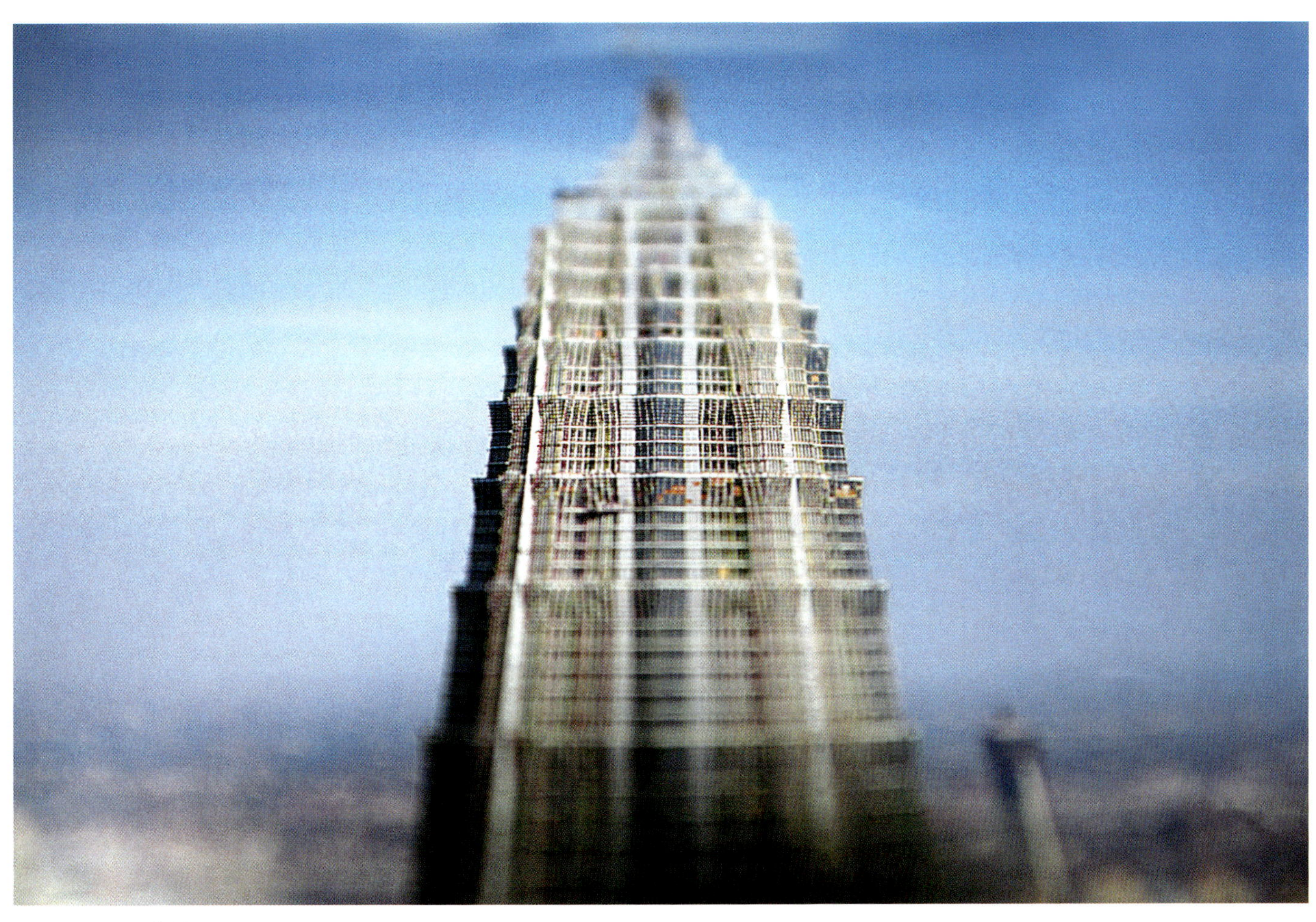

ZHU FENG 朱锋 *Top*, 2004

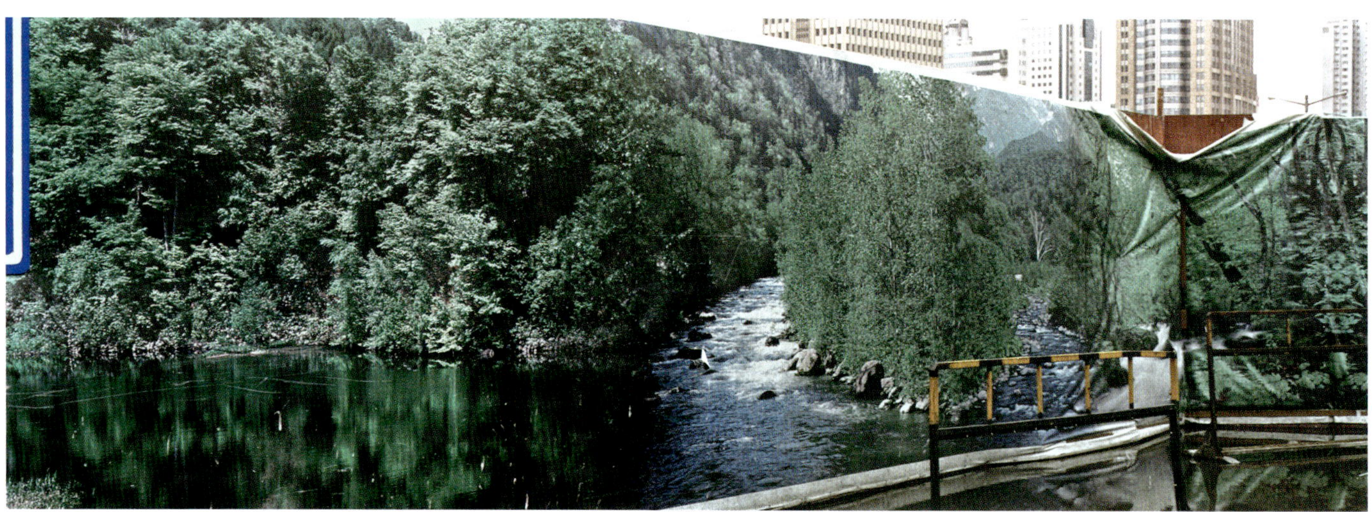

ZHU FENG 朱锋 *Untitled (0478-20)*, from the *Shanghai Zero Degree* series, 2004

AN
INTERVIEW WITH
LUO YONGJIN
罗永进,
XING DANWEN
邢丹文, AND
ZHANG DALI
张大力

RAECHELL SMITH

Each year, China gains momentum in its emergence as an active global participant and in its awakening to the influences of modernization and the West. During the march toward the Olympic games in Beijing in 2008, the world looked with eyes wide open to learn more about China's rush toward the future and its effects. As with any fundamental historical change, it brings both closure and opportunity. And so it is with China at the dawn of the twenty-first century.

If we look at the artwork presented in *Stairway to Heaven: From Chinese Streets to Monuments and Skyscrapers,* we see glimpses of how seventeen artists in China are capturing moments in time, drawing our attention to the old ways of life that are rapidly disappearing, some even say in the blink of an eye, and the similarly sudden emergence of new ways of life that are replacing them. While many of the manifestations of this so-called progress are familiar in terms of other regional encounters with the real-time effects of industrialization, urbanization, modernization, and globalization, these changes in China are made even more dramatic because they are compressed and compounded in time, in scale, and, certainly, in magnitude.

As I drew on my growing but somewhat troubled respect for present-day China and my already rich appreciation of contemporary Chinese art, I found myself aching with a sense of overload, trying to comprehend the enormity and complexity of the issues faced by these artists as they conceived and made the work now gathered for this exhibition. If I'm dizzy, then I can only imagine how they must feel as they attempt to grasp the recent and ongoing changes and articulate something of their experience with clarity and grace, inclusive of risks—even today—that we in the West can only imagine.

TECHNOLOGY, INFORMATION EXCHANGE, AND INSTANTANEOUS GLOBAL COMMUNICATION

There are certainly days when I struggle to keep up with e-mail, messages, and mail, not to mention information overload from traditional media and internet access. These are all incredibly useful and productive tools, though, that help me stay connected and do my curatorial work well. I imagine the same is true for you as an artist, regardless of where you live and work.

For example, I've just set the world clock on my laptop to the current time in

China, added your e-mail contact information to my address book, and have prepared myself by, among other things, spending time with your websites, all in order to have a very modern dialogue with you, two artists currently in China and one now en route from the Netherlands to New York, by email. Not so many years ago, such an exchange would have been virtually impossible.

Can you describe something about how recent advances in technology and global communication have affected your practice as an artist and how these developments may have impacted your career?

Luo Yongjin: New technology has a great impact on my works. I started in the early 1980s with film cameras, and now I have to use digital cameras for certain photos, for instance the *Night Watch* series, which is almost impossible for a normal camera in low light or at night. I can control the effect on the spot instead of finding the problems a few days later after the processing of film and coming all the way to the same place to take the same photos with corrections. Besides, I have to use the new technology of digital printing for large-format photos. Sometimes I can just carry a disc and print the photos in the exhibition place. As you said, global communication has made an easy and closer link to peoples from different corners of the world. It makes everything simple. I can instantly find all kinds of information I need from the internet. It is simple, convenient, and efficient.

Xing Danwen: I think that technology has really structured our new way of life, of doing things, and thinking—speed and efficiency. I think it's great but at the same time, it's exhausting. There is less time now to sense things because your senses are so governed by technology.

My artist website is something I do for me rather than for others. I hate administrative work, and since I receive requests for the same information from many people, I decided to publish information about my work on my website. Then, it becomes my own archive. So, when I get requests I just send a link to my website. It's easier and I can travel with free hands.

Zhang Dali: The new technologies have given me many convenient tools and can make more people know my work and the way in which I create my works. They also enable me to be aware of the latest trends on the international art stage. I think these tools have greatly influenced my artwork. For example, while I create a new work I do not only take into consideration the environment where I live, but I also imagine my work in a different situation and place. From a basic and essential point of view, I know I'm influenced by them, but they don't have a part in the decision-making process of creating an artwork. The convenience of these tools cannot change my understanding of art, but it can open me up to greater possibilities and different ways of doing things.

THE REALITIES OF URBANIZATION IN TODAY'S CHINA

China's urban population has changed drastically and grown exponentially in recent years with an influx of workers moving into the cities looking for work. The urgent need for more and more residential housing is met, in part, by the swift demolition of older residential areas to make way for a new types of buildings that are high-density and vertical in nature. The speed and scale at which this familiar, but painful cycle of urbanization is taking place in China makes it unique. I believe the current and recent changes to the physical and cultural landscape in China are comparable, in fact, to the kind of massive change that's happened all too frequently around the world as a result of the devastation and rebuilding that's most specific to times of war, extreme political upheaval, or natural disaster.

In a review of the exhibition *The Wall: Reshaping Contemporary Chinese Art,* published in the April 2006 issue of *Artforum,* art critic James Meyer stated: "China's transformation into a capitalist superpower and its rapid urbanization have been much touted, yet the actual effects of this transition on the Chinese population have yet to be fully assessed."

There are signs of this profound transformation in your work, but I wonder if you can give me a more personal account of how, for example, the city where you presently live and work differs from how it was in the recent past and how it might differ from the place where you grew up?

Luo Yongjin: Shanghai is, like all other Chinese cities growing bigger and higher every minute. Destruction and construction are taking place at the same time. As the old areas disappear the old traditions are also fading away. In the new areas people feel a distance from one another. You can hardly feel any warmth or intimacy in the cement buildings. Of course the living conditions are much better than before with spacious rooms, a bathroom in each apartment, a garden in the open space, convenient shops and other facilities in the neighborhood. But at the same time, the apartment buildings all look the same; as do the neighborhoods; as do the cities. My home town, Luoyang, in central China is, like all other Chinese cities, trying to imitate Shanghai and Beijing in all kinds of constructions, but the results are smaller in scale and of poorer quality. They are inferior copies. Chinese cities are loosing their identities.

Xing Danwen: I don't know if you've ever been to Chongqing. It's a city in China that's built on a mountain, with layers and layers going up; the city is built right into the side of the mountain. When I drive into my district in Beijing now, I see the layers and layers of buildings like the side of a mountain, like Chongqing, moving higher and higher. Going into downtown Beijing, it feels futuristic—the structures, the city. The highway has been built with several layers, going in many directions, with extensions that lead to different roads and the highway bridges are something like twenty stories high so you feel like the whole city is under you. You feel like you're driving a helicopter, not a car. From the ground looking up, the city can make an individual feel very fragile, very vulnerable. When you walk in the city, simply crossing a street can seem very far away. I think about my parents who do not drive and must take the bus to get around the city. That means they have to cross large, busy streets to transfer to a different bus. I can imagine the pressure for people living a simple, basic life now in this very advanced city.

Beijing has a lot of problems right now. If they had built the subway long ago, it would be better. Traffic jams are so bad. And most people think a city with a lot of cars is a sign of a rich and modern city. Just last year, we had a traffic test for the Olympics. They restricted cars with odd or even registration, but if they create a new policy, maybe it will reduce traffic for one month and then everyone will use two cars and there will be more traffic again. I know people who spend three or four hours by bus getting to work and back. Their whole life is work, going home to sleep, and then going back to work, nothing else. This is because the city is too big and public transportation hasn't kept up with the growth of the city.

Zhang Dali: Before coming to Beijing I lived in three different towns in China for about seven years each. They are quite different from Beijing. I think Beijing is a super-city. It is like a flat cake, without borders, and the population is also continuously increasing. I came to Beijing at the beginning of the 1980s, at that time there were about four million people; according to official statistics there are now thirteen million. At that time our main means of transportation were the bus and the bike. Now I can't ride a bike anymore; it's too dangerous and there are no more bike alleys, while cars are everywhere.

In these twenty-plus years many people have moved to Beijing. They wanted to live in this city, and they thought they could change their lives by their hard work. I'm happy for them, because before that time in China the population was not allowed to move from one place to the other; each person had a *danwei* (working unit), and the *danwei* was the entire world of one person, but now there is freedom to buy one's house and car. Before we were like a bird in a cage, but once the bird is set free it has to struggle to find food. Under these circumstances, I know, there is no security: danger, death, and destruction can be met at any step. For example a person might work hard and do well, but the boss may refuse to pay his salary. The advantage now is that that person can simply go somewhere else. The world of today is completely different from the past. At that time the sky was blue and the rhythm of life was very slow, but we can't go back. Last year I went back to one of the towns where I used to live. I didn't know it anymore; it was completely strange to me. It was like a model of Beijing in a smaller scale. I can't judge whether this is good or bad, I only know that I have gained a lot, and I have also lost a lot. I can only live in this way.

In your work, do you feel compelled or obligated to respond and comment on the changes brought about by urbanization and capitalism and your own experiences of these conditions?

LuoYongjin: Yes.

Xing Danwen: I grew up in Xi'an, in a Russian-built, three-story, gray brick building. At that time, I had only seen skyscrapers in films or in newspaper stories about the West. I really couldn't even imagine what life in that kind of place would be like. The first time I went to Manhattan, I felt very uncomfortable. My imagination of life in a city with skyscrapers was disconnected from my emotional experience of the place. It was similar when I went to Paris for the first time. I thought I knew Paris from studying nineteenth- and twentieth-century European paintings. But when I arrived, I couldn't find the Paris I knew. I think this happens to many people. So, I think that's how I connect myself to a new place, comparing my experiences from childhood about a city and how this idea compares with reality. This contrast is like a fantasy. This was an interest for me for a while and I knew I wanted to do a project with an urban subject. It all came together in the series *Urban Fiction*.

Urban Fiction comes out of my own experience of traveling to the West and comparing it to the old experiences, comparing it to where I come from and how much it has changed. At one time, everybody had said it was more of a struggle to live in the West, but from my experience, I didn't feel life was more difficult in the West. For a person living in a space with heat, a bathroom, a good kitchen, the living conditions were easier and more comfortable. With these things, the rest becomes secondary.

Where I grew up, people would use the public bathrooms. That was my life when I was a child. Even when I was a student in art school, we used a public toilet that was open-air and had no heat. In winter, it was so cold: I just could not go back there! We also had this open bathing area, and there was a schedule of certain times when you could get a hot bottle of water—the rest of the time the water was cold. And, in winter the cold water would freeze. In my dormitory, there was no heat in the room so in the morning my toothpaste and toothbrush would be frozen in the cup. Every morning, we would bring our duvets out into the sunshine to warm them.

I remember when I was a child, for New Year's my Grandmother would always prepare a lot of food, because she would want to share it with the neighbors. We were close to our neighbors, like a big family. She would make sweet rice balls for everyone. At that time, because we didn't have refrigeration, all our food was stored outside the window. She would dry meat and hang it outside on the balcony since Xi'an was cold. Just imagine, think of that kind of life, then you understand why I have this element of fantasy in my work . . . because it's such an extreme difference.

Zhang Dali: I think my work can't be separated from my reality; this reality is one of the forces intervening in the creation of my artwork. I have to respond to the reality, because I have no imagination or fantasy, but deeply in my heart I am very much against the demolition of the old architecture. I'm enraged, because the demolition makes me feel rootless. I also get very angry at the fact that the people coming into the city from the countryside receive such unequal treatment; I feel as if I'm one of them, in that I'm also an outsider in this city, and I run into the same kind of suffering. This city needs many people to build it, but at the same time, the city wants to keep these people at a distance. My artwork must reflect the situation of this reality, and only in this way can I feel that art and the making of art fulfills my responsibilities and obligations.

THE INTERNATIONAL ART WORLD AND ITS MYRIAD LOCATIONS OF PRACTICE AND CULTURE

Starting in the early 1990s, a handful of exhibitions outside mainland China began to introduce and contextualize contemporary art from China. These exhibitions followed closely on the heels of Mao Zedong's death in 1976, the end of the Cultural Revolution (1966–1976), and the significant shifts that would begin to occur, in 1979–80, under the economic reform and cultural opening to Western influences.

By 1999, when the internationally-renowned and influential exhibition maker

Harald Szeeman integrated contemporary art from China into the Aperto section of the Venice Biennale, and Cai Quo-Qiang was honored with the International Award of the Forty-Eighth Venice Biennale, the international art world began paying very close attention.

Since then, nearly a decade ago, contemporary art made by artists in China and elsewhere by those in the Chinese diaspora has become increasingly known and appreciated—internationally and, as I understand it, within China as well.

Chinese-born curators, art historians, and critics with innovative, influential practices in the East and the West working with the benefit of widespread connections have continued to organize exhibitions, conjure enlightening and meaningful thematic contexts, and introduce important experimental and avant-garde art by hundreds of artists born in or based in China to an increasingly international audience. I'm thinking of the important exhibitions organized and articles and essays written by, among others, Wu Hung, Gao Minglu, Fai Duwei, Hou Hanru, Gan Xu, and Gu Zheng.

With increasing frequency, Western-based curators, critics, collectors, and gallery owners have responded enthusiastically to the previously unfamiliar work by facilitating further explorations, discoveries, and exposure of new work by both recognized and underappreciated artists working in China and, in some cases, making work about China available to an ever-growing and more diverse audience.

Can you tell me what your own experience has been as the presentation and reception of your work has been expanded beyond the city where you live and work to a wider, more international audience?

Luo Yongjin: People are always as equally surprised at my works of architecture and at the changes in China. They are struck either by the scale of the new buildings or the phantom-like designs.

Xing Danwen: I worry about this as I get to the last stage of making new work, wondering how the work will speak to others. At the beginning, new work comes from a very personal perspective. If I have a feeling then I think maybe I can share this feeling with others. Then, I start to go beyond myself and slowly begin to consider how others will respond. The important thing is how my work will talk about something beyond myself to more than one person.

Zhang Dali: Personally I have lived in Europe for six years, therefore some of the reality outside of China is not completely unfamiliar to me. Beside this, I believe that my work can reach a greater audience by being in the hands of many collectors, galleries, and museums. This is very much related with the globalization of the market economy. The galleries I work with will present my work at the most important art fairs around the world. My creation process is described in the articles of many international journalists. This cannot be compared with the situation of the artist of two hundred years ago. If artists are not living and working within this tide of globalization then they will disappear and vanish. Globalization is not only about the contacts among more people and more cultures, it is also the globalization of the art market. Beside this, the rise of the Chinese economy has made many people more attentive toward China. Art is one of the many aspects, a small aspect, of the general attention that is given nowadays to what comes from China. The great change in contemporary Chinese art is that in the past it was underground, and it is now aboveground; it has become a part of the official art.

What relationships, connections, and experiences have been the most beneficial, most rewarding, or most challenging for you as an artist?

Luo Yongjin: The most rewarding and challenging is when I discover and create something that can best express myself in a very personal way.

Xing Danwen: It is hard but I am very lucky that I can make a living by selling my art. When I was studying art, I never expected I would be able to feed myself with my artwork. I thought if I was to be an artist, I would have to be prepared to starve or have other skills and do other jobs. The first challenge is to be selective, because we all have limited time and energy, and you must be able to concentrate. The second challenge is that it has become very difficult to be an artist because the art market is a bit crazy and messy. I know I'm not a big artist but it's hard to define yourself as an artist, especially when Chinese art has become so hot. More and more, you're not just struggling for basic survival; then I think you have to be aware of what kind of artist you want to be.

Zhang Dali: The curators of big exhibitions, when they choose a certain specific issue or title weaken my artwork. When you are an actor and you're on stage, you have to follow the rules dictated by the director. The same happens with the exhibitions. Artists need the stage; without the stage their art will remain in a warehouse. Sometimes the works in the big exhibitions can be easily misunderstood. There are also many advantages, because the artist is undergoing many new experiences, which are necessary for the artist to grow more mature.

The greatest challenge and reward I have received is from the galleries. At the end of the 1990s, around 1999, in the whole city of Beijing there were not more than 5 galleries dealing in contemporary art. Now, in the 798 art district alone, there are 200 galleries, not counting outside the 798, where there are even more.[1] At the same time there are now more and more galleries around the world dealing with Chinese contemporary art. These galleries need Chinese artists to supply a great number or quantity of work; therefore the artists are making artworks like mad, like in an assembly line of a big industry. As a result, many artists have no time to think and only copy themselves, endlessly repeating what they have done before. The artworks have lost their intellectual meaning and their spirit of criticism. From my point of view, this is something I want to avoid with all my strength. When their artwork becomes the pet vogue in the market, then the artists will become the manufacturers of a commodity; when artists are working to satisfy the market, they can easy forget their responsibility.

ART, CULTURE, AND POLITICS — CHINESE STYLE

There are aspects of your work that embody a cultural specificity that directly or indirectly reference Chinese cultural traditions and/or China's modern history. Are there artistic, cultural, or political references in your work that exhibition viewers may need to be familiar with in order to fully appreciate your work? How best can we, as the exhibition organizers, prepare and support the viewers' experience, including students at art schools and colleges and other viewers who may not have been to China or had an opportunity to study Chinese history and culture?

Luo Yongjin: It would be the best if they have some knowledge of Chinese history at least since the 1950s and, if possible, some general notions about traditional Chinese buildings.

Xing Danwen: With the urban subject matter, it would be good for people to understand how cities looked before so they can understand the difference between now and then. Big cities are all becoming similar, and I think the more developed cities all develop the same diseases.

Zhang Dali: Regarding *A Second History*, the content is actually related to contemporary Chinese history and China's political situation, but I also believe that the form of this work can be understood by any audience or any viewer with a bit of patience. I also believe that any artwork, no matter how difficult or complex, can be appreciated by any common person, in terms of feelings, of stimulation of

1. 798 Dashanzi Art District, located in the Chaoyang district of Beijing, is a former industrial zone (originally Factory #798), where the buildings have been adapted to accommodate artist studios, commercial galleries, bookstores, restaurants, and a variety of arts organizations. It has become the center of a growing art community in the city and is a vibrant cultural destination for residents and visitors to Beijing.

thought, etc. Just like I feel emotions while reading a book written in a foreign language and translated into Chinese, so too can my works elicit feelings or emotions or ideas to think about from any viewer in any place.

Luo Yongjin, what comes to mind in your work is the potential of images to convey powerful ideas that are embodied in political or cultural monuments and a history of ideologically motivated or idealistic architecture in China from previous eras, including the periods dominated by imperialism and Communism, and how these traditions seem to continue even after economic reform and cultural opening. Are the influences and inspirations to make monumental or imposing structures the same now or are they different? What do these buildings reveal about China's hopes for the future?

Luo Yongjin: In history throughout the world, the rich and powerful have always been building imposing structures to show their wealth and power, which does not bother me much because most of what we see today is quite pleasant to me. The point is that nowadays in China, so much architecture by both private citizens and government officials is so unbelievably ugly. It elicits in people only feelings of bad taste, ignorance, and lust. It has absolutely nothing to do with history. The owners are dreaming of building history with these structures. It is a side effect of the hundred-year modernization in Chinese culture that reached its peak during the Cultural Revolution when tradition was neglected and destroyed. There is no hope for our future if such structures keep on spreading throughout China.

Xing Danwen, in your work, there is evidence of the explosive growth and ambitiously marketed urban real estate developments in cities like Beijing and references to their positive/negative impact on communities, individual and collective identity, and the commercially motivated cultivation of personal desire, raw consumerism, projected realities, and hopeful sense of happiness/belonging, etc. I know that in previous interviews, you've talked about wanting to convey a sense of loneliness and isolation in this work as a facet of recent changes in living conditions in Chinese cities. As a young artist and perhaps even more so as a woman artist, what motivates you and benefits you in a such a successful attempt to capture some of this extraordinary complexity of the current living conditions and anxieties that are a very real part of living in China today?

Xing Danwen: I came to appreciate that living in this new way would be easier and more comfortable, but as the city started to change, I became concerned about the problem of the old city being demolished and the changes that were happening.

I worked as a photojournalist for five years. From 1995, Beijing began to change dramatically. The whole area of old *hutong* (courtyard) houses inside the first ring road, was taken down. The Forbidden City is in the north of Beijing, and the south is the poorer area. I did a story once with a journalist about the demolition of a family's home and their relocation.

During the Cultural Revolution, there was no private property, so many of the grander courtyard homes had been changed to accommodate the many workers who were assigned by the government to live there instead of one family, as they were originally built. Each assigned worker was given one room, and when they began to start a family, they would add on to their one room. The open spaces of the courtyards became filled with all the rooms that were added on by the forty or fifty families that were living there, leaving these narrow alleys in between them. Their life in that environment was like one big family; the neighbors become very close. Since they didn't have water pipes, they would share water from a common sink. It made it easy to communicate and share.

During the interviews for this story, when people were asked if they wanted to stay in this overcrowded courtyard house or move to a new apartment in the suburbs, most were happy to relocate. But I think at that time, before they moved out, I don't think they could really know what to expect, know how it would really feel to live in this new way. But from my perspective, I know how it is to live in one of these cubes, especially to work as an artist in a studio. Unless I go out, I just don't see people.

Zhang Dali, your documented actions in the work *Dialogue and Demolition* convey a sense of personal urgency regarding the push toward modernization and the subsequent/ensuing demolition and willing destruction (by government agencies as well as private developers) of historically and culturally significant public and private sites and, subsequently, the loss of familiar ways of life within these communities. Were your intervening actions motivated by a desire to give voice to or provoke reactions from your neighbors, to question the people responsible for the demolition and new building efforts, or by a personal effort to grasp the complexities of the drastic situation you encountered when you returned to China after living in Europe for a period of time?

Zhang Dali: I worked on this project for ten years. During those ten years, whether in terms of real life or in terms of intellectual/spiritual life, many important changes occurred. The title of this work is *Dialogue and Demolition*. In the process of creating this work I had two meanings in mind. At the time the art circles in China where mostly represented by artists working in their own studios, in private and closed spaces. The artist was talking to himself. There were artists with different opinions, but they sought no dialogue. The art circles at the time were very cynical. I wanted to move my art from the studio out into society; I wanted my art to be connected and related to the people. The second meaning was the change that occurred in the environment. That dramatic change gave me a kind of shock; it gave me the initial force to create such a work of art.

The profiles of the heads were appearing everywhere among the people and throughout their environment. They had the power to emanate their own sounds/voices. They had the power to make the people who had become used to being oppressed by the powers that be feel like they were still alive. I was forcing the people to speak and to express their rights. The silent majority had been thoroughly suppressed and dared not express themselves. But when your rights are expropriated, rebellion becomes the only effective weapon. The city would change overnight. An entire street could disappear all of a sudden. Who has the grounds to do this? Who is the real master of this city? And what is the aim of all this change? Are wider streets and higher buildings modernization? No one asked these questions. I think the modernization of thought is the only true modernization. My house may be small and tumbledown, the wind and the rain can enter inside, but the king cannot enter. I don't like when other people arrange and manage my life. I don't like when other people try to tell me what I have to do. I don't like when people beat me and at the same time try to tell me it is for my own good. I don't like to be fed like a dog with no dignity, only taking food from the master to fill my stomach. We have lost too much, but the administrators of the city will never take into consideration the opinions of the people living in the neighborhoods they are going to demolish.

The city is like an amusement park, the appearance is beautiful, but the people living inside have an empty heart. The pockets are full of money, but without a spiritual life, they are only a walking pieces of meat. I know that I alone can't change anything, but I refuse to remain silent. So I use my art to speak for me. My art is expressing what my opinions are. I hope that many more people will do the same.

There is a quote by the Danish philosopher Soren Kierkegaard that states, "It is perfectly true, as philosophers say, that life must be understood backward. But they forget the other proposition, that it must be lived forward." In the series *A Second History,* I wonder what your thoughts are on how a more thoughtful consideration of the past may enhance our current understanding of the past, present, and future. What do you wish to accomplish by drawing our attention to the skillful and artful manipulations of images overseen by the Communist Party, and are there lessons that can be applied to the present in terms of truth and deception?

Zhang Dali: I think that the life we live now, the situations and environment, are all the result of our past history. When I created this work I had a very clear understanding of the aesthetic of previous Chinese generations, their customs and the experiences that created such an aesthetic feeling. These experiences are passive and cannot be forced onto people; they are already in our blood. Now there is Photoshop, but we are still going along the same path, the only difference being that we leave no trace of the manipulation. I think most of the people are not adept at history, but history is nevertheless influencing the way people live and think. Only a minority of people who are very conscious and awake can see the way history functions. Nowadays the Chinese people are only concerned about the present. I think this is the most important work I have ever done. It was the first time that I had not added my emotions in the work I was doing; while I was doing the research and reviewing all the documents I kept myself cold and at a distance. I wanted to tell people what was hidden on the backstage of those images, I was not concerned with the way the images were doctored, but only with the meaning behind them.

ON THE ROLE OF ART HISTORY AND WHAT WE CAN LEARN FROM IT

Because I was trained as an art historian—not an economist, scientist, journalist, or urban planner—perhaps I have a greater awareness of how artists and artists' communities have responded historically to situations and conditions, both social and political in nature, by creating work that helps to shape our memory and understanding of significant events. One of the valuable contributions of artists, art, and art history is that we can gain from it a greater appreciation of different cultures and historical periods, either by looking back over time, or, if we are paying attention, by examining the art of our own time and what artists have to say about their experiences and their own political or cultural conditions. The work in this exhibition, made by seventeen contemporary artists who currently live and work in China, certainly addresses and considers some of the harsher and less appealing realities of globalism and, in particular, the rampant urbanization specific to China.

In an article published by the Asian *Wall Street Journal* in 2003, Shanghai-based cultural critic Lisa Movius, states:

> the rising profile of Chinese contemporary art in America is important beyond critical circles: as China's economic and political power grows, so does the value of Americans seeing a rawer, more accurate view of its realities than the popular stylized Chinoiserie. Chinese contemporary art, after all, may be one of the best reflections of China's enormous transformations over the past decade.

Let's project forward in time and consider your work and the work in this exhibition from the perspective of ten, fifty, or a hundred years from now. What might we gain by way of a greater appreciation and understanding of China at the beginning of the twenty-first century by looking at this art and knowing something of the artists who made it?

Luo Yongjin: I hope that people will understand that in the beginning of the twenty-first century, there were some sensitive artists who were both suspicious and sarcastic about the trendy architecture of the day. They were able to turn these tasteless structures into tasty works of art.

Xing Danwen: That's a difficult question. I've never thought about it like that. Actually, I would like to clarify that this work is not only about Chinese cities. The sources and the footage definitely come from China but, in the end, this work is talking about universal situations, humans and their living environments. Perhaps the work will give a historical perspective of architecture, because architecture is a historical witness. I think in ten, twenty, or even in one hundred years, people will continue to have problems. The basic human problems will be quite similar, but the particular problems may change.

Zhang Dali: All the art works, in the perspective of a future viewer, would help people to understand the past and also help those people to better understand the relations between their present lives and the life in the past. I believe there is continuity in history; the spirit of the people is not falling from the sky. Perhaps my work can bring to the Chinese people of the future some issues to think about, otherwise it will have no meaning at all.

These interviews took place in March 2008 in person in New York and by email while the participants were at or near their respective keyboards in Beijing, Shanghai, New York, Rotterdam, and Kansas City. I am most grateful for the sincere honesty and integrity extended by Luo Yongjin, Xing Danwen, and Zhang Dali over the course of this exchange, and I am in their debt for expanding my depth of understanding and appreciation for their work and the influences that shape their visions. My deep appreciation is also offered to all those who supported this seemingly simple exchange, among them, Mark Bessire, Andrea Flamini, Kris Ercums, Owen Martin, Donna Raskin and Walnut Street Transcription Services, Moti Hasson, Michael Schonhoff, Robert Heishmann, Gan Xu, Francis Gerstle, David Ford, Dr. John Kennedy, Bruce Ferguson, and Glenn Mott. Thank you all for making the conversations richer and more meaningful.

RAECHELL SMITH

中国作为全球参与者的地位逐年提高，它也开始越来越多地受到西方与现代化的影响。在2008年北京奥运会即将来临之际，全世界都在瞩目中国向未来匆忙迈进所造成的影响。如同任何基本历史变化一样，中国目前的急剧发展将带来机遇也会造成停滞。二十一世纪初的中国就是这样充满挑战。

从《通往天堂的阶梯：从中国的街道到纪念碑和摩天楼》这一影展的作品中，我们得以瞥见十七位中国艺术家是如何记录了历史长河中的这一时刻。他们把我们的注意力带到正在迅速消失的或者说转瞬即逝的传统生活方式，又将我们的目光吸引到同样迅速出现并取而代之的新的生活方式上。与许多其他地区我们称之为进步的表现相似，这种变化是工业化、城市化、现代化以及全球化的即时效应，而中国的这些变化因其浓缩的时间段和更为复杂的规模和幅度，无疑更加引人注目。

当我对今天的中国充满尊敬也颇有几分迷惑，对她的现代艺术的欣赏日益加深的时候，我发现我自己因为超负荷而感到周身不适。我试图理解艺术家们在为这个展览构思和拍摄作品时所面对的种种问题的庞大与复杂。如果我自己都感到头晕目眩，那么我完全可以体会到艺术家们在力图抓住这种全新的正在进行的变化，并冒着我们西方人只能想象的那些风险将自己的经历清楚而优雅地表现出来时，他们怀有一种怎样的情感。

技术、 信息互换与全球即时通讯

很多时候我尽量争取随时查阅电子邮件、留言和信件，更不用说随时浏览传统媒介和互联网上的信息了。这些信息当然都是实用而有价值的工具，使我得以与外界保持联络并帮助我做好博物管理工作。我想这一点对你这样的艺术家来说也同样适用，无论你在哪里工作和生活。

比如说，我刚刚把我电脑上的时钟调到中国时间，又将你的邮箱地址加入我的地址薄，还找时间浏览了你的网站。做这些都是为了能与你和两位身在中国的艺术家，用电子邮件与另一位正从荷兰赶往纽约的艺术家进行更有时效的交谈。以这种方式交流在几年以前是绝对不可能的。

你能否描述一下近期技术的进步和全球通讯如何影响了你的艺术创作，以及这些发展给你的职业带来了什么样的影响？

罗永进：新技术给我的工作带来很大的影响。八十年代初我开始使用胶卷相机拍照，现在我必须使用数码相机拍某些照片，比如说《夜巡》系列。这种光线暗

的或夜景的照片用老式相机很难拍好。我可以当场控制效果，不必象以前那样
等胶卷冲洗出来后才发现问题再回去重拍。除此之外，我还要依靠新的数码影
印技术来制做大幅照片。有时我甚至只带一张光盘到影展的地方去打印照片。
如你所说，环球通讯把世界各个角落的人们连接起来了。做什么都变得容易
了。我只要上网就可以立即找到我想要的任何信息。这些做起来非常容易，非
常方便，效率也非常高。

邢丹文：我认为技术为我们构建了新的生活方式和工作方式，也改善了我们的思考
速度和效率。我觉得这样很好，但这同时也让人疲惫。现在没有太多的时间去
感受什么了，你的感觉要受到技术的牵制。

　　我的艺术网站是我为自己，而不是为别人做的一件事。我不喜欢把时间花在
行政琐事上，可经常有人向我索取某些相同的信息。后来我决定把一些相关信
息都放在我的网站上。结果这些又成了我的档案。现在呢，如果有人向我索要
信息，我就给他们我个人网站的链接。这样做比以前容易，我可以毫无负担地
出门旅行了。

张大力：新技术给了我很多方便使用的工具，也让很多人了解了我的工作，以及
我的作品是如何制做出来的。新技术使我能及时了解到国际艺术舞台的最新潮
流。这些工具的使用很大程度上影响了我的艺术创作。比方说，当我创作一件
新的作品时，我不仅仅考虑我周围的生活环境，我还从另一个角度来设想我的
作品。　不过从本质上来看，我知道我虽然受到影响，但是这些技术在我的艺术
创作中并不起决定性作用。这些工具带来的方便不会改变我对艺术的理解，却
让我看到了不同的方法和更多的可能性。

当前中国城市化的现实

中国的城市人口近年来随着大批民工的涌入而急剧变化并呈指数级增长，拆除老房
以让位于新型的高密度高楼层住宅部分地满足了居民对住房的迫切需要。这种熟悉
却让人痛苦的中国城市化进程速度之快，规模之大使这个变化过程独具特色。我相
信中国近期和目前的自然与文化景观上的变化，与世界各地频繁发生的那种大规模
的，常常是对战争、政治动乱或自然灾害造成的破坏进行重建时出现的那些巨变很
有可比性。

　　2006年4月出版的《艺术探索》刊载了艺术评论家詹姆斯·梅耶（James Meyer）
对题为《墙：当代艺术的历史与边界》的展览的评论。他在评论中说：　"中国走
向资本主义超级大国的变革与它快速的城市化被过分吹捧了，不过这种过渡对中国
民众的实际影响仍然有待于我们进行全面的评估。"

　　我在你的作品中看到了这一深刻变革的迹象，你能否从你个人的角度告诉我，
例如，你目前生活和工作的城市与不久以前相比有什么不同，与你从小长大的城市
又有什么不同？

罗永进：上海就象中国其他城市一样，每分钟都在变大变高。拆迁和建设同时进行。老区越来越少了。古老的传统也随着老居住区的拆除而消失了。在新的住宅小区里人与人之间有了距离。当然，居住条件比以前好多了，房间大了，每个公寓里都有卫生间，室外有花园，居民区里有便利店和其他设施。但是同时，公寓楼与居民区看起来都很相似，整个城市也如此。我的家乡洛阳在华中地区，它看起来跟中国的其他城市没有区别，建筑都尽量模仿上海和北京，但是规模相对要小，模仿得极差，质量低劣。中国的城市正在失去特色。

邢丹文：我不知道你是否去过重庆，它是一座山城，一层高过一层，整个城市正好建在山坡上。现在我开车进入我住的小区时，会看到一层比一层高的楼房，就象在山上一样，象重庆一样，越来越高。　去北京市中心，感觉就象走进未来世界，建筑、城市都给你这种感觉。高速公路也有很多层，通往不同的方向，延伸到不同的路径。高速公路桥有二十层楼那么高，整个城市仿佛都在你的脚下。你感觉好象在开直升飞机，而不是在开汽车。从地下往上看的时候，城市让你感觉自己非常微不足道。当你走在城市中，仅仅过一条街也要走很远。我想到我的父母，他们不开车，到哪里都要坐公共汽车。这就是说，他们要穿过很大很忙的街道去换车。我想象得到过着普通生活的人们在这样发达的城市中生活所承受的压力。

北京目前存在很多问题。如果很久以前建地铁就好了。交通堵塞非常严重。很多人认为城市富有和现代化的标志就是道路上有很多车。刚好在去年，我们为奥运会做了交通检验。他们限制了单双号车出行。但他们如果制定一个新政策，交通也许会减少一个月，然后每个人又得开两辆车，交通又会更忙。我知道有些人每天要花三、四个小时坐车上下班。他们的全部生活就是上班，回家睡觉，然后再去上班，其他什么也做不成。这都是因为城市太大了，交通却没有跟上城市的发展。

张大力：来北京以前我在中国三个不同的城镇生活过，每个城镇生活过七年左右的时间。它们跟北京很不一样。我觉得北京是个超级城市。它就象一块又扁又平的大饼，没有边界，人口不断增长。我八十年代初来北京，那时北京有大约四百万人口；现在据官方统计已经有一千三百万人口了。那时我们的主要交通工具是公共汽车和自行车。现在我不再骑自行车了，太危险了，也没有骑自行车的路了，到处都是小汽车。

在最近的二十多年里很多人来到北京，他们想住在城里，他们相信努力工作能改变他们的生活。我为他们高兴，因为在那之前中国人口不能自由流动，每个人都有<u>单位</u>，<u>单位</u>就是一个人的全部世界。现在人们可以自己买房子和汽车了。以前我们象笼子里的鸟，鸟一旦自由了就会出去找食吃。在这种状况下，我知道，没有安全感，每一步都有可能遭遇危险、死亡或毁灭。比如，一个人可能努力工作，做得很好，但雇主却拒付工资。好处是这个人可以再去找工作。今天的世界跟过去完全不同。那时候天是蓝的，生活节奏是慢的，但我们不能再回到从前了。去年我去了我以前生活过的一个城镇。我几乎认不出来了，城镇看起来很陌生，象个小型的北京城。我不能判断这样是好是坏。我只知道我得到了很多，也失去了很多。我只能这样生活。

在你的作品中，你觉得有义务或者说不得不对城市化和资本主义带来的变化和你自身对这些变化的感受有所反映并做出评论吗？

罗永进：是的。

邢丹文：我生长在西安，小时候住在一栋三层俄式灰色砖楼里。那时我只在电影里和报纸上看到过西方的摩天楼。我甚至想象不出大楼里的生活是什么样子的。第一次来曼哈顿的时候，我感觉很不舒服。我对这种摩天楼鳞次栉比的城市生活的想象跟我感情上对这种地方的感受脱节了。第一次去巴黎时我也有这种感觉。原以为我通过学习十九和二十世纪欧洲绘画已经对巴黎有所了解。但是当我置身其中时，却找不到我心目中的巴黎。我想很多人都有过这样的感觉。所以，我是这样把自己同新的地方联系起来的，我把自己童年时期关于城市的经历同现在看到的真实情况做比较。这种对比就象幻想。很长时间我一直对这种比较感兴趣，我知道我想做一个关于城市主题的项目。这就是《都市演绎》系列的由来。

《都市演绎》来自我自身的经历。我去西方旅行，把新的经历与过去的经历相比较，把它与我生活过的地方想比较，看过去的地方变化了多少。有一段时间，人人都说生活在西方更艰难。但以我自己的经历，我觉得生活在西方并不困难。对一个生活在有暖气、卫生间和厨房的地方的人来说，居住条件更方便更舒服。有了这些，其他的都不重要了。

在我长大的地方，人们要去公共浴池洗澡。我小时候就是那样生活的。在艺术学院上学的时候，我们要使用露天的公共厕所，没有暖气。冬天很冷，我不能再回到那里。我们有公共浴池，在固定的时间供应饮用热水，其他时间水是凉的。还有，冬天水会结冰。我的宿舍没有暖气，早上起来牙膏和牙刷都冻在杯子里了。每天早晨我们都要把被褥拿到外面晒暖。

我记得小的时候，过年时奶奶总要准备好多吃的，因为她要送一些给邻居。我们跟邻居走得很近，象一家人一样。奶奶会做很多汤圆送给别人。那时没有冰箱，吃的东西都放在窗户外面。她把肉晾干挂在阳台上，因为西安很冷。想象一下，想起那样的生活，你就会明白为什么我的作品中会有这种幻想作祟，因为现在的经历与过去差别太大了。

张大力：我认为不能把我的作品与我的现实情况分离开，这种现实促使我创作了这样的作品。我必须反映现实，因为我没有想象和幻觉，但在心灵深处我对拆除旧建筑非常反感。我被激怒了，因为拆迁让我感觉如同失去了根基。我对农村

人在城市里受到如此不公平的待遇也非常气愤，我觉得我自己就是他们之中的
一员。在城市里我也是外来者，我也有相同的遭遇。城市的建设需要很多人的
付出，但同时城市却把这些人拒之千里。我的艺术作品必须反映这一现实，只
有这样做我才能感觉到艺术和创造艺术让我承担起了我的责任和义务。

国际艺术界及其众多的文化与实践场地

自九十年代开始，　　　中国境外的很多展览开始介绍中国现代艺术，并将中国现代
艺术还原于中国文化背景之中。这些展览紧紧追随毛泽东逝世的1976年，那时也
是"文化大革命"（1966－1976）结束的时期。随之而来的是即将开始的重大转
变，在1979年到1980年这段时间，　经济改革和文化对外开放开始实施。

到1999年，国际知名且颇具影响力的艺术展览策划人哈罗德·塞曼（Harald
Szeeman）将中国的现代艺术与威尼斯双年展的开放展接轨，蔡国强在第四十八届
威尼斯双年展获得国际奖。　国际艺术界开始密切关注中国。

从那以后，也就是从十多年前开始，无论在国外还是国内，按我的理解，海内外
中国艺术家所创作的现代艺术作品越来越多地得到国内外观众的了解与欣赏。

活跃于东西方，富有创新意识又具备影响力的那些中国出生的策展人、艺术史学
家和评论家们，凭借他们联络广泛的优势，不断组织展览，并且巧妙地变幻着兼具
启迪性和深刻含义的主题背景，把数百名立足中国的艺术家们的创新与前卫作品介
绍给越来越多的海外观众。我能想到的、曾经组织过重要展览和写过评论文章的人
有巫鸿、　高名潞、费大为、侯瀚如、徐淦和顾铮。

同样与日俱增地，西方的策展人、评论家、收藏家和画廊主也对他们以前不太熟
悉的这些作品付出极大的热情。他们进一步发掘和曝光这些工作在中国的已获承认
或仍被低估的艺术家的作品，把这些作品展现给为数更多更具多元化的观众群。

你能否告诉我，当你的作品被宣传介绍到你工作和生活以外的地方，被越来越多
的更为国际化的观众所接受，你自身经历了怎样的过程？

罗永进：人们对我所拍摄的建筑作品的惊异程度不亚于他们对飞速变化的中国的惊
　　　异程度。他们都感受到了新型建筑的规模或者幻影似的设计所带来的冲击。

邢丹文：在最后完成作品的时候我很担心。我不知道我的作品会给别人传达什么样
　　　的信息。作品最初来源于个人观察。如果那时我有所感觉，我就会与别人分享
　　　我的感受。然后，我开始超越自我，并慢慢开始考虑别人会如何做出回应。最
　　　重要的是，我的作品如何同除我以外的更多的人交谈。

张大力：　我本人在欧洲生活了六年多，所以国门之外的世界对我来说并非完全陌
　　　生。除此之外，我相信我的作品能通过许多收藏家、画廊和博物馆之手让更多
　　　的观众看到。这与市场经济全球化有很大关系。与我合作的画廊会把我的作品

打入世界各个重要的艺术展览中。我的创作历程在很多国际刊物上被提及。这一点是不能与二百年前艺术家的情况同日而语的。如果一个艺术家不能将自身置于全球文化浪潮上，他迟早会从人们的视线中消失。全球化不只是人与人和文化与文化之间越来越多的接触，它也是艺术市场的全球化。还有，中国经济的崛起也让人们更加关注中国。人们对中国的方方面面都很关注，艺术只占了其中一个方面。中国现代艺术的最大变化是，以前它是地下的，现在它浮出地面，成为官方允许的艺术形式。

作为艺术家，一些什么样的关系、联系和经历使你受益最大，或者说对你最具挑战性？

罗永进：我觉得使我受益最大，最具挑战性的是发现和创作一些能让我最好地表达我自己的作品。

邢丹文：以销售自己的作品为生是一件很困难的事，但我庆幸我做到了。学习艺术的时候我从未指望我将来会以此为生。我原以为如果想成为一个艺术家，我就要准备好忍饥挨饿，或者找个第二职业。最初的挑战就是一定要善于选择，因为我们的时间和精力都有限，我们一定要专注。第二个挑战是，做为一个艺术家是很艰难的，因为艺术市场疯狂而凌乱。我知道我不是个大艺术家，不过把自己定义为艺术家其实很难，特别是在中国艺术这么火的时候。更重要的是，你并非仅仅为了生存。你一定要弄清楚你想做一个什么样的艺术家。

张大力：大型展览的策展人在选择某个题目时，往往让我的作品显得微不足道。当你作为一名演员站在舞台上时，你不得不听从导演的指挥。参加展览也会有这种感觉。艺术家需要这个舞台，没有这个舞台他们的作品就只能堆在仓库里。有时大型展览中的展品很容易被误解。不过这也带来很多优势，因为艺术家会有新的经历，这些经历让艺术家更成熟。

　　我获得的最大挑战，也是最大的收益，来自画廊。九十年代末，即1999年前后，整个北京城大概只有五家画廊经营现代艺术作品。现在仅仅在798艺术区[1]就有二百多家画廊，798以外的地方就更多了。同时，目前世界范围内经营中国现代艺术作品的画廊也越来越多。这些画廊需要中国的现代艺术家们提供大量的作品，艺术家们为此疯狂地工作着，就象在大工厂的装配线上工作一样。结果很多艺术家没有时间思考，他们只能模仿他们自己，没完没了地重复以前的创作。作品已经失去了知识性和批评精神。在我看来，这就是我想尽最大努力去避免的事情。当艺术成为市场上的时尚宠物，艺术家就变成了货物制造者；当艺术家仅仅为了满足市场需要而创作，他们就会很轻易地忘掉自己的责任。

1. 798大山子艺术区位于北京市朝阳区，曾为工业区（原来的798厂）。那里的房子被改建成艺术家工作室、商业性画廊、书店、餐馆和各种各样的艺术机构所在地。现在该区作为北京正在成长的艺术社区，成为市民和参观者向往的文化活跃地。

艺术、文化和政治 — 中国风格

你们的作品一定在某些方面包含了一些文化特征，这些文化特征直接或间接地涉及
到中国文化传统或者中国现代历史。有没有哪些艺术、文化或者政治上的相关知识
是参观你们展览的人应该具备的，以便于他们更充分地欣赏你们的作品？我们做为
展览的组织人，要做些什么来帮助那些可能从未去过中国，也没有机会学习中国历
史和文化的的艺术院校的学生和其他参观者？

罗永进：如果他们能了解一些至少五十年代以来的中国历史的相关知识，以及，
　　　　如果可能的话，关于传统中国建筑的基本知识，那再好不过了。
邢丹文：就城市主题来说，最好能让人们知道以前的城市是什么样子的，他们就能
　　　　看出现在和过去的不同之处。大的城市变得越来越类似，比较发达的城市现在
　　　　都滋生出共同的毛病。
张大力：关于《第二历史》，其内容与现代中国历史和中国政治环境有关。但我
　　　　相信，这种形式的艺术品可以为各种各样的观众所理解，只要他们有一定的耐
　　　　心。我也相信，任何艺术作品，不管它有多么难懂多么复杂，都能为任何一个
　　　　普通人所欣赏，无论从感觉上或是从引导思维上来说。就象我在读一本由外文
　　　　翻译成中文的小说时能感受到那种激情一样，我的作品也能引发来自任何地方
　　　　参观者的感觉或激情，并促使他们思考。

罗永进，　你的作品中，有些影象潜在地传达着一种隐含在政治和文化纪念性建筑
中的强烈的意念，同时也讲述着一部中国历史，它包含了前几个时代，包括共产主
义和帝国主义统治时期的一些意识形态式或者理想主义类型的建筑物，所幸这些历
史传统得以在改革开放之后延续下来。目前在建设纪念碑和某些大型建筑时人们受
到什么观念的影响？他们的灵感来自哪里？这些影响以及灵感同以前比起来是相同
的还是不同的？这些建筑向我们揭示了哪些关乎中国的希望和未来的东西？

罗永进：在中外历史上，富裕和权力阶层经常修建一些宏伟的建筑物，借以炫耀
　　　　他们的富有和特权，对此我并不反感，因为多数我们今天能看到的这样的建筑
　　　　物在我看来都很美。问题在于目前在中国，很多建筑，不管是私人或是政府官
　　　　员筹建的，都难以置信地丑陋不堪。人们看到的就是低级趣味、愚昧无知和赤
　　　　裸裸的欲望。它们与历史毫不相干。拥有这些建筑物的人梦想着用这些建筑来
　　　　塑造历史。这是曾在文革时达到高峰的中国文化一百年的现代化的副作用。传
　　　　统被忽视和摧毁了。如果这样的建筑在中国继续修建下去，未来将没有任何
　　　　希望。

邢丹文，在你的作品中，处处可以看到在象北京这样的城市中，房地产业爆炸性的增长和房地产市场贪婪的加剧，以及由此给社区、个人和集体造成的正面和负面的影响，还有以商业为动机滋生出的个人欲望、不成熟的消费至上主义、规划好了的现实，以及充满希望的幸福感和归属感，等等。我知道在以前的采访中，你谈过你力图借作品表达一种孤独感和孤立感，来触及中国改善城市住房条件进程中的一个层面。作为一名年轻的艺术家，特别是一名女性艺术家，是什么促使你做出这样非常成功的尝试，去捕捉存在于目前中国住房条件以及作为人们生活一部分的焦虑感中的那种非常明显的复杂性，并使你受益非浅？

邢丹文： 我逐渐认识到，以这种新的方式生活可能很方便很舒适，但是当城市开始改变的时候，我开始担心旧城市被破坏所带来的问题和正在发生的变化。

我做过五年的摄影记者工作。从1995年开始，北京开始发生剧烈的变化。一环内的整个老胡同住宅区都拿掉了。紫禁城在北京的北部；南部是相对贫困的地区。 有一次我和一位记者报导了一件关于一个家庭动迁的事。

在文革期间，没有个人受穷的问题。很多大宅院由政府重新安置给工人们居住，不象以前那样只住一家人。每个工人分到一间房子，他们成家时，会在原来房间基础上再加一间。宅院的空间盖满了四、五十家人新加的房子，中间的过道非常窄。他们生活在那样的环境中，就象一个大家庭一样。邻居间来往密切。他们没有自来水，他们会共用一个水池。这样交流和分享都很容易。

在那次采访中，当人们被问及他们喜欢留在拥挤的大杂院还是喜欢搬到新开发的郊区公寓时，很多人都表示喜欢搬迁。但我认为，在他们搬走以前那个时候，他们并没有真正意识到将来会是什么样子，也想不到住在新的地方是 一种什么感觉。在我看来，我知道住在这些新的小方块里，特别是身为艺术家工作在这样的工作室里意味着什么。如果我不走出工作室， 就见不到人。

张大力，你的《对话与拆》记录行为传达了一种个人的紧迫感，你担忧着人们过于急切地推进现代化进程所导致的的拆除行动和随之而来的政府机构或个体发展商对一些著名的公共和私人历史文化场所的人为破坏，使社区失去了熟悉的生活方式。你的干涉行为是否来自一种意愿，要让你的邻居们说话，促使他们反抗，质问对拆除和新建负有责任的人，或者是你在欧洲生活过一段时间后回到北京，自己在付出努力想挖掘出这种激烈局面的复杂性所在？

张大力： 这个项目我做了十年。 其间无论从物质生活还是从知识生活和精神生活上来讲，都发生过很多重大的变化。这部作品的题目是"对话" 与"拆"。创作这部作品的过程中我有两个意思。那时中国的艺术圈子主要代表人物是一群在自己工作室工作的艺术家，他们的空间是私人的，封闭的。艺术家自己同自己交谈。 有很多艺术家有自己的不同见解，但他们却不寻求与人对话。艺术圈是愤世嫉俗一族。我想把自己的艺术从工作室搬到现实生活中，我要把我的艺术与人民连接和联系起来。第二个意义，就是环境中出现的变化，那种非常剧烈的变化震撼了我， 让我有了最初的动力去创作这样的艺术作品。

那些大头像出现在各色各样的人群和环境中。他们有权利发出自己的声音。他们有权利让习惯了上层势力压迫的人意识到他们的存在。我强迫这些人说话，表达他们的权利。大多数沉默的人习惯于抑制自己的感情和想法，他们不敢表达意见。然而，当你的权利被剥夺了的时候，反抗就成了唯一有效的武器。这个城市在一夜之间就变了样，整个一条街转眼就会消失。谁有理由这样做？ 谁是城市真正的主人？做出这些改变的目的何在？现代化难道仅仅是拓宽的街道和建高了的大楼吗？从没有人问过这样的问题。我认为只有头脑的现代化才是真正的现代化。我的家可以很小而且摇摇欲坠，遮挡不住风雨，可即使是国王也不能随便进来。我不喜欢别人来安排和干预我的生活。我不喜欢让别人告诉我怎么做。我不喜欢别人在鞭打我的同时还试图告诉我他们这样做是为了我好。我不喜欢被人当做狗养着，没有尊严，只能从主人那讨食吃。我们已经失去了很多，但是，城市的当权者们永远不会考虑那些居住在他们将要毁坏的居民区里的人们的意见。

城市就象一个娱乐园，它看起来很漂亮，但是住在里面的人心灵是空虚的。口袋里装满了钱，却毫无精神生活可言，这样的人如同行尸走肉。我知道我个人改变不了什么，但我拒绝保持沉默。因此我让我的作品为我说话。我的作品表达了我的想法。我希望有更多的人能够这样做。

丹麦哲学家索伦·祁克果（Soren Kierkegaard）有一句名言说，"哲学家所说的生活只有向后看才能理解好，这是绝对正确的，但是他们忘掉了另一个命题，那就是生活必须向前过。" 在《第二历史》这个系列中，我想知道，你是如何看待这一点的，即对过去更好的反思如何增进我们目前对过去、现在和将来的了解。当你将我们的注意力吸引到在共产党监督下精心巧妙地制作的视觉影象上面时你想达到什么目的呢？ 在诚实与欺瞒这一点上有没有教训我们现在可以借鉴？

张大力：我认为，目前我们所过的生活，周围的形势和环境，都是历史的结果。在创作这个系列的时候，我对中国以前几代人的审美观有很清楚的了解，他们的习俗和经历很有美感。这些经历是被动的，不能强加于人，它早已流淌在我们的血液中。现在有了Photoshop这样的图象处理软件， 可是我们还要走同样的程序。唯一的区别是我们不会留下加工的痕迹。我觉得大部分人对历史都不内行。尽管如此，历史依然影响着我们的生活和思维。只有少数的人非常觉悟非常清醒，他们能看清历史如何发挥作用。如今中国人只关心现在。我认为这是我创作过的最重要的作品。这是我第一次没有把我的感情因素掺杂到作品中去，我在研究这个项目和浏览文件的时候非常冷静非常客观。我想告诉人们那些影象后面隐藏着什么。我不在意这些影象是如何被处理的，我只关心它们后面隐藏的意义。

关于艺术史的角色以及我们能从中学到什么

因为我是学习艺术史出身的，而不是学经济学、科学、新闻和城市规划学的，所以我能比较强烈地意识到艺术家和艺术群体如何对社会和政治形势及环境做出历史性的反映，他们由此而创作的作品定型了我们的记忆和对重大事件的理解。艺术家、艺术和艺术史最有价值的贡献之一就是能使我们从中更好地理解不同的文化和不同的历史时期，无论是通过回顾过去，还是，如果我们用心的话，通过审视我们所处时代的艺术和艺术家们对自身经历和他们的政治文化环境所表达的意见。　这次展览中由十七位目前居住和工作在中国的现代艺术家创作的作品确实触及和思索了全球主义中比较残酷的不太让人满意的一面，尤其是中国特有的猖獗的城市化进程。

2003年《亚洲华尔街日报》发表了一篇文章，旅居上海的文化评论家Lisa Movius在文中说：

> 中国现代艺术在美国的形象日渐上升，其重要性已经超出了艺术评论的范畴：在中国的经济与政治力量增长的同时，美国人对她的评价也越来越高，他们对中国的现实情况有了较之以往流行的那种程式化的中国观更为新颖更为准确的看法。中国的现代艺术毕竟有可能成为中国过去十年来巨大转变的最好的见证之一。

让我们及时展望未来，用十年、五十年甚至一百年以后的眼光来看待你们的作品和这次展览中的作品。通过透视这些艺术和了解这些艺术家而更深入地评价和理解二十一世纪初的中国，我们将得到什么样的启示？

罗永进：我希望人们能够理解在二十一世纪初期，有一些感觉敏锐的艺术家，他们对今天时髦的建筑持着嘲讽和怀疑的态度。他们得以将这些无味的建筑物变成了精美的艺术品。

邢丹文：你的问题很难回答。我从没那样想过。事实上，我想说明这些作品不只是关于中国城市的。作品的原始资料和镜头取自中国，但是最终，这些作品讨论的是全球的形势，以及人类和他们居住的环境。可能这些作品会从历史的角度看待建筑，因为建筑是历史的见证。我想在十年、二十年，甚至一百年之后，人类还会遇到问题。人类的基本问题是相似的，只是具体的某一问题可能会变化。

张大力：从将来的观众的角度来看，所有的艺术品都会帮助人们了解过去，它们还会帮助那些人更好地理解他们现在的生活与过去生活的关系。我相信历史有它的连续性，人类的精神不会倒下。也许我的作品会给将来的中国人留下一些问题去思考，否则这些作品将没有任何意义。

这些采访是2008年3月在纽约通过面谈和电子邮件完成的，被采访者身在北京、上海、纽约、鹿特丹和堪萨斯城他们各自的键盘边。我非常感谢罗永进、邢丹文和张大力在这次采访过程中所表现出的真挚、诚实与正直。他们也使我对他们的作品有了更深的评价与了解。我也衷心感谢所有对我提供支持的人士，他们是：Mark Bessire，Andrea Flamini，Kris Ercums，Owen Martin，Donna Raskin 和沃纳特街誊写服务公司 （Walnut Street Transcription Services），Moti Hasson，Michael Schonhoff，Robert Heishmann，徐淦（Gan Xu），Francis Gerstle，David Ford，Dr. John Kennedy，Bruce Ferguson，和 Glenn Mott.

Ai Weiwei 艾未未

1957   Born in Beijing

1978   Studied at Beijing Film Academy

1981   Attended Art Student League, New York, N.Y.

Attended Parsons School of Design, New York, N.Y.

2008   Lives and works in Beijing

SELECT EXHIBITIONS

2008   *New Vista—The Phenomenon of Post-Tradition in Contemporary Art*, White Space Beijing, Beijing, China.

Under Construction, Sherman Contemporary Art Foundation, Sydney, Australia; Campelltown Arts Center, Campelltown, Australia.

2007   *Documenta 12*, Kassel, Germany.

China Welcomes You, Kunsthaus Graz, Graz, Austria.

Made in China: The Estella Collection, Louisiana Museum of Modern Art, Humlebæk, Denmark; The Israel Museum, Jerusalem, Israel.

We Are the Future, Second Moscow Biennale of Contemporary Art, Former Lenin Museum, Moscow, Russia.

The Real Thing: Contemporary Art from China, Tate Liverpool, Liverpool, England; Institute Valencia d' Art Modern, Valencia, Spain.

2006   *Altered, Stitched and Gathered*, P.S. 1 Contemporary Art Center, Long Island City, N.Y., United States.

Art in Motion, Museum of Contemporary Art Shanghai, Shanghai, China.

Fifth Asia–Pacific Triennial of Contemporary Art, Queensland Museum of Art, Brisbane, Australia.

Detours: Tactical Approaches to Urbanization in China, Eric Arthur Gallery, University of Toronto, Toronto, Canada.

China Power Station: Part I, Serpentine Gallery, London, England.

Zones of Contact, 2006 Biennale of Sydney, Sydney, Australia.

2005   *The Second Guangzhou Triennial*, Guangdong Museum of Art, Guangzhou, China.

Regeneration: Contemporary Chinese Art from China and the U.S., Arizona State University Art Museum, Arizona State University, Tempe, Ariz., United States.

A Strange Heaven: Contemporary Chinese Photography, Tennis Palace, Helsinki City Art Museum, Helsinki, Finland; Galerie Rudolfinum, Praha, Croatia.

2004   *Between Past and Future: New Photography and Video from China,* Smart Museum of Art, University of Chicago, Chicago, Ill., United States; International Center of Photography, New York, N.Y., United States.

2002   *Reinterpretation: A Decade of Experimental Chinese Art, 1990–2000*, First Guangzhou Triennial, Guangdong Museum of Art, Guangzhou, China.

2000   *Fuck Off*, Eastlink Gallery, Shanghai, China.

1999   *Aperto All Over*, Forty-Eighth Venice Biennale, Venice, Italy.

1989   *The Star-Group from Beijing*, State University of New York, Albany, Albany, N.Y., United States.

Chen Shaoxiong 陈劭雄

1962   Born in Shantou, Guandong Province

1984   Received B.F.A., Guangzhou Fine Art Academy (Print Department)

1984   Begins teaching at Guangdong Art Normal School

1990   Co-founder of Big Tail Elephant Group

2008   Lives and works in Guangzhou

SELECT EXHIBITIONS

2006   *China Power Station: Part 1*, Serpentine Gallery, London, England.

Guangdongtokyo, Ota Fine Arts, Tokyo, Japan.

Regeneration, Williams College Museum of Art, Williamstown, Mass., United States.

2005   *Second Guangzhou Triennial: Beyond—An Extraordinary Space for Modernization*, Guangdong Museum of Art, Guangzhou, China.

Third Tirana Biennale: Go Inside, National Art Gallery, Tirana, Albania.

Follow Me! Chinese Art at the Threshold of the New Millennium, Mori Art Museum, Tokyo, Japan.

Chen Shaoxiong: Ink City—New Works, Courtyard Gallery, Beijing, China.

2004 *Zooming into Focus: Contemporary Chinese Photography and Video from the Haudenschild Collection,* San Diego State University Art Gallery, San Diego, Calif., United States; Shanghai Art Museum, Shanghai, China.

Between Past and Future: New Photography and Video from China, Smart Museum of Art, University of Chicago, Chicago, Ill., United States; International Center of Photography, New York, N.Y., United States.

2003 *Anti-C.S.X.,* Vitamin Creative Space, Guangzhou, China.

Zone of Urgency, Fiftieth Venice Biennale, Venice, Italy.

2002 *Shanghai Biennial: Urban Creation,* Shanghai Art Museum, Shanghai, China.

First Guangzhou Triennial: Reinterpretation: A Decade of Experimental Chinese Art, Guangdong Museum of Art, Guangzhou, China.

1999 *Fast Forward: New Chinese Video Art,* Contemporary Art Center, Macau, China.

1998 *Inside Out: New Chinese Art,* Asia Society and P.S. 1 Contemporary Art Center, Long Island City, N.Y., United States; San Francisco Museum of Modern Art, San Francisco, Calif., United States.

Big Tail Elephant, Kunsthalle Bern, Bern, Switzerland.

Gu Wenda 谷文达

1955 Born in Shanghai

1976 Received B.F.A., Shanghai School of Arts and Crafts, 1976

1981 Received M.F.A., China Academy of Fine Arts, Hangzhou

1981–87 Taught at China Academy of Fine Arts, Hangzhou

2008 Lives and works in Shanghai and Brooklyn, N.Y.

SELECTED EXHIBITIONS

2007 *united nations: the green house* and *united nations: united colors,* Baker Library, Dartmouth College, Hanover, N.H., United States.

forest of stone stelkes: retranslation and rewriting tang dynasty poetry, Hood Museum of Art, Dartmouth College, Hanover, N.H., United States.

2005 *The Wall: Reshaping Contemporary Chinese Art,* Albright-Knox Museum of Art, Buffalo, N.Y., United States; University at Buffalo Art Gallery and University at Buffalo Anderson Gallery, State University of New York, Buffalo, Buffalo, N.Y., United States.

2003 *Wenda Gu: from middle kingdom to biological millennium,* University of North Texas Art Gallery, Denton, Tex., United States; H&R Block Artspace at Kansas City Art Institute, Kansas City, Mo., United States; Institute of Contemporary Art at Maine College of Art and Bates College Museum of Art, Lewiston, Maine, United States.

2002 *New Way of Tea,* Asia Society, New York, N.Y., United States.

2001 *First Chengdu Biennale,* Chendu, China.

1999 *Transience: Chinese Experimental Art at the End of the Twentieth Century,* Smart Museum of Art, University of Chicago, Chicago, Ill., United States; University of Oregon Museum of Art, Eugene, Ore., United States; Hood Museum of Art, Dartmouth College, Hanover, N.H., United States.

1998 *Inside Out: New Chinese Art,* P.S. 1 Contemporary Art Center, Long Island City, N.Y., United States; Asia Society, New York, N.Y., United States; San Francisco Museum of Modern Art and Asian Art Museum, San Francisco, Calif., United States; Museo de Arte Contemporaneo, Monterrey, Mexico; Tacoma Art Museum and the Henry Art Gallery, Seattle, Wash., United States; National Gallery of Australia, Canberra, Australia; Hong Kong Museum of Art, Hong Kong, China.

Gu Zheng 顾铮

1959 Born in Shanghai

1998 Received Ph.D., Osaka Prefecture University, Osaka

Became Professor and Vice Director of Research Center for Visual Culture, Fudan University, Shanghai

2008 Lives and works in Shanghai

SELECT EXHIBITIONS

2008 *Foto Ophoto,* OFOTO Gallery, Beijing, China.

2006 *Rumor and Legend,* OFOTO Gallery, Shanghai, China.

2000 *The Associated Exhibition of Black-and-White Photographs, Fifth Shanghai International Photography Exhibition,* Shanghai Exhibition Center, Shanghai, China.

1995 *My View of Japan*, YMCA Gallery of Kobe, Kobe, Japan.

1986 *Exhibition of the Beihe Association*, Beijing and Shanghai, China.

Hong Lei 洪磊

1960 Born in Changzhou, Jiangsu Province

1987 Received B.F.A., Nanjing Academy of Arts, Nanjing

1993 Studied at Central Academy of Fine Arts, Beijing

2008 Lives and works in Shanghai

SELECT EXHIBITIONS

2007 *Whispering Wind: Recent Chinese Photography*, Frist Center for the Visual Arts, Nashville, Tenn., United States.

Convection, Three Shadows Photography Art Center, Beijing, China.

2006 *Fever Variations*, 2006 Gwangju Biennale, Gwangju, Korea.

City Skin: Images of the Contemporary Metropolis, Shenzhen Art Museum, Shenzhen, China.

Right Here: Photographs by Chin-San Long/Ain't Here: Photographs by Hong Lei, Zhu Qizhan Art Museum, Shanghai, China.

2005 *Regeneration: Contemporary Chinese Art from China and the U.S.*, Arizona State University Art Museum, Arizona State University, Tempe, Ariz., United States.

Re-viewing the City, First Guangzhou International Photo Biennial, Guangdong Museum of Art, Guangzhou, China.

2004 *Between Past and Future: New Photography and Video from China*, Smart Museum of Art, University of Chicago, Chicago, Ill., United States; International Center of Photography, New York, N.Y., United States.

Spellbound Aura, Museum of Contemporary Art, Taipei, Taiwan.

Young Artists from Korea, China and Japan, National Museum of Contemporary Art, Seoul, South Korea.

2003 *Alors, la Chine?*, Centre Pompidou, Paris, France.

2002 *China Century*, 2002 Pingyao International Photography Festival, Pingyao, China.

2001 *Cross Pressures: Contemporary Photography and Video from Beijing*, Oulu Art Museum, Oulu, Finland; Finnish Museum of Contemporary Photography, Helsinki, Finland.

1992 *Oil Painting in the 90s*, First Guangzhou Biennial, Guangdong Exhibition Center, Guangzhou, China.

Liang Weiping 梁卫平

1960 Born in Shanghai

2008 Lives and works in Shanghai

SELECT EXHIBITIONS

2006 *2006 Contemporary Photography*, Shanghai, China.

2005 *Liang Weiping: Suzhou Creek Photography*, Shanghai, China.

Liu Bolin 刘勃麟

1973 Born in Shandong Province

1995 Received B.F.A., Shandong Art College, Shandong

2001 Received M.F.A., Central Academy of Fine Arts, Beijing

2008 Lives and works in Beijing

SELECTION EXHIBITIONS

2008 *Liu Bolin: China Report 2007*, Eli Klein Fine Art, New York, N.Y., United States.

Out of Place, Robischon Gallery, Denver, Colo., United States.

Face East: Chinese Contemporary Art, Robischon Gallery, Denver, Colo., United States.

2007 *Liu Bolin*, Galerie Bertin-Toublanc, Paris, France.

Made in China: Chinese Contemporary Art, Shanghai Duolun Museum of Modern Art, Shanghai, China.

Chinese Performance Art Photography, Ying Gallery, Dashanzi Art Zone, Beijing, China.

2006 *Satellite 06 Contemporary Art & Design*, Vanguard Gallery, Shanghai, China.

Red Star, Red Star, Red Star, 751 Factory, Dashanzi Art Zone, Beijing, China.

2005 *Post-calligraphy*, Maside Art Center, Beijing, China.

Lu Yuanmin 陆元敏

1950 Born in Shanghai

Became Executive member, Shanghai Photographer's Association

2008 Lives and works in Shanghai

SELECT EXHIBITIONS

2005 *Peace and Progress*, 2005 Pingyao International Photography Festival, Pingyao, China.

Re-viewing the City, First Guangzhou International Photo Biennial, Guangdong Museum of Art, Guangzhou, China.

Shifting Views: Chinese Urban Documentary Photography, University of Michigan, Ann Arbor, Mich., United States.

2004   *Documenting China: Contemporary Photography and Social Change,* Bates College Museum of Art, Lewiston, Maine, United States; China Institute, New York, N.Y., United States; Weisman Art Museum, Minneapolis, Minn., United States.

Dreaming of the Dragon's Nation: Contemporary Art from China, Irish Museum of Modern Art, Dublin, Ireland.

2003   *Shanghainese 1990–2000,* Shanghai Literature & Art Publishing House, Shanghai, China.

Humanism in China: A Contemporary Record of Photography, Guangdong Museum of Art, Guangzhou, China; Shanghai Museum of Art, Shanghai, China; China National Museum, Beijing, China.

2002   *East Meets West: China Contemporary Art Exhibition,* Vienna, Austria.

2001   *2001 Pingyao International Photography Festival,* Pingyao, China.

2000   *Fifth Shanghai International Photography Exhibition,* Shanghai, China.

Luo Yongjin 罗永进

1960   Born in Beijing

1982   Received B.A., English, P.L.A. University of Foreign Languages, Luoyang

1986   Studied oil painting, Zhejiang Academy of Fine Arts, Hangzhou

1992   Received M.A., History of Art, Guangzhou Academy of Fine Arts, Guangzhou

2000   Became Professor of Photography, Shanghai Institute of Design, China Academy of Fine Arts

2008   Lives and works in Shanghai

SELECT EXHIBITIONS

2008   *Luo Yongjin,* Ofoto Gallery, Shanghai, China.

Luo Yongjin, Hexiangning Art Museum, Shenzhen, China.

2007   *Cina, West of California?,* Centro Trevi Kuoturzentrum, Bolzano, Italy.

Moving Closer: Luo Yongjin, Bangkok University Gallery, Bangkok, Thailand.

2006   *Luo Yongjin Photography,* Eidos, Barsano, Italy.

Luo Yongjin: Points of View, Allsopp Contemporary, London, England.

2005   *Faces in Time,* Sala del Granaio, Grimaldi Foundation, Modica, Italy.

Guangzhou Photo Biennale, Guangdong Art Museum, Guangzhou, China.

2004   *Documenting China: Contemporary Photography and Social Change,* Bates College Museum of Art, Lewiston, Maine, United States; China Institute, New York, N.Y., United States; Weisman Art Museum, Minneapolis, Minn., United States.

Between Past and Future: New Photography and Video from China, Smart Museum of Art, University of Chicago, Chicago, Ill., United States; International Center of Photography, New York, N.Y., United States.

2002   *Shanghai Biennale,* Shanghai, China.

2001   *First Chengdu Biennale,* Chengdu, China.

Ma Liuming 马六明

1969   Born in Huangshi, Hubei Province

1991   Received B.F.A., Hubei Academy of Fine Arts, Oil Painting Department, Hubei Province

2008   Lives and works in Beijing

SELECT EXHIBITIONS

2007   *Art Taipei 2007,* Star 85 Art Space, Taipei, Taiwan.

2006   *Re-Excavate the Contemporary Realism,* Soka Art Center, Beijing, China.

2005   *Mahjong,* Kunstmuseum Bern, Bern, Switzerland.

2005   *Expanded Painting and Acción Directa,* Prague Biennale 2, Prague, Czech Republic.

2004   *Between Past and Future: New Photography and Video from China,* Smart Museum of Art, University of Chicago, Chicago, Ill., United States; International Center of Photography, New York, N.Y., United States.

2002   *Reinterpretation: A Decade of Experimental Chinese Art, 1990–2000,* First Guangzhou Triennial, Guangdong Museum of Art, Guangzhou, China.

Pingyao International Photography Festival, Pingyao, China.

2001   *Hot Pot,* Kunstnernes Haus, Oslo, Norway.

Translated Acts: Body and Performance Art From East Asia, Haus der Kulturen der Welt, Berlin, Germany; Queens Museum of Art, Queens, N.Y., United States.

1999   *Aperto Over All,* Forty-Eighth Venice Biennale, Venice, Italy.

1998   *Inside Out: New Chinese Art*, Asia Society, New York, N.Y., United States; P.S. 1 Contemporary Art Center, Long Island City, N.Y., United States; San Francisco Museum of Modern Art, San Francisco, Calif. United States.

1997   *Another Long March: Chinese Conceptual Art and Installation Art in the Nineties*, Foundament Foundation, Breda, Netherlands.

1992   *The First Guangzhou Biennial: Oil Painting in the Nineties*, Guangdong Exhibition Center, Guangzhou, China.

Wang Jing 王净

1972   Born in Shanghai

1996   Received B.A., Department of Oil Painting, Anhui Normal University

2000   Received M.A., Central Academy of Fine Arts, Beijing
Became Lecturer, School of Art and Design, Shanghai Institute of Technology

2008   Lives and works in Shanghai

SELECT EXHIBITIONS

2008   *Wang Jing*, Boulder Museum of Contemporary Art, Boulder, Colo., United States.

2006   *Different Impression: Young Artists Contemporary Art Exhibition*, Today Art Museum, Beijing, China.

2005   *Awakening: La France Mandarine*, National Art Museum of China, Beijing, China.

2003   *The Eighteenth Asian Art Exhibition; Mapping Asia: P.R. China*, Hong Kong Heritage Museum, Hong Kong, China.
Turning: First Annual Invitation Exhibition of Contemporary Artists 2003, Chongqing Art Museum, Sichuan, China.
Transformation of Art: Semantic Meaning and Displacement of Culture, Taikang Art Museum, Shanghai, China.

2002   *Wang Jing: Toy*, Moganshan Lu, Shanghai, China.

2001   *Wang Jing: Flora and Fauna*, Art Scene China, Hong Kong, China.

Weng Fen 翁奋

1961   Born in Hainan Province

1985   Received B.A., Guangzhou Academy of Fine Arts, Guangzhou

2008   Lives and works in Haikou City

SELECT EXHIBITIONS

2008   *Red Aside: Chinese Contemporary Art of the Sigg Collection*, Fundacio Joan Miro, Barcelona, Spain.

2007   *RED HOT: Asian Art Today from the Chaney Family Collection*, Museum of Fine Arts, Houston, Tex., United States.

2005   *Re-Viewing the City*, First Guangzhou International Photo Biennale, Guangdong Museum of Art, Guangzhou, China.
The Second Guangzhou Triennial, Guangdong Museum of Art, Guangzhou, China.
Follow Me! Chinese Contemporary Art at the Threshold of the New Millennium, Mori Art Museum, Tokyo, Japan.
A Strange Heaven: Contemporary Chinese Photography, Tennis Palace, Helsinki City Art Museum, Helsinki, Finland; Galerie Rudolfinum, Praha, Croatia.

2004   *Between Past and Future: New Photography and Video from China*, Smart Museum of Art, University of Chicago, Chicago, Ill., United States; International Center of Photography, New York, N.Y., United States.
Spellbound Aura, Museum of Contemporary Art, Taipei, Taiwan.

2003   *Zooming into Focus: Contemporary Chinese Photography and Video from the Haudenschild Collection*, San Diego State University Art Gallery, San Diego State University, San Diego, Calif., United States.
Alors, la Chine?, Centre Pompidou, Paris, France.
Peripheries Become the Center, First Prague Biennale, National Gallery, Prague, Czech Republic.
New Zone: Chinese Art, Zacheta National Gallery of Art, Warsaw, Poland.

2002   *China Century*, 2002 Pingyao International Photography Festival, Pingyao, China.
Reinterpretation: A Decade of Experimental Chinese Art (1990–2000), First Guangzhou Triennial, Guangdong Museum of Art, Guangzhou, China.
Urban Creation, Fourth Shanghai Biennale, Shanghai Art Museum, Shanghai, China.
Chinese Modernity, Museu de Arte Brasileira, Sao Paulo, Brazil.
New China Photography, Courtyard Gallery, Beijing, China.

2001   *Virtual Future*, Guangdong Museum of Art, Guangzhou, China.

First Chengdu Biennial, Chengdu Contemporary Art Museum, Chengdu, China.

2000　*China Avant-Garde Artists Documents Exhibition*, Fukuoka Museum of Art, Fukuoka, Japan.

1999　*Post-Sense Sensibility: Distorted Bodies and Delusion*, Basement of Building No. 2, Peony Residential District, Beijing, China.

Xing Danwen　邢丹文

1967　Born in Xi'an, Shaanxi Province

1992　Received B.F.A., Central Academy of Fine Arts, Beijing

2001　Received M.F.A., School of Visual Arts, New York

2008　Lives and works in Beijing

SELECT EXHIBITIONS

2008　*China Design Now*, Victoria and Albert Museum, London, England.

2007　*Roland Fischer/Xing Danwen*, Galerie Sollertis, Toulouse, France.

　　　City of Expiration and Regeneration, 2007 Shenzhen & Hong Kong Bi-City Biennial of Urbanism and Architecture, Shenzhen, China.

2006　*disCONNEXION/duplication*, Chinese Museum, Melbourne, Australia.

　　　C on Cities, Tenth Venice Architecture Biennale, Venice, Italy.

　　　Made in China, Museum of Contemporary Photography, Chicago, Ill., United States.

2005　*The Wall: Reshaping Contemporary Chinese Art,* Albright-Knox Museum of Art, Buffalo, N.Y., United States; University at Buffalo Art Gallery and University at Buffalo Anderson Gallery, State University of New York, Buffalo, Buffalo, United States

　　　Re-Viewing the City, First Guangzhou International Photo Biennale, Guangdong Museum of Art, Guangzhou, China.

2004　*Between Past and Future: New Photography and Video from China,* Smart Museum of Art, University of Chicago, Chicago, Ill., United States; International Center of Photography, New York, United States.

2003　*The American Effect,* Whitney Museum of American Art, New York, United States.

2002　*Reinterpretation: A Decade of Experimental Chinese Art (1990–2000),* First Guangzhou Triennial, Guangdong Museum of Art, Guangzhou, China.

2001　*Living in Time: Contemporary Artists from China,* Hamburger Bahnhof Museum for Contemporary Art, Berlin, Germany.

1999　*Transience: Chinese Experimental Art at the End of the Twentieth Century,* Smart Museum of Art, University of Chicago, Chicago, Ill., United States. Oregon Museum of Art, Eugene, Ore., United States; Hood Museum of Art, Dartmouth College, Hanover, N.H., United States.

　　　BEIJING—The Revolutionary Capital, Institute of Contemporary Arts, London, England.

Yang Yongliang　杨泳梁

1980　Born in Shanghai

1999　Received B.F.A., Shanghai Fine Art Institute

2003　Received M.F.A., Shanghai Institute of Design, China Academy of Fine Arts, Shanghai

2008　Lives and works in Shanghai

SELECT EXHIBITIONS

2007　*Phantom Landscape Series 2 & 3*, OFOTO Gallery, Shanghai, China.

　　　Art Now, Danwon Arts Festival, Gyeonggido Museum of Modern Art, Korea.

　　　2007 Pingyao International Photography Festival, Pingyao, China.

　　　Celebrating, epSITE, Epson Imaging Gallery, Shanghai, China.

2006　*Phantom Landscape Series I*, OFOTO Gallery, Shanghai, China.

Yening　也宁

1978　Born in Dunhua, Jilian Province

2001　Received B.A., Photography Department at Luxun Academy of Fine Arts, Shenyang, China

2001　Began teaching at Sichuan Fine Arts Academy, Chongqing, China

2008　Lives and works in Beijing and Chongqing

SELECT EXHIBITIONS

2008　*A Point of View: Women Artists*, Songzhuang of Beijing, Beijing, China.

2007　*Made in Songzhuang*, Shangshang Art Museum, Beijing, China.

2006　*Shanghai Mandarin Palace Art Events*, Shanghai, China.

Plan of Coincidence: Exhibition of Chinese and Slovene
Photographers, Art Reflect, Ljubljana, Slovenia.
Only Child: Art Documentary Exhibition, Park 19 Art Gallery,
Guangzhou, China; Chinese Contemporary, Beijing, China.

2005 *100 Artists for a Museum*, Casoria International Contemporary
Art Museum, Casoria, Italy.

2000 *Cross-Straits Three Ground*, Art Museum of Luxun Academy
of Fine Arts, Shenyang, China.

Zhang Dali 张大力

1963 Born in Harbin, Heilongjiang Province

1987 Received B.F.A., National Academy of Fine Arts and Design,
Beijing

2008 Lives and works in Beijing

SELECT EXHIBITIONS

2006 *A Second History*, Walsh Gallery, Chicago, Ill., United States.
Fever Variations, 2006 Gwangju Biennale, Gwangju, Korea.
Sublimation, Beijing Commune, Beijing, China.

2005 *The Wall: Reshaping Contemporary Chinese Art*, Albright-Knox
Museum of Art, Buffalo, N.Y.; University at Buffalo Art
Gallery, University at Buffalo Anderson Gallery, Buffalo,
N.Y., United States.

2004 *Zhang Dali,* Chinese Contemporary Gallery, London, England.
*Between Past and Future: New Photography and Video from
China,* Smart Museum of Art, University of Chicago,
Chicago, Ill., United States; International Center of
Photography, New York, N.Y., United States.
*Over One Billion Served: Conceptual Photography from the
People's Republic of China*, Museum of Contemporary Art,
Denver, Colo., United States.
Regeneration, Samek Art Gallery, Bucknell University,
Lewisburg, Penn., United States.

2003 *The Logan Collection,* Denver Art Museum, Denver, Colo.,
United States.

2002 *Reinterpretation: A Decade of Experimental Chinese Art
(1990–2000),* The First Guangzhou Triennial, Guangdong
Museum of Art, Guangzhou, China.

2001 *China Art Now,* Singapore Art Museum, Singapore.
*Cross Pressures: Contemporary Photography and Video from
Beijing,* Oulu Art Museum, Oulu, Finland; Finnish
Museum of Contemporary Photography, Helsiniki,
Finland.

2000 *Fuck Off*, Eastlink Gallery, Shanghai, China.

1999 *Revolutionary Capitals: Beijing-London*, Institute of
Contemporary Art, London, England.
Food for Thought: Insight into Chinese Contemporary Art,
De Witte Dame, Eindhoven, Netherlands (coproduced
with Canvas Foundation, Amsterdam, Netherlands; Royal
Tropical Institute, Amsterdam, Netherlands; MU Art
Foundation/Artic Foundation, Eindhoven, Netherlands;
and Canvas Foundation, Amsterdam, Netherlands).

Zhu Feng 朱锋

1974 Born in Shanghai

2000 Received B.A., Fine Art Department of East China Normal
University, Shanghai

2008 Lives and works in Shanghai

SELECT EXHIBITIONS

2008 *Hills and Rivers*, Epsite, Epsom Imaging Gallery, Shanghai,
China.
Streets Are Ours, Shanghai Zendai MoMA, Shanghai, China.
Celebrate, China Contemporary Photography, Epsite, Epson
Imaging Gallery, Shanghai, China.

2007 *Shanghai Zero Degree*, Weima Gallery, Shanghai, China.

2005 *Selfhood—Absent Minded*, Yiyun Town Art Saloon,
Guangzhou, China.
Harvest, Art Scene Warehouse, Shanghai, China.
Guangzhou Photography Biennial, Guangdong Museum of
Art, Guangzhou, China.
Re-Viewing the City, 2005 Guangzhou Photo Biennial,
Guangdong Museum of Art, Guangzhou, China.

2004 *Urban New Generation Image*, Xingguang Photography
Gallery, Shanghai, China.

2003 *Paradise Lost*, 2003 Pingyao International Photography
Festival, Pingyao, China.

2002 *Images and Variations*, Shanghai Normal University,
Shanghai, China.
China Century, 2002 Pingyao International Photography
Festival, Pingyao, China.

2000 *The Night of Shanghai*, Weima Gallery, Shanghai, China.
The Fifth Shanghai International Photography Exhibition,
Shanghai Exhibition Center, Shanghai, China.

WORKS IN EXHIBITION

Ai Weiwei 艾未未

From the series *Study of Perspective*,
1999–2003
(*White House, Eiffel Tower, San Marco,
Hong Kong, Long Island City, Mona Lisa,
Tiananmen*, and *Berne*)
Eight black-and-white photographs
Each 20 × 24 inches (51 × 61 cm)
Collection AW Asia, New York

"June 1994," 1994
Black-and-white photograph
47 × 61 inches (119 × 155 cm)
Collection AW Asia, New York

Chen Shaoxiong 陈劭雄

Ink City, 2005
Video
3:01
Collection of the artist: courtesy Boers-Li
Gallery, Beijing

Gu Wenda 谷文达

*Fragment (United Nations: The Great Wall of
People)*, 2008
A hair brick fragment from the site-
specific installation with 1,500 solid
human hair bricks and hair curtains
made of one ton of Chinese hair. *United
Nations: The Great Wall of People* (2000)
was originally commissioned by the
Millennium Museum, Beijing and Albright
Knox Museum of Art, Buffalo, N.Y.
Collection Bates College Museum of Art

Gu Zheng 顾铮

From the series *Shanghai*, 2004
Untitled (no. 1, 4, 5, 6, 7, and 10)

Gelatin silver print
9¼ × 11¾ inches (23.5 × 30 cm)
Collection Bates College Museum of Art
From the series *Shanghai*, 2004
Untitled (no. 2, 3, 8, and 9)
Gelatin silver print
11¾ × 9¼ inches (30 × 23.5 cm)
Collection Bates College Museum of Art

Hong Lei 洪磊

Autumn in Forbidden City, East Veranda, 1997
C-print
23½ × 29½ inches (60 × 75 cm)
Collection AW Asia, New York
Chinese Garden Landscape, 1998
C-print
19½ × 23½ inches (50 × 60 cm)
Collection of Anne Riesenberg and Andy
Graham, Portland, Maine

Liang Weiping 梁卫平

Untitled (no. 2), 2006
Ink jet print
11 × 16½ inches (28 × 42 cm)
Collection Bates College Museum of Art
Untitled (no. 4), 2006
Ink jet print
12 × 16½ inches (30.5 × 42 cm)
Collection Bates College Museum of Art
Untitled (no. 3), 2006
Ink jet print
16½ × 12⅝ inches (42 × 32 cm)
Collection Bates College Museum of Art
Untitled (no. 1), 2006
Ink jet print
16 × 11½ inches (40.5 × 29 cm)
Collection Bates College Museum of Art

Liu Bolin 刘勃麟

From the series *Hidden in the City*
Laid Off, 2006
C-print
38½ × 47¼ inches (98 × 120 cm)
Collection Bates College Museum of Art
From the series *Hidden in the City*
Suo Jia, 2006
C-print
31¹⁄₁₆ × 39¼ inches (79 × 99.5 cm)
Collection Bates College Museum of Art

Lu Yuanmin 陆元敏

From the series *Shanghainese*
Untitled (no. 2)
Black-and-white photograph
11 × 16 inches (28 × 41 cm)
Collection of Anne Riesenberg and Andy
Graham, Portland, Maine
From the series *Shanghainese*
Untitled (no. 1)
Black-and-white photograph
16 × 11 inches (41 × 28 cm)
Collection of Anne Riesenberg and Andy
Graham, Portland, Maine

Luo Yongjin 罗永进

From the series *Government Buildings*
Luoyang (no. 2), 2005
Epson ink jet print with pigment ink on
fine art paper
24 × 24 inches (61 × 61 cm)
Collection Bates College Museum of Art
From the series *Government Buildings*
Shanghai (no. 4), 2006
Epson ink jet print with pigment ink on
fine art paper

24 × 24 inches (61 × 61 cm)

Collection Bates College Museum of Art

From the series *Government Buildings*

Pinglu (no. 7), 2005

Epson ink jet print with pigment ink on
fine art paper

24 × 24 inches (61 × 61 cm)

Collection Bates College Museum of Art

From the series *Government Buildings*

Lishui (no. 8), 2005

Epson ink jet print with pigment ink on
fine art paper

24 × 24 inches (61 × 61 cm)

Collection Bates College Museum of Art

From the series *Gas Stations*

Hangzhou (no. 01), 2006

Epson ink jet print with pigment ink on
fine art paper

24 × 28½ inches (61 × 72 cm)

Collection of the artist

From the series *Gas Stations*

Yixing (no. 03), 2006

Epson ink jet print with pigment ink on
fine art paper

22⅛ × 24¼ inches (56 × 62 cm)

Collection of the artist

From the series *Gas Stations*

Xinzhou (no. 06), 2005

Epson ink jet print with pigment ink on
fine art paper

24 × 24 inches (61 × 61 cm)

Collection of the artist

From the series *Gas Stations*

Zhengzhou (no. 08), 2004

Epson ink jet print with pigment ink on
fine art paper

24 × 24 inches (61 × 61 cm)

Collection of the artist

From the series *New Residence Hangzhou*

Hangzhou (no. 24), 2003

Epson ink jet print with pigment ink on
fine art paper

24 × 23½ inches (61 × 60 cm)

Collection of the artist

From the series *New Residence Hangzhou*

Hangzhou (no. 31), 2003

Epson ink jet print with pigment ink on
fine art paper

24 × 21 inches (61 × 53 cm)

Collection of the artist

Ma Liuming 马六明

Fen-Ma Liuming Walks The Great Wall, 1998

Gelatin silver print

47¾ × 72½ inches (121 × 184 cm)

Collection AW Asia, New York

Wang Jing 王净

From the series *Toy Piece*

The China Food in 2008, 2008

Installation

39⁷⁄₁₆ (h) × 51¼ × 51¼ inches (100 ×
130 × 130 cm)

Collection Bates College Museum of Art

Weng Fen 翁奋

On the Wall, Haikou 6, 2003

C-print

22¾ × 26¾ inches (57.8 × 68 cm)

Collection Bates College Museum of Art

Staring at the Sea, No.6, 2003

C-print

42½ × 34⅝ inches (108 × 88 cm)

Collection Bates College Museum of Art

Xing Danwen 邢丹文

From the series *Urban Fiction*

Image 0, 2004

Photography with digital manipulation

Light-jet C-print

67 × 95 inches (170 × 241.77 cm)

Collection of the artist

From the series *Urban Fiction*

Image 3, 2005

Photography with digital manipulation

Light-jet C-print

31½ × 41⅝ inches (80 × 105.5 cm)

Collection of the artist

From the series *Urban Fiction*

Image 9, 2004

Photography with digital manipulation

Light-jet C-print

31½ × 39½ inches (80 × 100.3 cm)

Collection of the artist

From the series *Urban Fiction*

Image 14, 2006

Photography with digital manipulation

Light-jet C-print

31½ × 39¹⁵⁄₁₆ inches (80 × 101.3 cm)

Collection of the artist

From the series *Urban Fiction*

Image 21, 2004

Photography with digital manipulation

Light-jet C-print

31½ × 45½ inches (80 × 115.7 cm)

Collection of the artist

Yang Yongliang 杨泳梁

From the series *Phantom Landscape I*

Untitled (no. 5), 2006

Ink-jet print on Epson fine art paper

63 × 23⅝ inches (160 × 60 cm)

Collection Bates College Museum of Art

From the series *Phantom Landscape I*

Untitled (no.3), 2006

Ink-jet print on Epson fine art paper

52¹³⁄₁₆ × 23⅝ inches (134 × 60 cm)

Collection Bates College Museum of Art

Yening 也宁

From the series *Dream in the Deserted Peking*

Untitled (no. 1), 2006

39⁷⁄₁₆ × 78¹¹⁄₁₆ inches (100 × 200 cm)

Digital C-print

Collection Bates College Museum of Art

From the series *Dream in the Deserted Peking*

Untitled (no. 2), 2006
39⁷⁄₁₆ × 78¹¹⁄₁₆ inches (100 × 200 cm)
Digital C-print
Collection Bates College Museum of Art

Zhang Dali 张大力
Dialogue Forbidden City, 1999
C-print
31 × 43 inches (80 × 110 cm)
Collection AW Asia, New York
From the series *A Second History*
*The First Sports Meeting of the National
Army, 1952, 2006*
Digital C-print
45 × 25 inches (114.3 × 63.5 cm)

Collection of the artist; courtesy Walsh
Gallery, Chicago
From the series *A Second History*
*Chairman Mao Reviewing Red Guards,
1966, 2006*
Digital C-print
45 × 25 inches (114.3 × 63.5 cm)
Collection of the artist; courtesy Walsh
Gallery, Chicago
From the series *A Second History*
*Organizing a Study Class Is a Good
Method, 2006*
Digital C-print
45 × 25 inches (114.3 × 63.5 cm)
Collection of the artist; courtesy Walsh
Gallery, Chicago

Zhu Feng 朱锋
*The Old and New: The Red Guard Parade at
Tiananmen Square and Chang'an Street on
November 11, 1966, 2007*
Banner
35½ × 98⁷⁄₁₆ inches (85 × 250 cm)
Collection of the artist
Top, 2004
C-print
26 × 39 7/16 inches (66 × 100 cm)
Collection Bates College Museum of Art
From the series *Shanghai Zero Degree*
Untitled (0478-20), 2004
C-print
27⅝ × 78¹¹⁄₁₆ inches (70 × 200 cm)
Collection Bates College Museum of Art

ACKNOWLEDGMENTS

The power of *Stairway to Heaven* resides within a cadre of dedicated friends and colleagues whose commitment to art, excellence, and scholarship and love for contemporary Chinese art permeated every decision made to manifest this book and exhibition. It has been a privilege and honor for all of us to work with the artists Ai Weiwei, Chen Shaoxiong, Gu Wenda, Gu Zheng, Hong Lei, Liang Weiping, Liu Bolin, Lu Yuanmin, Luo Yongjin, Ma Liuming, Wang Jing, Weng Fen, Xing Danwen, Yang Yongliang, Yening, Zhang Dali, and Zhu Feng.

The advice and knowledge of the field of Chinese contemporary art provided by Gan Xu and Gu Zheng was paramount in the organization of this project. They work tirelessly and unselfishly to find and support marginalized, young, and overlooked mature artists through their scholarship and interest in making connections with older generations and traditional Chinese art.

This is the third exhibition I have co-curated with Raechell Smith of the H&R Block Artspace at the Kansas City Art Institute. The project's attention to every detail is consummated in her tireless search for artists whose work strengthens and challenges the curatorial themes. Her team at the Artspace led by Owen Martin has been invaluable.

It is with great pleasure and pride that I thank Larry Warsh and Taliesen Thomas of AW Asia. Larry's commitment and knowledge of Chinese art and willingness to loan the art of Ai Weiwei, Hong Lei, Ma Liuming, and Zhang Dali, gave the project a much greater level of historical perspective and resonance. All of these works are now iconic within the field of Chinese contemporary art, and we are honored to present them to our audiences.

We extend our gratitude to Aura Gallery and Boers-Li Gallery in China, and the Walsh Gallery in Chicago for their support of Chinese art and generous loans to this exhibition.

I was fortunate to travel in China with Andy Graham and T. W. Eglin, who offered great insight during studio visits and lengthy late-night banquet conversations. I thank Will for his suggestion for the title of the exhibition and to Andy and Anne Riesenberg for their generous loans to the exhibition.

China's cultural presence is so large today that it is hard to imagine that the first major presentation of Chinese art outside China was in the 1993 exhibition *China's New Art, Post-1989*, which was followed by the 1998 exhibition *Inside Out: New Chinese Art*. Bates College is proud to be a leader in supporting the emerging field of Chinese contemporary art. *Stairway to Heaven* is the fourth exhibition of Chinese art, including the *Xu Bing: Calligraphy for the People*, *Wenda Gu: From Middle Kingdom to Biological Millennium*, and *Documenting China*, presented at the Bates College Museum of Art.

At Bates I would like to thank museum colleagues Bill Low and Anthony Shostak as well as Dean Jill Reich, Kerry O'Brien, Professor Maggie Maurio-Fazio, museum interns Alana Corbett '07, Forbes S. Litcoff '09, Emily Monty '10, and Rachel Tofel '10, and the Friends of the Bates College Museum of Art.

Working with Richard Pult and his colleagues at University Press of New England reinforces my trust in the strength of great publishers. Their passion for scholarship complemented with extreme professionalism and brilliant creativity provide the ingredients to make a great book.

Mark H. C. Bessire, Director
Bates College Museum of Art

The H&R Block Artspace at the Kansas City Art Institute is pleased to collaborate, once again, with Mark H. C. Bessire and the Bates College Museum of Art to realize the traveling exhibition and catalogue for *Stairway to Heaven: From Chinese Streets to Monuments and Skyscrapers*. Inspired partnerships such as this create profound impact as they extend resources and aspirations and serve to enrich the dialogue that each of our institutions facilitates in our own communities about contemporary art and culture.

For the Kansas City presentation, we are grateful for the important financial support provided by the Richard J. Stern Foundation for the Arts, Missouri Arts Council, H&R Block Foundation, and the Kansas City Art Institute. The project has benefited, in so many ways, from the contributions and inspired commitment of many individuals. At the Artspace, our appreciation is extended to staff members Michael Schonhoff, Owen Martin, Robert Heishman, and Jaimie Warren. A special thanks to Donna Raskin and Walnut Street

Business Services for invaluable and timely assistance with the artist interviews. We are also grateful for the expertise and collaboration we enjoy with our colleagues at the University of Kansas: Kris Imants Ercums and Saralyn Reece Hardy at the Spencer Museum of Art and Dr. David Cateforis in the Department of Art History.

Raechell Smith, Director
H&R Block Artspace at the
Kansas City Art Institute